THE LIVING WORD OF GOD

THE LIVING WORD OF GOD

Rethinking the Theology of the Bible

Ben Witherington III

BAYLOR UNIVERSITY PRESS

Cover Design by Jeremy Reiss

Library of Congress Cataloging-in-Publication Data

Witherington, Ben, 1951-
    The living Word of God : re-thinking the theology of the Bible / Ben
Witherington III.
        p. cm.
    Includes bibliographical references (p.   ) and index.
    ISBN-13: 978-1-60258-017-6 (hardcover : alk. paper)
    1. Bible--Theology. I. Title.
    BS543.W58 2007
    230'.041--dc22
                                                    2007034701

Printed in the United States of America on acid-free paper with a
minimum of 30% pcw recycled content.

For Richard and Judy

Faithful friends and faithful servants of our Lord

It is the doctrine of inspiration, that God inspired not only the people who spoke but also the words they spoke, that distinguishes the evangelical view of Scripture, and also forces us to wrestle with issues of hermeneutics. Inspiration maintains that God indeed "spoke these words and said. . . ." But it does not maintain that he dictated all these words. To the contrary it recognizes, indeed argues, that these words are also the words of people in history. . . . None of the words was spoken in a vacuum. Rather they were all addressed to, and conditioned by, the specific historical context in which they were spoken. . . .

To see Scripture as both human and divine creates its own set of tensions. . . . God did not choose to give us a series of timeless, non-culture-bound theological propositions to be believed and imperatives to be obeyed. Rather he chose to speak his eternal word this way, in historically particular circumstances, and in every kind of literary genre. God himself, by the very way he gave us this word, locked in the ambiguity. . . . The issue is whether one is wont to begin with a theological a priori and conform historical questions to that a priori (= telling the exegetes what God could or could not have done before one looks at the data), or whether one starts with historical investigation and expresses one's theological constructs in light of that investigation (= telling the theologian what God in light of historical probabilities seems to have done).

–Gordon D. Fee, Gospel and Spirit: Issues in
New Testament Hermeneutics (*Peabody, Mass.:*
Hendrickson, 1991), 30–34

The question of biblical authority, of how there can be such a thing as an authoritative Bible, is not, then, as simple as it might look. . . . A regular response to these problems is to say that the Bible is a repository of timeless truth. There are some senses in which that is true. But the sense in which it is normally meant is certainly not true. The whole Bible from Genesis to Revelation is culturally conditioned. It is all written in the language of particular times, and evokes the cultures in which it came to birth. It seems, when we get close up to it, as though, if we grant for a moment that in some sense or other God has indeed inspired this book, he has not wanted to give us an abstract set of truths unrelated to space and time. He has wanted to give us something rather different, which is not (in our post-enlightenment world) nearly so easy to handle as such a set of truths might seem to be. The problem of the gospels is one particular instance of this question. And at this point in the argument evangelicals often lurch towards Romans as a sort of safe place where they can find a basic systematic theology in the light of which one can read everything else. I have often been assured by evangelical colleagues in theological disciplines other than my own that my perception is indeed true: namely, that the Protestant and evangelical tradition has not been half so good on the gospels as it has been on the epistles. We don't quite know what to do with them. Because, I think, we have come to them as we have come to the whole Bible, looking for particular answers to particular questions. And we have thereby made the Bible into something which it basically is not . . . into a set of abstract truths and rules–abstract devotional doctrinal, or evangelistic snippets here and there.

–Bishop Tom Wright, "How Can the Bible be Authoritative?"
http://www.ntwrightpage.com/Wright_Bible_Authoritative.htm
(accessed April 23, 2007)

CONTENTS

PREFACE

I was watching a movie not long ago, and one of the central characters was getting passionate about something he was saying. In order to punctuate and emphasize what he was saying, he added the phrases, "Word of God, hand to my heart." He of course was using these phrases to indicate the absolute truthfulness of what he was saying. This incident led me to ponder the question: when people hear the phrase "word of God," what ideas and images does it conjure up in people's minds? For example, is it seen as a synonym for the Bible, or even a particular translation of the Bible? Does the use of the phrase "word of God" even in casual conversation conjure up notions of some truth or truths that have been revealed to human beings by God? Does the phrase then mean a word from God, and also at least, some of the time, a word about God? Does the phrase presuppose a certain theory of inspiration or even a theology of revelation? Behind those questions is a larger question: do such questions presuppose a certain image of God and how God operates?

At least in traditional and orthodox Christian circles, the discussion about the inspiration and authority of the Bible or the "word of God" often begins and sometimes even ends with a sort of deductive and syllogistic logic that goes like this:

1. God is all-knowing and all powerful and completely truthful.
2. God then is capable of truthfully and accurately revealing his mind, plan, and nature.
3. God has inspired certain human authors to write down his words.
4. They have accurately and perspicuously done so. Therefore,
5. The Bible is the word of God and is accurate and truthful in all it intends to assert.

Now what is interesting about this whole deductive line of thinking is that it is based not only on certain assumptions about the nature of God—assumptions that are in fact well grounded in what the Bible says about God's character—but also it is presuming a good deal about the nature of inspiration and revelation, and how inspiration works out in practice. In fact, an empirical study of inspiration suggests that while prophets sometimes took dictation, becoming mouthpieces who simply spoke the oracle they heard in a "thus sayeth the Lord" kind of fashion, inspiration does not seem to have worked this way in other forms of literature that made it into the Bible.

Notice as well that the five-point theory enunciated above says precious little if anything about the human contribution to getting God's words down on paper. This omission is quite odd, since throughout the history of Christianity, the church has not viewed the Bible in the same way as, say, Muslims view the Qur'an—as something that simply involved the human agent taking mechanical dictation from the deity, or in the way Joseph Smith claimed he received the material he put into the Book of Mormon—by simply translating and copying materials from discovered golden tablets that came directly from God.

In a panel discussion we were both on recently at the 2006 Society of Biblical Literature annual meeting, Barbara Brown Taylor set up a taxonomy of ways the Bible is viewed in the modern era. First, Scripture is seen as divine creation, rather like the golden tablets Joseph Smith allegedly found in upstate New York. Little if any human contribution is involved with this model, except that God used a human language to speak to us. Second, there is Scripture as divine inspiration. On this model there is a strong sense that the Bible is a revelation from God, but that humans are inspired to speak God's word and so make some contribution to what is said, reflecting their own style, thought patterns, interests, and the like. This view has a lot of variations, and is perhaps the one most often discussed within the context of the church. Third, Scripture has been viewed as something rather like Shakespeare at his best—a form of exalted human speech involving human inspiration. On this view the concept of revelation falls out of the picture by and large. The Bible is seen as a human product from stem to stern, though perhaps reflecting the apex of human literary achievement. A step further down the ladder is the view that the Bible is simply a human creation with occasionally an inspiring thought or memorable idea, which may well be the view of the majority of those who are not biblical monotheists (Jews, Christians, or Moslems). Sometimes they will be a little more charitable and say that the Bible is a literary classic or masterpiece. Finally there is the view that Scripture is human machination, that the book was written to deceive, mislead, or be an opiate to the masses.

This study focuses on the most prevalent of these views, listed as the second option above. The vast majority of Christians have held this view about the Bible down through the ages, and in my opinion it does the most justice to both the divine and human dimensions to Scripture. The Bible is not merely another attempt by humans to describe the Ineffable One or speak about their own religious thoughts and experiences of the Transcendent. The Bible claims to be and is a word from, not merely a word about, God.

In fact, the Bible, including the New Testament—our primary concern in this study—has always been seen as the word of God in the words of human beings, and the contribution of the latter has normally been recognized to be considerable. For example, Luke tells us in Luke 1:1-4 that before writing his Gospel he did research. He consulted eyewitnesses and the original preachers of God's message. In other words, he did not just sit in his study and take divine dictation. Various normal human processes were involved, and when Luke wrote things down they reflected his own style, vocabulary, ways of expressing things, and the like.

Sometimes analogies have actually been usefully drawn in the church, with the incarnation of God's Son who was recognized as being fully human and also fully divine.

But what would it actually mean to say that the Bible is both fully human and fully divine? In a subsequent chapter, we dialogue with Peter Enns's discussion of the incarnational analogy. We need to ask: What does the Bible actually have to say about its own character? What additional conclusions could we draw from inference from such texts?

Oddly, enough, most discussions about God's word do not actually involve a careful investigation of what the Bible has to say about itself, nor is the theory of inspiration usually promulgated based on an investigation of what is actually going on in the various texts within the canon. In this study I wish to ask, wouldn't it be better to take an inductive approach to this subject and actually examine biblical texts in all their historical contexts, and then draw some conclusions about our theories of inspiration, authority, canon, and our theology of the Bible as God's word? Wouldn't it be better to say that the text of the New Testament as originally given is what inspiration actually looks like? Wouldn't it be better to assess the nature of the New Testament's truth claims *after* delving in depth into a close study of the meaning of various relevant texts, asking how they work and what sorts of information they are trying to convey?

These questions are not rhetorical, but real, and my answer to all of them is yes. I am both a historian and an exegete, and I am also a theologian. But I take it as a fundamental axiom that I should not bring my theology to the text, and then tell the text what it must say in order to be consistent with my presuppositions about the Bible being God's word and being truthful. I also do not think I should begin with a later theology of Scripture or a later creedal or confessional doctrine of God and use those things anachronistically to determine what this or that New Testament text must say. Such an approach leads to all sorts of distortions, false harmonizing of the text, and other exercises in futility, where instead of actually explaining the text, one is attempting to explain it away or make it say something it actually does not say. Rather my theology should be drawn from the biblical text, even my theology of Scripture, after the hard work of interpretation and reflection on meanings has taken place. And hard work it is because we have to fight off many modern misconceptions of what an ancient text must say or do if it is to be seen as veracious.

I ask my students in our introductory NT class a basic question: How many times according to each of the Gospels did Jesus cleanse the temple? How many times in Mark? They usually dutifully answer, "Just once." Then I ask, when and where in the Markan narrative does this take place? Some bright spark answers, "In the Passion narrative." "Right you are," I respond. The same question is asked again about Matthew and Luke, with the same response, but then I ask them about the Gospel of John. "How many times does Jesus cleanse the temple in John?" Some immediately say "Twice," and then they add "Once at the beginning and once at the end of ministry." I respond, "Really?" Does the Fourth Gospel say anything about Jesus cleansing the temple during the last week of his earthly life? In fact, on closer inspection it does not. The Fourth Gospel also, like the first three, only records one cleansing of the temple, but the placement of the narrative is near the beginning of the story, not near its end. Is this a contradiction or a discrepancy between the accounts?

Well, in fact, it is not. Under inspiration, the Gospel writers appear to have followed the conventions of their own day when it came to writing a biography of Jesus, and one of those conventions was that they had a certain freedom to arrange their material. Sometimes it might be a chronological arrangement, sometimes it might be a more topical arrangement, or in the Fourth Gospel even a theological arrangement of materials. In other words, we have just learned that strict chronology is a modern hang-up that we should not impose on ancient texts. We need to read such texts in their original contexts and in light of the methodologies followed in that age. This approach, of course, requires actual historical study of the texts. Hard work, detailed research in the original languages, and the like are involved.

Inevitably at this juncture in the conversation, some student will raise a hand and say, "But isn't the Bible clear in itself? Shouldn't the truth be immediately apparent to anyone who picks up and reads this book?" I respond, "Veracity must always be judged on the basis of what a person is intending to say and trying to convey." Modern notions about chronological or verbal precision equaling inerrancy are not helpful if the inspired author was intending to give us the gist of something in a way that was user friendly for his audience, arranging the material so it would do a better job of persuading the audience about the truths the author most wants to convey. In other words, if the author wants to convey something in a general way, then he should not be faulted for imprecision! This is not a question of the author being mistaken, but rather us being too picky and demanding more of the text than the author intends to give. The greatest causes of misunderstanding of the Bible are the modern expectations and the presuppositions we bring to the text that lead us to assume that the text must be understood in a way that makes common sense to any of us in the twenty-first century.

Of course, the underlying issue behind the student's question about clarity is that he or she assumes that the truth of such issues should be apparent to laypersons simply by examining the surface of these texts, even in translation. This assumption is false. Every translation is already an interpretation, so the intermediary role of scholarship cannot be escaped, unless one already has a knowledge of the original languages, the original contexts of the Bible, ancient writing conventions, and more. The essence of the salvation message of the New Testament can, of course, be understood without such sophistication, but the Bible speaks to a plethora of subjects and often speaks at a depth and in ways that moderns would naturally find puzzling or confusing.

The issue of the perspicuity of Scripture is an important one, but one must ask, Clear to whom, and with what background study required? We are not in the position of the early Christians, language-wise or otherwise. I assume these texts were clear to the human authors who wrote them, and probably clear to many in the audience as well. But for them to be clear for us, we must imaginatively enter into their worlds, their forms of discourse, their ways of conveying important truths. It is not enough to roughly translate their words into our common parlance and then just assume we should be able to understand what they say and mean.

What we have begun to discuss in this preface is a foretaste of what is to come. In order to make progress in understanding the New Testament as God's word, we must seek to understand it on its own terms, and on its own turf, not merely in the comfort of our own terms and turf. We must tease our minds into active thought. We must examine the particulars of particular texts and ask hard questions. And having undertaken such a historical exercise, then perhaps we will be ready to ask and answer various theological questions about the inspiration, authority, and truthfulness of the New Testament, and the sense in which it can be called the word of God.

In other words, we need to go forward in our discussion of such matters, not backward, and so we will not be debating something like

B. B. Warfield's old classic study, *Inspiration and Authority of the Bible*, as good as it was in its day, nor will we be examining various modern statements on biblical inerrancy. These are not the appropriate places to start our discussion. We should start with and stick closely to the Bible itself, assuming that as was the case with Jacob, if we wrestle with the divine long enough, we will obtain a blessing, even if we walk with a limp for a while thereafter.

Easter 2007

Chapter 1

SEEKING THE WORD OF GOD

*For since you came when called for my salvation, how would you not come
for your own honor? So taking heart I proceed to what remains, knowing
that this encomium is on the one hand by the mind of a god but on the other
hand written by a human being (nous men Theou, cheipes de graphousin
anthrôpou).*

—*Aretology of Isis, lines 11–12*

HOLY GOD AND HOLY WORDS

Ours is a culture of texts. The written word is king, as is clear enough
from the fact that we now have a whole line of intellectual property
lawyers prepared to go court in an instant if a client's words have
been begged, borrowed, or stolen without permission. It is therefore
difficult for those of us who are surrounded by texts to wrap our
minds around the fact that the New Testament was written in and for
a predominantly oral culture—a culture where the spoken word took

precedence over the written, and the written word simply supported or at least served as a surrogate for the spoken word.

When I call the world of the New Testament an oral culture, I don't merely mean that most people couldn't read and write, which of course was true. The best that we can tell, the literacy rate was never over about 10 to 20 percent in the age in which the New Testament was written. In fact, in many places it would have been less than that. Literacy was usually a sign of someone being of higher social standing and better education, and was more likely to be the privilege of males in a male-dominated culture. Remarkably the early Christian movement was guided, goaded, and guarded by a series of texts in its most crucial period of development—the second half of the first century A.D. when every one of the NT books was written.

In the battles over whether and in what sense the Bible in general or the New Testament in particular can be called God's inspired word, very little ink has been spilled discussing the issue of the power and authority that texts had in an oral culture. In fact, especially in cultures that had, and cherished, certain sacred texts that provided source material about one's religion, the text took on an almost magical quality. This feature is understandable especially in a Jewish context, for texts about biblical religion were normally kept in sacred spaces—in the temple, or in the synagogue. They were carefully and lovingly copied by scribes, who often were full-time employees of priests or Levites, or the temple hierarchy.

But Judaism was not the only culture in which texts were kept in sacred places. If one chooses to make the arduous climb up to Delphi, where the oracle was in southern Greece, you will discover many buildings called treasuries, just like the treasury in the temple in Jerusalem. These treasuries were not just where money and valuables were kept. They were also places where important and crucial documents were stored, indeed kept, it was believed, under the watchful eye of one deity or another. Similarly, in Rome one deposited for safe keeping with the Vestal Virgins wills, property deeds, treaties, and sacred documents. No wonder, then, that many people in antiquity were convinced that texts themselves, especially religious texts, might well be invested with some of the divine qualities of the deity they were placed near. People believed, for example, that curse tablets (tablets on which one wrote a curse formula against someone) themselves might engender a curse on someone, especially if the tablet was placed near or in the divine presence.

Many such examples as these could be given, but I want to offer one more that is crucial to the biblical tradition. The stories in the Old Testament about the ark of the covenant are interesting for many reasons. Take a moment to read 1 Samuel 4–6 and then 2 Samuel 6. The ark of the covenant was constructed so that it not only contained the written covenant document in its lower part, but on the top of the ark itself there were cherubim and angels, and between the two sections it was believed that the divine presence rested. The divine presence, the divine power, and the divine word were all right there together. So present was God with his word that when Uzzah reached out to prevent the ark from falling when an oxen stumbled and he actually touched the ark itself, he was immediately struck down and died on the spot (2 Sam 6:6-7). Uzzah's punishment of course scared David to death, and thereafter David was afraid of the Lord.

That Israelites like David would associate God's word with power and inherent authority is not surprising, nor indeed is it surprising that they would think that God's Words were living things that themselves had power. After all, did the Israelites not have a creation story telling them that God created the world simply by speaking words? Hadn't they learned the tale of how God himself wrote down the essence of the Torah, the Law, on a tablet for Moses?

My point in this discussion is simple: ancients did not think words, and especially divine words, were mere ciphers or sounds. The ancients believed words partook of the character and quality of the one who spoke them, especially when talking about God's words, and not surprisingly oral culture puts a premium on the oral word. The living voice was generally preferred, except when it came to holy words spoken to unholy people. Then there might well be a preference for a mediated conveying of God's word, a reading or proclaiming of his word by a spokesperson—a prophet, a priest, or a king, or an apostle, prophet, or elder if we are talking about the Christian community. As the author of Hebrews says, the Israelites at Sinai heard "such a voice speaking words that those who heard it begged that no further word be spoken to them" (Heb 12:19). When the living Word was proclaimed by a living voice, whether God directly or through God's messenger or emissary, things were likely to happen. Imagine what would be the conclusion if it was thought that God's special anointed one, the Messiah, was doing the proclaiming of God's word as well? Would they not have expected the words of the Messiah to be clearly from God, having especial divine power and efficacy? And I would suggest that Jesus himself had, and conveyed a particular theory of inspiration if we examine closely a text like Mark 12:36. Here Jesus says that David spoke Psalm 110 through the prompting or by means of the Holy Spirit. Notice that Jesus is not just referring to an inspiration of persons, like David himself, but an inspiration that results in an inspired text which Jesus could quote as still having divine authority—a Holy Scripture, not merely sacred speech or oral tradition. No wonder Jesus contrasts mere human traditions with the Word of God in Mark 7:13. All of this helps us to begin to understand the use of the phrase "word of God" in the New Testament.

THE VIVA VOCE—THE MESSAGE ABOUT JESUS AS THE SPOKEN WORD OF GOD AND JESUS AS THE WORD MADE FLESH

By general consensus among New Testament scholars (and that sort of nearly universal agreement is rare in the guild), 1 Thessalonians is one of the very first, if not the very first of all the New Testament documents to be written. From near the very beginning of this discourse we hear about the word of God. First Thessalonians 2:13 says: "When you received the word of God, which you heard from us, you accepted it not as the word of humans, but as it actually is—the word of God."

This verse deserves some unpacking. In the first place, Paul equates the message he proclaimed to the residents of Thessalonike with the word of God. Clearly the phrase refers to an oral proclamation here that was heard. If we ask what message Paul proclaimed, whatever else it contained, it surely contained the good news about Jesus, and perhaps in addition some quoting and exegeting of OT texts.

Then Paul makes a remarkable statement. The Thessalonians received this proclamation as it actually was—not merely the words of human beings, cooked up or contrived by mere mortals, but they received it as a word from God, indeed as the word of God to and for them. This echoes the contrast we mentioned above found in Mark 7:13. We see already in Paul's words at least one expression of a theology of God's word. God's word, though spoken in human language, should never be confused with mere human speech, or even mere human words about God, however accurate. Rather we are talking about divine speech that changes human lives. But then Paul adds another remarkable phrase: "which is [still] at work in you who believe." The word of God is seen as something living and active, having taken up residence in the life of Paul's converts, and still is in the process of working on and in them.

The implications of these statements are enormous. (1) Paul believes that he adequately and accurately speaks God's oral word and has the authority to do so. (2) Paul is not only a good reader of OT texts, though certainly he sees the OT as God's word written down. (3) Included in the phrase "word of God" here is what later came to be called "the Gospel," or the good news of and about Jesus Christ, which was the heart and soul of Paul's message wherever he proclaimed it in the empire. (4) In and through these words that Paul proclaimed, God was speaking, and such speech should never be seen as merely the words of human beings. A profound theology of revelation and a clear conception of Paul being an inspired person who could truthfully convey God's message of salvation is presupposed. In this regard, Paul seems little different from Jesus when it comes to a theology of God's

Word. Ancients had little trouble in believing in the idea of divine revelation. Moderns are the ones who have trouble with the idea.

Another early Pauline text of relevance to this discussion is 1 Corinthians 14:36-37 where Paul asks his audience if the word of God originated with them or if they were the only ones it had reached. Again, he is not talking about the Corinthians having received a shipment of Bibles from the Gideons. He is talking about their having heard and received the oral proclamation of God's word from Paul and others. But what Paul goes on to say in verse 37 is more than a little important. He adds, "If any think they are prophets or are spiritually gifted, let them acknowledge that what I am writing is the Lord's command." Here finally we have a reference to a text being "the Lord's command" and not just any text. In this case, the reference is to Paul's own letter written to the Corinthians. Here we have the nodal idea of an inspired text being God's word, in this case involving some imperatives.

Paul is not the only one who has this concept that the word of God is an oral proclamation that includes telling the story about Jesus, and that the word of God is a living and active thing. We see this concept in various places in the book of Acts. Several texts deserve brief mention. First we notice Acts 4:31, which speaks of the fact that the Holy Spirit of God filled all who were present (men and women) and they all "spoke the word of God boldly." In this text we begin to see the connection, which is already obvious in various OT prophetic texts (cf., e.g., Isa 61:1—the Spirit of God prompts the preaching of the good news), that the Holy Spirit, not merely the human spirit, inspires the speaking of God's word. Here already the concept of prophetic inspiration and revelation is transferred to the followers of Jesus, apparently to all of them, and all on this occasion and in this place are prompted to speak God's word boldly. Again, we are not talking about preaching from a text or preaching a text. We are talking about an oral proclamation of a late word from God.

So much is the word of God (in this case, the proclamation about Jesus) seen as a living thing in Acts that remarkably we have texts like Acts 6:7 where we hear how the word of God itself grew and spread, which is not merely a personification of an abstract idea. The author believes that God's word is alive, and when it is heard and received it changes human lives and takes up residence in them; thus, the very next sentence in this verse says. "The number of the disciples in Jerusalem increased." Note also Acts 12:24, in which it is stated that God's word grew and spread.

We see this same sort of concept of the word of God in the book of Hebrews. Hebrews 4:12-13 is worth quoting in full: "for the word of God is living and active. Sharper than any two-edged sword it penetrates even to the dividing of the soul and spirit, joints and marrow; it judges the thoughts and attitudes of the heart. Nothing in all of creation is hidden from God's sight." Here again the subject of the phrase "word of God" is an oral proclamation. The focus is not on the after-the-fact literary residue of that proclamation, as is perfectly clear because the author speaks of it sinking into the inner being of the listener. But more remarkably, the "word of God" inside the believer is said to be analogous to God's eyes—it penetrates the innermost being of a person and judges the thoughts of one's heart or mind, laying everything bare. Our author, however, is not the originator of these ideas. We can fruitfully compare what is said here with Psalm 139, where the focus is on the work of God's presence or Spirit. What is said in Psalm 139 about the Spirit is said here about the living and active word. These two things are seen as going and working together. We have already seen the connection of word and Spirit in Acts 4 as discussed above.

Another text of relevance to this discussion is 1 Peter 1:23, which speaks of believers being born anew by "the living and abiding word of God." This can certainly refer to the oral proclamation, but the term "living" may also convey the sense of life giving as it does in the phrase "living bread" in John 6:51; we may compare this as well to 1 Peter 1:3, which speaks of a living hope and surely means more than merely an extant hope. Or we may consider 1 Peter 2:4-5, which speaks of believers as living stones of the new spiritual house of God. Stephen Llewelyn is right to point out that the phrase "living image" was applied to a king who was said to be the living image of some deity.[1] When we hear the phrase "the living word of God," then, we are meant to think of something that is actually God's word and as such has life-giving potential. Normally the phrase also connotes an oral proclamation of God's word in some form.

Notice that thus far we have said nothing about the other use of the phrase "Word of God" in the NT to refer to Jesus himself (John 1), nor about the concept that the written OT is the word of God as well. The logos theology of the prologue to John's Gospel is often thought to be distinctive of this book, but we may well see it also in 1 John 1:1-2 where we hear of the Word of Life, which seems to be synonymous with both Jesus (who could be touched) and with the message about Jesus as God's incarnate Word. Similarly in Revelation 19:13 the name of God's Son is said to be "the Word of God." We have seen some hints already of the notion that texts could be the Word of God, and now we must turn to more evidence by looking in detail at 2 Timothy 3:16 and some texts in Hebrews.

THE WORD MADE SCRIPTURE

Because of the enormous significance of 2 Timothy 3:16-17 for this particular study, we must necessarily go into considerably more detailed explanation of these verses, since whole theories about the nature of God's word and of inspiration have been derived from these verses. Here, clearly enough the subject matter is a written text, in this case what Christians now call the Old Testament. The Old Testament was in fact the Bible of the earliest Christians, because of course the New Testament had not yet been written, collected, or canonized. Indeed, even the OT canon, or list of included books, was not completely settled before the waning decades of the first century A.D. Here we must make an important distinction between "the Bible" as one form that God's word took (the written form), and the "word of God" which is, as we have already seen in this chapter, a much broader category. The "word of God" in the first instance refers to inspired and powerful spoken words. The earliest Christians were neither without a Scripture (the OT) nor without the living voice, the oral word of God, which in their view now included Christian proclamation, especially the good news about Jesus.

Interestingly the NT writers tend to say more about the inspiration of the OT than the OT writers themselves. For example, in Mark 12:36 Jesus tells his audience that David "in the Holy Spirit said. . . ," and then a portion of a psalm is quoted. Or in Acts 1:16 we hear that the Holy Spirit through the mouth of David predicted what would happen about Judas. Second Peter 1:21 can be compared at this point. We are thus not surprised to hear about the inspiration of OT figures in the NT, but 2 Timothy 3:16-17 goes a step beyond that in talking about an *inspired text itself*. It would appear that the inspiration of persons who could write could entail the inspiration of particular texts, though no one would claim that everything they ever said or wrote was the inspired word of God.

Second Timothy 3:16 is surely the most famous of the verses of 2 Timothy, cited over one hundred times in the patristic literature. However, various translations are possible, and each causes a variable in its meaning. It could read, for instance, "Every *graphé* (i.e., Scripture) is God-breathed and profitable/useful . . . so that/with the result that the person of God is ready, equipped for good works." Usually when *pas* (all/every) is used with a noun without the definite article, it means "every" rather than "all." Thus, the meaning seems likely to be "every Scripture" or perhaps "every passage of Scripture." Paul does use *graphé* in the singular to refer to the whole of Scripture in Romans 11:2, but there we have the definite article (cf. also Gal 3:22), meaning that "all Scripture" is included, but the emphasis would be on each one being God-breathed. Paul does not envision any Scripture that is not God-breathed.[2] One could also read the verse to mean "Every inspired Scripture is useful. . . ," but against this view is the more natural approach of taking the two qualifying adjectives as relating to the noun in the same way as in 1 Timothy 4:4.

A further issue is what to make of the adjective *theopneustos*. Its literal meaning, "God-breathed," is a term used in pagan literature—for example, in reference to the Sibylline oracles (cf. *Sib. Oracles* 5.308, 406; Plutarch, *Or. at Delphi* 7; Pseudo-Phocylides, 121), and in the papyri (SIG 95; CMRDM 2.A8). We may compare, for example, an aretology to Isis written in Macedonia which reads at one point "this encomium is written not only by the hand of a man, but also by the mind of a god" (line 14).[3] Greek words with the *-tos* ending tend to be passive rather than active, so we should not take this to mean "every Scripture is inspiring," but rather "every Scripture is inspired," meaning that God speaks through these words. God breathed life and meaning and truth into them all (see similarly Num 24:2; Hos 9:7; cf. Josephus, *Against Apion* 1.37-39; Philo, *Moses* 2.292; *Spec. Leg.* 1.65; 4.49; 2 Pet 1:21).

We are not given an explanation of how inspiration works. This text by itself does not explicate a theory of inspiration or its nature. Does the Spirit lift the mind of the writer to see, understand, and write, or is it a matter of mechanical dictation? These questions are not answered here. Rather, whatever the process, the product is God's word, telling God's truth.

The emphasis here is on what it is good or profitable for—as a source of teaching about God and human beings and their ways, as a means of refuting false arguments or errors and offering positive proofs and rebuking sin, and as a means of offering constructive wisdom and teaching on how to live a life pleasing to God. The OT, then, is largely viewed here as a source for ethical instruction and exhortation, which is not surprising given the emphasis in this letter. No emphasis appears here on it being a sourcebook for Christian theology, which would come more from the Christian kerygma and Christian tradition. We may also want to consult other places where Paul speaks about the nature of the OT Scriptures, such as Romans 15:3-4 or 1 Corinthians 10:11, which confirms that Paul thinks that what we call the OT is very suitable for Christian instruction, especially for training in righteousness and other ethical matters.

There is debate about verse 17 as to whether we should see it as a purpose or result clause. Is the purpose of Scripture to fit a person of God for ready service, or is it the result and effect of Scripture that that happens? Probably this is a result clause. The result of learning Scripture is that one is equipped. It seems likely as well that since this clause is directed specifically to Timothy, "person/man of God" here refers to a minister of some sort. Paul then would be talking about equipping the minister by means of studying the Scriptures.

Using the rhetorical device of *gradatio*, Paul brings to a climax the list of what Scripture is useful for and concludes with the phrase "training in righteousness." Here righteousness surely has an ethical rather than a forensic sense, in keeping with the ethical focus of the rest this statement about of Scripture's usefulness. Chrysostom puts it this way: "This is why the exhortation of the Scripture is given: that the man of God may be rendered complete by it. Without this he cannot grow to maturity" (*Hom. 2 Tim.*). Clearly, with this text, we are well on the way to a full-blown theology of inspired written texts being God's word, being God-breathed. Neither Paul nor the author of Hebrews views the OT as an example of what God *once* said, relegating the revelation and speaking to the past. No, God's word still has the life and power and truth of God in it, and it still speaks in and to the present.

Especially striking are the formula quotations in Hebrews, by which I mean the ways that the author of Hebrews introduces OT quotations in his quotation-filled sermon. In that sermon, God the Father, Jesus Christ, and the Holy Spirit are all said to be the speakers of various OT texts! A few examples must suffice. As our author introduces a quotation from Deuteronomy 32:43 at Hebrews 1:6, we find the phrase "when God brings his firstborn into the world *he says*"—noting the present-tense verb of saying here. But in Hebrews 2:11-12, in introducing a quotation from Psalm 22:22, we hear, "So Jesus is not ashamed to call them brothers and sisters. He says . . ." (cf. Heb 10:5). Now Christ is depicted as speaking an OT text. And on multiple occasions we hear in Hebrews "as the Holy Spirit says" used to introduce various OT quotes (see Heb 3:7; 10:16).

Two things stand out here. First, our author already has the beginnings of a Trinitarian theology. What Scripture says, God says, and the God who is said to be speaking these OT texts is Father, Son, or Spirit. We do not yet have a text where all three of them are said to speak one particular passage of Scripture. Equally telling is the fact that the present-tense verb keeps cropping up. The OT is not just for God's original chosen people. It is viewed as a text that speaks directly and pertinently to Christians in the present. Furthermore, the OT is seen as speaking about a whole host of subjects including God's Son, not only about ethics. The author of Hebrews takes up stories, laws, covenants, as well as ethical material from the OT in order to convey to the audience the living word of God about Jesus and Christian life.

Second, the author enunciates a hermeneutic of progressive revelation from the very beginning of the book. He says that God revealed himself in various times and ways, or partially and piecemeal in the past, but now God has revealed himself fully and finally in the person of his Son (Heb 1:1-2). Clearly the incarnate Word is seen as the most crucial revelation of God, to which all early revelations prepare, foreshadow, or foretell, but this by no means causes the author to suggest that the OT ceases to be God's word when the Incarnate Word shows up. To the contrary, Jesus and the Christ event are seen as the hermeneutical keys to understanding the OT, but also the OT is understood as crucial to understanding the Christ event. Some sort of symbiotic relationship is envisioned between the word written, the word proclaimed, and the Word Incarnate.

One more text directly relates to this sort of discussion, particularly in regard to the issue of inspiration and revelation. Second Peter 1:20-21 says, "Above all you must understand that no prophecy of Scripture came about by the prophet's own interpretation. For prophecy never had its origin in the human will, but prophets, though human, spoke from God as they were carried along by the Holy Spirit." It is indeed normally about prophets and prophecy that we hear about the notion of inspiration, and this text seems to add a bit more to the discussion than 2 Timothy 3:16. First of all, here there is a contrast between prophecy that made it into Scripture and other prophecies. The author says that whatever may be the case about other prophecies, OT prophecy cannot be a matter of purely private or individual interpretation or explanation. That is, the author thinks there is a meaning in the prophecy itself that makes a claim on the listener, and it is not for the listener to determine the meaning of the text but rather to discover it. Indeed he even means it wasn't up to the prophet to interpret or add his own interpretation to it. He was constrained by the source of the information to speak another's words and meaning—namely God's. This is made clearer in what follows in verse 21. This latter verse speaks about the origins of true prophecy and insists that it does not originate as a matter of human will or ingenuity. To the contrary, it is the Holy Spirit that inspires the prophet. In fact, the text literally says the prophet is carried along or forcefully moved by the Spirit to say what he or she does. The prophet is so led by the Spirit that his or her words can be said to be God's Words, originating from a divine source.

Much more could be said along these lines, but these comments will need to suffice as we draw this first chapter to a close. The living word of God is seen as an oral message, an Incarnate person, and finally as a text, in particular the text of the OT. Its life, power, and truth are a derived life, power, and truth if we are talking about the oral or written word. The source is God who inspires, speaks, and empowers the words with qualities that reflect the divine character. Paul thinks that what he says, God is saying. Both Paul and the author of Hebrews think that what the OT says, God says. These same writers think that what Jesus says, God says. Indeed, the author of Hebrews is audacious enough to suggest that the preexistent Christ actually spoke some of the OT texts into existence! The emphatic center and focus of the proclamation of "the word of God" by early Christians were Jesus and the Christ event in general. Some NT writers even reached the point of being able to talk about Jesus being the Word of God incarnate, come in the flesh, such that when Jesus spoke on earth, he not only spoke for God, he spoke as God and indeed spoke about himself. The message and the messenger are one in this case. There is also a case to be made that Jesus provided the precedent, as Mark 12:36 suggests, for early Christians to see written OT texts as both inspired and as speaking to and for them.

    C. S. Lewis once said that when the author of a play comes out on the stage, the play is over. The authors of the Johannine literature, but also the other NT writers, all believed that when Jesus came, history, particularly salvation history, had reached its zenith; they were now in the eschatological era when all the promises and prophecies of God were coming true in and through Jesus and his followers. Jesus was seen as the climax of revelation and the climactic revelation. He was seen as God's Word, God's Purpose, God's Salvation, God's being come in person. What was previously predicated of Wisdom (Prov 3; 8; Wisdom of Solomon) and of Torah (Sirach), is now predicated of a historical person—Jesus, or in Revelation 19:13 of the returning exalted Christ. However inspiring all this may be, and it is, we have not even scratched the surface of talking about the nature of inspiration which turns ordinary words into God's word. We turn to that subject in the next chapter.

Chapter 2

INSPIRATION WITHOUT AN EXPIRATION DATE

For God to reveal himself means that he accommodates himself.

—Peter Enns

Without question, millions of people have found the Bible to be an inspiring book, in part or in whole. And sometimes there is some confusion as to what is meant by the idea of the inspiration of the Bible or the word of God. To be clear from the outset, I am not talking about the inspiring effect of the Bible on readers in any age. I am dealing with the issue of whether the Bible itself is inspired and what that might mean. Let me also offer another caveat. I am also not merely talking about certain persons—say, prophets—being inspired by God to speak. I am asking are their words in some sense God's Words, whether oral or written, such that they can be considered true and trustworthy? Is the literary residue, written texts that made it into the Bible, inspired? The author of 2 Timothy 3:16 would answer that question with a resounding yes! Literally, he says, every writing (i.e., in this case sacred text or Scripture) is God-breathed. But before exploring these concepts some more, we should quickly review several items we have learned already in this study.

In our last chapter we established several important facts. First, at least some writers of the NT saw their own words as "the word of God" whether orally spoken or written down in a document of some sort. Second, we demonstrated that the phrase "word of God" was used to refer to oral proclamation, the written surrogate of an oral proclamation (for example, a letter), and of Jesus himself. Third, we noted the difference between "the Bible," which means "book" and always refers to a book, and "the word of God," which has a broader scope of meaning, even including the story of Jesus. The Bible, by which I mean in this case the OT (which was the only Bible in the time of the NT authors), was certainly regarded as the inspired word of God, as was especially clear from our examination of 2 Timothy 3:16-17. In that text, we began to see the concept called "inspiration" fleshed out. In this chapter, we need to study this concept in some detail.

In 2 Timothy 3:16 there is an interesting—indeed, some would say peculiar—statement about inspiration. We noted that the word *theopneustos* literally means "God-breathed," referring to the activity of God, and the claim is made that every single Scripture (in the OT) is God-breathed. Of course, Paul does not give us a list of books that he would include under the heading of Scripture, but since he elsewhere cites as authoritative texts from the Law, the Prophets, and the Writings, all three major divisions of the Scripture, we may assume that he would have had a rather full OT canon list. In Paul's day, in any case, very few books were still being debated in regard to whether they belonged in Torah or not (e.g., Esther, and perhaps a books like Ecclesiastes or Daniel).

Returning to 2 Timothy 3:16, one could say this statement is about the cause of human words becoming God's word, rather than the effect—the words become "inspired." There is no theory of a process or how inspiration happens or the nature of its effects here, simply a didactic statement: that God breathed his life, power, meaning, and message into these words. Should we take this to mean that some sort of mechanical dictation process happened where the human writer was superseded (ruled and overruled) by a Divine Author's iron hand? Two things need to be said about this idea. First, the Bible doesn't claim that this is how all these texts in the OT became the word of God. Second, the idea could only possibly apply to certain prophetic revelations, as we shall see. In the last chapter we also saw in 2 Peter 1:20-21 the clear claim that prophets did not originate their own prophecies, for a true prophecy has its origins not in the human will, imagination, or interpretation, but rather the prophet spoke as he was led and carried along by the Holy Spirit, which resulted in the outcome that what the prophet said, God said. Clearly in that passage we are dealing with the prophet as simply the divine mouthpiece who says what God's Spirit leads him or her to say. But this remark is made about a specific kind of OT literature—the prophetic oracle.

MECHANICAL DICTATION OR TRUE REVELATION?

Howard Marshall, in an influential study on biblical inspiration, strongly warns against assuming that mechanical dictation is the means by which human words became God's word or even Scripture. The effect of making such a claim is that "biblical writers have been depersonalised—and indeed God himself has been depersonalized, since he no longer acts as a person dealing with persons, but as a workman using a tool. [On this view of inspiration, the] Bible is no longer regarded as in any real sense a human book; it is simply a heavenly telegram. In short, the theory not only does not correspond to what the biblical writers tell us about themselves; it also leads to a false view of God's relationship with human persons."[1] In this quotation, Marshall is in essence rejecting the first of the views of Scripture enunciated in Barbara Brown Taylor's taxonomy of possible views of Scripture that we referred to earlier.[2]

In that last quoted sentence, Marshall is referring to the prima facie evidence of the Bible itself. For example, he rightly points out that in a text like Ezra 7:11-26 we find a biblical writer quoting a source from the Persian archives. He adds, "It is impossible to think of such sources as being dictated by God, and it is farcical to suggest that they became inspired when they were copied out by Ezra."[3] While I certainly grant his point in the first half of the statement, the second half is problematic, if indeed "every Scripture is inspired by God." I doubt Paul or other NT writers would want to write texts like Ezra 7:11-26 out of the canon simply because they came from a Persian archive originally.

It would be better to suggest that perhaps God providentially guided the biblical author to choose material which, while not originally part of inspired Scripture, nevertheless was true, and so could be included in a sacred text like Ezra's. This phenomena shows up in numerous places in the OT. Another good example would be the sayings of Agur and Lemuel, two nonbiblical sages, that show up at the end of the book of Proverbs (Prov 30–31). This same point could be made about NT authors' use of extracanonical material. For example, in Acts 17:28 Greek poets or writers are quoted; in Titus a Cretan "prophet" is cited (Titus 1:12), and in Jude 9 a Jewish apocryphal story about the body of Moses is recounted. Obviously those who included such materials in their books, speeches, or letters must have thought they conveyed some wisdom or truth of some kind.

But we must agree with Marshall's main point: the theory of mechanical dictation of the Scripture does not account for *all* of what we find there. Indeed, one could argue it accounts for perhaps only a minority of what we find there. The exception to this rule comes in regard to certain kinds of prophetic experiences, where the prophet or another sort of emissary is simply a mouthpiece for God. So at this juncture we need to say something about prophetic inspiration and mechanical dictation.

In another study, I have written at length and in detail about the nature and character of prophecy in the ancient Near East, in the OT, in the Greco-Roman world, and in the NT.[4] In that study I pointed out the difference between the prophetic experience, which is a top-down experience where someone receives a revelation from outside themselves, and divination, which is a religious procedure initiated by a human being to try and extract an answer from some deity. A prophet is someone who receives a revelation and is prompted to do something with it. Sometimes these revelations are merely auditory in character; sometimes they are both visual and auditory (hence the term "seer"). Sometimes ecstasy seems to have been involved in the process of receiving the revelation. Two biblical examples can illustrate this point.

First Samuel 10:5-12 refers to a band of prophets, speaks of the role of music in the process of inspiration, and refers to the ecstasy experienced in the process of receiving a revelation, an ecstasy that even overcomes King Saul himself. We may compare this to the experience of John of Patmos as recorded in Revelation 1:10 where John says he was "in the Spirit" (notice he does not say the Spirit was in him, though that was also true) on the Lord's day, and he heard and saw various things. In my detailed study on prophecy, I pointed out that while being in an ecstatic state was a common phenomena cross-culturally, when it comes to a prophet receiving a revelation, the experience is not universal. Some prophets received late words from God in a quiet manner without ecstasy or spiritual transport. But what is interesting about such experiences is that those people who became ecstatic believed that God's Spirit had taken over their minds and bodies, and whatever they uttered in such a state was purely from God. This surely is a sort of mechanical communication theory of what leads at least to an oracle, an oral proclamation of God's word, though we could not call it mechanical dictation theory since the divine intervention comes at the juncture of the experience, not at the later juncture of writing down what was said and happened.

In the case of John of Patmos, however, something more needs to be said. When a prophet hears a word from God in his own language, that prophet can indeed, if she or he has heard it clearly, simply repeat it. No human contribution is added to the content of the message in such cases, only to its public enunciation. However, when a prophet or seer "sees" a revelation, then the prophet can apparently describe it using his or her own vocabulary, style, and the like, which is why in the case of visionary or apocalyptic prophecy, we repeatedly hear the phrase, 'It was like. . . .'"

Two examples must suffice. In Ezekiel's throne chariot vision the prophet says, "The center of the fire looked *like* glowing metal, and in the fire was what looked *like* four living creatures" (1:4-5). Revelation 1:14 states, "His head and hair were white *like* wool, as white *as* snow, and his eyes were *like* blazing fire." Obviously the seers are not attempting a literal description, but rather one that involves analogy and metaphor, which is where the human element comes into the picture. The seers are groping for words large, bold, and descriptive enough to related what was an overwhelming if not almost ineffable experience. The prophetic experience is one thing; the prophetic expression or explanation of the experience is another, and when it involves visions the prophet must use and often expand his own vocabulary to describe what happened. Only when a prophet has an overwhelming ecstatic experience that involves involuntary speech can we talk about mechanical communication. In these cases, inspiration does seem to lead to a somewhat mechanical transfer of God's exact words., but even when a verbatim transfer of God's words is required, it usually is not a case of mechanical dictation. Let us consider one example, the story of Jeremiah's call to be a prophet.

Jeremiah 1:4-10 recounts how the "word of the Lord" came to Jeremiah. But notice right away that Jeremiah is not experiencing ecstasy; he is having a conversation with God. When God tells him that he is appointed to be a prophet, Jeremiah laments, "Ah sovereign Lord . . . I do not know how to speak; I am only a child." To this God rejoins, "Do not say, 'I am only a child.' You must go to everyone I send you to and say whatever I command you." Jeremiah then adds: "Then God reached out his hand and touched my mouth and said to me, 'Now I have put my words in your mouth.'" Notice that this exchange happens in the context of a personal relationship, and while Jeremiah has his marching orders and must relay exactly what God tells him to say, God has not taken away his faculties or overridden them. Rather God has enabled Jeremiah to have a gift of speech so he can clearly and accurately convey God's word. This story does not portray mechanical dictation, but rather divine enablement in the context of a personal relationship. Let there be no doubt: the text also makes very clear that God has enabled and inspired Jeremiah to speak God's word, not merely Jeremiah's interpretation of God's word. Jeremiah is not portrayed here as a mere witness to God's revelation. He is depicted as conveying God's revelation to an audience that does not have the prophet's unique direct access to the God-whispered words. Jeremiah would likely have agreed with what 2 Peter 1:20-21 says.

At this juncture we are helped by the balanced treatments of the issue of the inspiration of the Scriptures by both Howard Marshall and Paul Achtemeier. Marshall sums things up well: "The weakness of the liberal view is that it views the Bible too much in terms of human religious genius and progressive discovery of truth . . . and ignores the elements of its inspiration and authority which are rightly stressed by conservative scholars. The weakness of the conservative view is that it sees the Bible too one-sidedly as a book produced directly by the Spirit of God and ignores the elements of human composition . . . in the Bible."[5] I agree with both sides of this critique; we do not know what inspiration looks like until we actually examine the texts and their problems and promise. What we can agree upon at this juncture is that there are claims in the Bible that both individuals and texts are inspired, and that when an individual is inspired he or she is inspired to speak God's word in the words of human beings, which sometimes involves a verbatim transfer of an oracle heard, and sometimes involves more of a human component. Sometimes it can even involve God giving a person a miraculous (and presumably temporary) ability to speak in a foreign language that they have never spoken before, as we see in Acts 2:4-12.

What we have also seen at this juncture is that the theories of mechanical communication or even mechanical dictation of inspiration do not suit the majority of biblical texts. In only a few cases do we hear of God overwhelming or taking over the control center of a person's being and speaking through them. Rather, the prophet must consciously convey God's word, which he has seen or heard. The impression left, especially when we are dealing with visionary prophecy, is that the prophet must make some decisions as to how to describe what he or she has seen. The prophetic *experience* of inspiration is one thing. The prophetic *expression* is yet another, and can involve verbatim repetition, but the prophetic *corpus of writings* is yet a third thing, as it involves the writing down of some or all of what has been seen or heard. Inspiration as a theory, to have meaning and do justice to texts like 2 Timothy 3:16, must refer not only to what has happened to the recipient of divine revelation (he or she is inspired), nor only to the oral proclamation of God's word, but also to the inscripturation or writing down of the revelations as well. The written word is God breathed as well as the oral word, according to the author of 2 Timothy 3:16. Revelatory experience, revelatory expression, and revelatory writings are all involved in this process.

"LET GOD BE TRUE, AND ALL THE WORLD A LIAR"

A variety of theories address the relationship of "the Word of God" to the Bible, and most of these theories appear to have been suggested because of the book's problem passages. For example, one theory holds that the Bible "contains the word of God." This theory would allow a person to distinguish some divine passages from the nondivine ones. The problem with this approach is that the interpreter becomes the final authority about what is and isn't divine in the Bible, not the Bible itself.

Another theory is that the Bible "becomes the word of God" when the reader encounters it. There is some truth to this dynamic and experiential approach, if one is talking about when God's word becomes a word on target for this or that particular hearer or reader. But once again, a subjective or reader-oriented element of this sort of approach seems to suggest that if the Bible doesn't do it for you, then it is not the word of God for you. This theory ignores the fact that God, and

God's word, can make an objective claim on human beings without our recognizing it or responding to it.

Perhaps an analogy will help. A person is driving along in England and is pulled over by the police for driving on the wrong side of the road. The person protests that they just came out of the Chunnel from France and they did not realize that left-hand drive was the rule in the United Kingdom. They may well have been ignorant of this fact, but the law does not cease to be the law for them just because they are not cognizant or responding to it. Ignorance is no excuse.

Similarly, the Bible as God's word is making not only a truth claim but an objective claim on human beings in general, whether they are aware of it or respond to it or not. Theories about the Bible that try to finesse or diminish the object quality of the claim made in 2 Timothy 3:16 do not help us all that much. As Johannes Bengel suggested, we do not stand over the word of God. Rather it makes a claim on us—hence, his famous slogan, "Apply the whole of yourself to the text; apply the whole of the text to yourself." Claims that the Bible contains or becomes the word of God are far from the claim made in 2 Timothy 3:16 that every Scripture is God-breathed, and therefore, because of *the very character of the document itself that it is truthful as God is truthful*, the Bible is the Word of God written.

Yet another theory is that the Bible involves or contains witnesses to revelation, witnesses to the word of God, and witnesses to the truth, but not revelation or the word of God itself. It is as if the writers were saying, "We have seen his glory," but they don't see their own reflections about that event as themselves glorious or solid gold or revelation. As popular as this view may be in some circles, texts like 2 Timothy 3:16 and others make clear that the NT authors would not agree that the words in the Bible are merely pointers to a revelation that took place elsewhere or a word of God that somehow did not get written down. They think that the written text of the Bible is God-breathed and so itself can be called "word of God" and a revelation.

I doubt that Paul, Luke, or whoever wrote 2 Timothy was unaware of the problems and interpretive issues involved in various passages of the OT, which makes the claim in 2 Timothy 3:16 more audacious, as if the writer were saying "The Bible is the inspired word of God in every passage, despite its warts, wrinkles, and problems." Surely such a keen and knowledgeable interpreter of the OT as the author of the Pastorals had to struggle with some of its texts.

For example, when the psalmist says, "Blessed are those who dash the heads of the Babylonian babies on the rocks" (Ps 137:9), surely ancient readers of the text pondered the question of how this comports with the idea of a God who loves all of humankind and is especially concerned for the weak, the vulnerable, and the young (cf., e.g., John 3:16). Could that psalm verse be a word of God not in the sense that it reveals the character of God, but in this case because it truly and truthfully reveals what was in the heart of the psalmist and what he was praying for?

Could calling something the word of God simply mean calling it a true revelation about some subject, whether in some cases it is telling the truth about God, in others about the fallen human heart, in still others about history, in still others about ethics, and so on? Perhaps part of the problem is that moderns seem to assume that when you call something "the word of God," then one assumes in every passage it reflects God's character and will, rather than simply being a true revelation about some subject that God wanted us to know about, including our fallible selves.

Maybe we have been thinking about Scripture all wrong and asking it the wrong questions. Maybe we should not have been asking how does a text like Psalm 137:9 comport with the character and will of God, when we should have been asking in what sense, and in regard to what subject, is this text telling the truth? Maybe the Bible is meant to be as much a revelation of human character as of divine character, and of how the two do and should interact. Maybe we should see God's breath or inspiration as a sort of truth serum that prompts the human speaker or writer to tell the truth about some subject.

If this is the character of inspiration and the resulting word of God written, then perhaps the most essential question to ask of any biblical text is, what truth is it trying to teach us or address? There is a difference between what Scripture teaches and what it touches. For example, what do we do when the Bible reports a lie—for example when Isaac, out of fear, tries to pass off his wife as his sister (Gen 26:7)? Obviously this verse is not the word of God in the sense that it is telling God's truth about Isaac's wife, but we could indeed say that it gives us a true or accurate report of the lie that Isaac spoke. Again the primary issue seems to be, what sort of truth is this text trying to tell us? Asking the text the right sort of questions, and avoiding asking the wrong ones, is a key not only to understanding the Bible as a written expression of God's word, but it also prevents us from creating more troubles in interpretation than are necessary. In oracles, which are one form of truth telling, we can expect the will and character of God to be most clearly reflected. Prayers and songs that come from the human heart may well tell us the truth about ourselves rather than about God's character. And narratives can reveal both of these sorts of truths, and others. Much depends on the genre of literature, and the genre affects how the truth is being told and in some cases what truth is being told. But one additional text—2 Peter 1:19-21—can really help us understand the biblical concept of inspiration and its relationship to truth.

PROPHETABLE AND INSPIRED SPEECH: 2 PETER 1:19-21

To begin with, 2 Peter 1:19 should be seen as an allusion to the prophetic word in Psalm 2. Peter is probably not suggesting here that it has greater certainty than his own personal experience, but that the prophetic word has very great certainty and is something on which one can firmly rely. The prophetic word then is seen here as a second witness to the truth of the Parousia's historicity. The debate has been as to whether Peter is saying that Scripture confirms his experience or that the apostolic witness fulfills and thus authenticates Scripture. But, the translation "made more sure" for *Bebaioteron* with *exomen* is doubtful. It is not the Scripture that needs to be made more sure.

Nor is there likely a comparison between the value of prophecy vis-à-vis the value of personal experience. The point rather seems to be that Peter is introducing a second and objective witness here that people can check out for themselves. The drift of the argument seems to be, "If you do not believe me, check out the OT messianic prophecies, here especially Psalm 2:9. The prophetic word has unquestionable clarity and certainty. You can rely on it." Verse 19b indicates that the audience must heed this word, for it is their only light in an otherwise dark and murky world; it can guide them through the darkness as nothing else can. Verse 19c must be seen as a reference to the Parousia, which causes no problems if the author had said only "when the day dawns." Notice he says these prophetic words, "Guide us until then." There is a time-conditioned element even in Scripture. To be sure, it is eternal truth, but only applicable in and to situations in time, and when time expires we will no longer need a guidebook to walk through the dark. Believers will have in fact the day star in their very hearts to illumine them (cf. 1 Cor 13:8-13; prophecy and knowledge cease, and the general thought of Jer 31 about God's word written on the heart comes true). *Phôsphoros* means literally "light bearer" and may be a reference to Venus, the day star, which accompanies dawn. However, we should not puzzle for long about it because Numbers 24:17 (LXX) seems to be in the background here—"a star shall rise out of Jacob," and the reference is to the Messiah. The point then is that Christ will illumine the believer not just from the outside in, but from the inside out on the day of Parousia, because his day of revelation will be their day of transformation. Hence the phrase "in your hearts" is natural and understandable. It is not a reference to believers being currently and slowly illuminated by God's presence or word.

Verses 20-21 express why we may so firmly rely on OT prophecy, or why it has such great certainty. Peter says that, above all, his audience ought to know the truth about these things. Verse 21 gives the reason for verse 20, and we will tackle it first. Biblical prophecy was never brought about by the will of a human being, but rather humans borne (carried) along by the Holy Spirit, spoken from God. We find in these words a definition of inspiration and how the prophetic Scriptures came to be.

First, the author insists that true prophecy never is a purely human product that results from mere human will. The *ou* ("not") in verse 21a contrasts with verse 21b's *alla* ("but"). Instead these persons were borne along, carried, and compelled by the Holy Spirit so that they spoke not merely human words but "from God." The key verb here, *pherō*, can be used of the wind moving something along or driving it in a certain direction, or it can be used figuratively of God's Spirit moving or motivating human beings (cf. Job 17:1 LXX). The phrases here suggest that God is the primary author of prophetic Scripture. These prophets, though they spoke in their own words, spoke from God. What do "carried along," "borne along," "impelled," and "moved" by the Holy Spirit mean? We should probably not see any mechanical dictation theory. These terms are intended to indicate that the human authors were guided, directed, and motivated by the Holy Spirit so that what they said was not their own creation or imaginings but the very word of God—the truth. Thus, the Spirit is the motivator or originator, the guide or guard of the words of the human author so that what the author says can be said to be spoken from God. Michael Green adds:

> It is interesting that in this, perhaps the fullest and most explicit biblical reference to the inspiration of its authors, no interest should be displayed in the psychology of inspiration. The author is not concerned with what they felt like, or how much they understood, but simply with the fact that they were the bearers of God's message. The relative parts played by the human and the divine authors are not mentioned, but only the fact of their cooperation. He uses a fascinating maritime metaphor in verse 21. . . . The prophets raised their sails, so to speak (they were obedient and receptive), and the Holy Spirit filled them and carried their craft along in the direction He wished. Men spoke: God spoke. Any proper doctrine of Scripture will not neglect either part of this truth. Certainly those who

are convinced of God's ultimate authorship of Scripture will take every pain to discover the background, life situation, limitations, education and so forth of the human agent who cooperated with God in its production. For revelation was not a matter of passive reception: it meant active cooperation. The fact of God's inspiration did not mean a supercession of the normal mental functionings of the human author. The Holy Spirit did not use instruments; He used men. God's way is ever one of truth through personality, as was perfectly demonstrated at the incarnation. Moreover, He did not use any men, but holy men, those who were dedicated and pledged to His service. And even with such men, He did no violence to their personalities, but co-operated with them while revealing Himself through them. "He says they were *moved*, not because they were out of their minds (as the heathen imagine *enthousiasmos* in their prophets), but because they dared nothing by themselves but only in obedience to the guidance of the Spirit, who held sway over their lips as in his own temple" (Calvin).[6]

So then, we should not see here an overwhelming of human nature. It is too obvious that God used human beings and their own character and characteristics to produce Scripture. Thus, biblical inspiration for the most part is to be distinguished from pagan ecstatic utterance in which the human being is a purely passive vessel through which "the god" speaks. What Peter says comports with what the OT prophets themselves say (cf. Jer 14:13; 23:16; 18:21-22, 26; Ezek 13:3). A prophet speaks on God's initiative, not his own (Amos 3:8; Jer 20:9), and it is God's word the prophet proclaims in his or her own words.

Now we must ask what verse 20 means. *Idias* can mean either one's own or the prophet's own. *Epiluseōs* usually means explanation or interpretation.[7] The question then is, do we read "no prophecy is a matter of one's own interpretation" or "no prophecy arises from the prophet's own interpretation"? Either one of these is possible. Richard Bauckham argues for the second view saying:

This conforms to a widely accepted view of the nature of prophecy, according to which the prophet is given a sign (e.g. Amos 7:1; Jer. 1:11, 13), a dream (e.g. Zech. 1:8; Dan. 7:2) or a vision (e.g. Dan. 8:1), and then its interpretation. In true prophecy this interpretation is not the prophet's own explanation of his vision, but an inspired, God-given interpretation. Thus, it is possible that 2 Pet. 1:20 counters a view which held that the prophets may have received visions, but that their prophecies, found in the OT, are only their own interpretation of the visions, mere human guesswork. This was one way of denying the divine origin of scriptural prophecy.[8]

Against this, however, must be that verses 20-21 then come to mean the same thing said in two ways—that is, it is not prophetic interpretation because it is God's Spirit that caused it. This seems somewhat tautological, whereas we would expect verse 21 to give us a real reason that it is not this sort of interpretation. More likely then, it is saying, "It is not a matter of one's own interpretation, because it derives from God and is objective truth, not subjective opinion."

J. B. Mayor says:

> When St. Peter says that "it was revealed to them that not unto themselves but unto us they did minister the things now reported unto us" he does not surely mean to deny that they ministered to their own generation also, although not exclusively nor in the highest degree. The prophets never cast themselves as it were into the midst of the ocean of futurity; their view reaches over the ocean, their hearts it may be are set on the shore beyond it, but their feet are on their own land, their eyes look upon the objects of their own land; there is the first occasion of their hopes, and there lie their duties. They are prophets in both senses of the term, preachers of righteousness to their own generation, as well as foretellers of blessing for generations yet to come.[9]

Perhaps then Peter is refuting an argument of his opponents which said, "So he says there is going to be a Parousia and that the OT says so. Well, that's just his interpretation of the matter." J. N. D. Kelly says:

> Much the most natural meaning, and the one which suits the context best as well as agreeing with the lexical evidence for *epilusis*, is the one implied by the printed translation (so too RV; RSV; NEB; etc.) viz. that no individual is entitled to interpret prophecy, or Scripture generally, according to his personal whim. It is precisely this, as we shall later see (iii.16), that the troublemakers are guilty of, and it leads in the writer's view to disaster. But if one's own interpretation is excluded, what is the approved alternative with which "Peter" contrasts it? The next verse makes this clear: it is the interpretation intended by the Holy Spirit, whose inspiration lies behind prophecy.[10]

Peter has thus left us on the high ground here—with the witness of Scripture. Both Scripture and apostolic experience and testimony are on the side of the teaching in this discourse. It is interesting that Paul, in texts like Galatians 3 and 1 Corinthians 11 also appeals to experience first, and then to Scripture to support his argument. Also, Peter has stressed that when it comes to interpreting Scripture, it is not just a matter of my opinion against your opinion. The Holy Spirit is viewed as the "hermeneut" who interprets the words in and for the prophet. Teachings that were at variance with apostolic teaching and interpretation of Scripture were to be rejected. Needless to say, this implies a very high view of the word of God spoken and written.

TOM WRIGHT'S LAST WORD

Recently there has been an interesting and fresh attempt to shift or deflect this kind of discussion about the inspiration or authority of God's Word to a "higher court" by suggesting that the real issue is the authority and character of God who is speaking in and through the

Bible. We find this suggestion in Bishop N. T. Wright's most recent book *The Last Word.*

Wright begins his study by properly complaining that all too often when we discuss the Scriptures, and whether and in what sense they can be called the word of God, it turns into a dialogue of the deaf. We don't really listen to the text. Moreover, we don't really listen to each other, especially when we disagree on something fundamental, and the end result is that nothing much is accomplished.[11] The dialogue is unfortunately not helped by books like John Webster's *Holy Scripture,*[12] where the Bible itself and in particular its content are not engaged. As Wright rightly complains, "One would never have known, from reading this book, anything at all about what the Bible contains," a very odd thing given that Webster is arguing the Bible itself is the central source for all Christian thought, except apparently for dogmatic and philosophical thoughts about the character and nature of the Scriptures themselves! As the old saying goes, "these things ought not to be."[13]

Wright seeks to help us move the discussion of the nature and authority of Scripture forward by suggesting that the phrase "the authority of Scripture" is actually shorthand for God's and Christ's and the Spirit's authority exercised through Scripture. In other words, Wright wants to stress that the word of God written at most has a mediated or derived authority. He then stresses that most of the Bible's content, and all of it when it was put together as a canonical collection of books, can be best described as story—indeed the grand story of creation, fall, and various acts of redemption or salvation.

So Wright then wishes to press the question, how can a story be authoritative? The commandments in the Bible, the songs, the hymns, the proverbs, and the oracles are all to be seen as functioning within the larger hermeneutical category of story, and furthermore a story that continues to develop over a long period of time. For example, the function of the Ten Commandments in Moses' day and under the Mosaic covenant might differ considerably from the way some of those commandments functioned in a later part of the story, after the Savior has come. One of the things that most concerns Wright is that the story be heard as a whole, and that the parts be judged in relationship to the design, trajectory, climax, and intended ends of the whole story. He rightly protests the chopping up of the text into little snippets on the way to making the text say something else than what it appears to be saying on the whole. Again, Wright wishes to insist that even the grand narrative of Scripture—Scripture as a whole from Genesis to Revelation—must be set in the larger context of the authority of God.

Part of what Wright means by all this is that we need to ask what part Scripture plays in God's enacting of his works of creation and redemption. Of course, a simple, if simplistic, answer would be that God uses the Bible to change lives, not only of individuals but also of communities and whole cultures. In this regard we are thinking primarily of the word proclaimed orally and its effect. The word of God is not just a repository of true information or, as Wright puts it, even just "an accurate running commentary upon the work of God in salvation and new creation,"[14] but something that is itself a change agent. We saw in the last chapter the passage in Hebrews about the word of God, in this case in its oral form, penetrating and exegeting the soul of the listener. It is seen as a living thing.

Wright then mainly wants to talk about the function and purpose of Scripture as a change agent, an instrument of transformation. I applaud this as the correct larger framework in which the word of God both oral and written should be seen, and one could draw fruitful analogies again between Jesus as the Word of God incarnate, whose mission was to come and be the savior, and the role of the word of God orally proclaimed and written, which has as its function transforming and saving human lives. However, and it is a big however, this finesses and in effect dodges the truth question, or at least lays it aside for another day.

It is not all that helpful to tell us that the Bible is the way God exercises God's authority among human beings to bring them to a saving knowledge of Jesus Christ if we don't first ask the question, but are all these claims true? Is it true that God speaks in and through the Bible? Is it true that the word of God is a genuine revelation of God's mind, nature, and character, as well as the character of human beings? Is it true that Jesus died and rose again for our sins and salvation? To be like Pilate, shrugging our shoulders and querying "What is truth?" in a cynical way, is no more helpful than ignoring the fact that the Bible has no divine authority at all unless it is in some sense a truthful revelation from God. One might even ask, why would God use the Bible at all to exercise authority or transform people if God did not see it as a suitable, helpful, faithful, truthful instrument? Western culture is suffering from enough truth decay as it is—particularly when it comes to matters of theology, spirituality, and religion—for us not to address the issue of truth when discussing the inspiration and authority of the Bible, or more broadly of the word of God oral, written, and incarnate.

Bishop Wright understands this problem. His little book *The Last Word*, an ironic title if there ever was one, was not in any way intended to be the last word on God's word. It was more a brief exercise to help us think through what our starting point and larger framework for discussion ought to be. Fair enough. But a discussion of truth claims might have served us better than a review of the history of how the Bible was used and interpreted through the centuries, though that is a quite useful exercise to help us understand how we arrived where we are in terms of our views of the Scripture. It is accordingly left to this study to deal with this large issue, and so a couple of chapters hence we turn to the question about the kind of literature we are actually dealing with in the New Testament. As we shall see, truth telling becomes something of an art form, and if one doesn't recognize the genre, one will certainly be asking the wrong questions of the right documents. First, however, we attend to Peter Enns's provocative suggestion about the incarnational analogy.

Here I will simply add what Isaiah 40:8 says: "the grass withers, the flower fades, but the Word of God stands forever." In other words, God's word is indeed so God-breathed that it has no expiration date! It never ceases to be God's word, it never ceases to be true, it never ceases to be relevant; as Isaiah 55:11 puts it, God's word never ceases to accomplish what it intends, for "my Word which goes out from my mouth, . . . will not return to me empty." If this is supposed to be the character and caliber of God's word, then the issue of the nature of its truth claims is an urgent question indeed, especially in an age when so many believe and indeed many openly claim that the Bible is riddled with errors and cannot be trusted.

Chapter 3

THE ENDS OF ENNS: THE DANGERS OF AN ANALOGY

*The search for truth and the advance of human knowledge are inseparable:
comprehension and civilization are one.*

                                                                    —Rodney Stark

*It has become quite fashionable today . . . to assume that the major obstacle
in reclaiming the Bible for the church is "the historical-critical method" of
biblical study. [But] since all Christians, including especially preachers and
theologians, must be subject to the control of the written, canonical text,
historical biblical criticism . . . becomes an indispensable tool. . . . this critical task remains foundational for the entire theological enterprise since the
treasure that is ours in Scripture is contained "in earthen vessels" (2 Cor.
4.7, RSV) that are shaped and transmitted by ancient Israel and the first-
century church.*

                                                                —Karl P. Donfried

Sometimes analogies can be stretched too far. For example, the author
of Hebrews is sometimes quoted as saying that Jesus was like us in

all respects, save without sin. Well, in the first place that's not what Hebrews says or suggests. The text in question, Hebrews 4:15, actually reads, "He was tempted in every way like us, save without sin." That is a different matter. There are ever so many ways that Jesus was not like us. For example, he had an unfallen human nature and also a divine nature. In his divine identity he preexisted all of creation. We could go on. But my point is that it is always a dodgy and even dangerous thing to draw analogies with a unique being like the Son of God, all the more if the analogy is between a thing, namely the Bible, and a person, namely the Son of God.

THE INCARNATIONAL PRINCIPLE

The incarnational principle is the rubric that Peter Enns uses to explain the character and nature of the Bible.[1] In fact he is willing to put it this way: "The long-standing *identification* between Christ the word and Scripture the word is central to how I think through the issues raised in this book. How does Scripture's full humanity and full divinity affect what we should expect from Scripture?"[2] "Identification" is much too strong a word here; "analogy" would be better. Furthermore, books do not have either humanity or divinity. We can talk about the books of the Bible being divinely inspired but not about their divinity, or for that matter about their humanity. All of the Son of God is not "fully human"; only his human nature is. Nor is all the Son of God fully divine; only his divine nature is. According to the classical Chalcedonian formulation, the two natures should not be fused or confused. This is very different from the nature of the Bible.

If I understand 2 Timothy 3:16 correctly, the whole Bible is suffused with divine inspiration, while also the whole thing is composed of human words. Some of it is more directly the word of God (e.g., the oracles), some of it more indirectly, but it is always the word of God in human words whether it involves oracles where God speaks directly or some more indirect means of communication.

What Enns wants to argue most vociferously about, however, is the "humanness" of Scripture. Put another way, he wants to insist on the historical givenness of Scripture—that it is written in a particular language in a particular cultural setting, reflecting particular cultural customs and conventions and ways of thinking in order to be a word on target for the original intended audiences. "The Bible, at every turn, shows how 'connected' it is to its own world [which] is a necessary consequence of God incarnating himself. . . . It is essential to the very nature of revelation that the Bible is not unique to its environment. The human dimension of Scripture is essential to its being Scripture."[3] Missing entirely is any discussion about how this human givenness of Scripture may or may not affect the truth claims of the book. Are we being told that incarnation requires a full participation in wide-ranging human ignorance, errors of various sorts, misjudgments, misrepresentations, mishandling of scriptural texts, and the like?

"To err is human," as Alexander Pope reminded us, but do we need to turn that equation around and say "To be human, one must err"? If one says that, one has a rather large theological problem, as we shall see. To say that incarnation involves certain limitations of time and space manifested in historical particularity is one thing. It is quite another to suggest that incarnation involves participating in human fallenness, including in its fallen understanding of things. Revelation or even revelation incarnate does not in the first instance *mean* historical givenness, though Enns puts it that way. Revelation means God's truth expressed in particular ways that humans can understand.

But let us allow Enns to flesh out what he wants to claim. In his discussion of "myth," particularly in regard to ancient Near East parallels to the creation and flood stories in Genesis, Enns settles for a definition of myth as follows: "It is an ancient, premodern, prescientific way of addressing questions of ultimate origins and meaning in the form of stories: Who are we? Where do we come from?"[4] This definition is problematic. In the first place, it is not what the term *mythos* means in the NT (cf., e.g., 1 Tim 4:4), where it is a pejorative term referring to something that is not true. In the second place, even where the term "myth" was used in a positive way in antiquity, it meant something like a story about a god or the supernatural. On this definition, lots of the Bible is myth as it recounts the mighty salvific acts of God, but that tells us nothing about whether it records historical events or not, unless you believe that there can't be any kind of supernatural incursion into the realm of the natural. Isn't it ironic that Enns spends so much time in his study arguing for the historical givenness of these ancient texts, but he wants to define terms in a wholly modern way that the biblical audience would not recognize or grant? What's wrong with this picture?

Yet Enns, rightly in my judgment, asks, should the Bible be judged on the basis of modern standards of historical inquiry and scientific precision? Surely the answer is no. But these texts *should* be judged on the basis of ancient standards of historical inquiry and truth telling. Let us suppose the author of Genesis is making historical claims of an ancient nature. They are more general and less precise than we perhaps would want to make today, but nonetheless, historical claims are being made. Taking the nature of ancient historiography into account, we must still assess the resulting historical truth claims. Is the author of Genesis claiming there was a historical Noah and a historical flood of great magnitude during his era? Surely the answer to this question is yes, and even more tellingly NT writers—and Jesus—also thought the answer to this question was yes (cf. Matt 24:37-39; 1 Pet 3:20). Revelation, as it turns out, doesn't just mean incarnational speech. It means truth telling in incarnational speech.

A second point that Enns wants to make is that the situatedness of the biblical record should not pose a problem for the definition of revelation. Enns is right that something does not need to be unique to be true, or to be a divine revelation. Special revelation could in part be based on general revelation, for all truth is God's truth. For example, that some of the proverbs in Proverbs actually are revamped versions of Egyptian proverbs is not a problem. This would only be a problem if we were suggesting that revelation can only come to a biblical author directly from God, and never through human sources of information. But why should we have thought this about a historical religion for which history, archaeology, and the like are crucial and indeed are the means and places where God has chosen to reveal the truth? A biblical statement does not need to be unique to be true. The same can be said about various ancient stories of the flood. Instead of trying to play source criticism with this material and argue about which is the chicken and which the egg, it would be wiser to recognize that all these very ancient stories are reflections on even earlier, very ancient events—namely a large flood in the ancient Near East.

But what about the issue of scientific claims? Enns confidently says, "We do not protect the Bible or render it more believable to modern people by trying to demonstrate that it is consistent with modern science,"[5] which is precisely what creationists have tried to do, over and over again, all the while redefining scientific timetables and terms. Here Enns could have been helped by recognizing the difference between what Scripture teaches and what it touches. In my view, the biblical authors do presuppose some things about the rising of the sun and the like. But just as clearly the Bible is not a scientific textbook, nor do I think it is trying to teach us about such matters any more than Paul in 1 Corinthians 15 is trying to instruct us about the practice of baptism for the dead. The creationists are mistaken to read Genesis in some of the ways they do, such as trying to judge the age of the earth. This is not merely unnecessary, it is obscurantism, ignoring the empirical evidence we do have. The author(s) of Genesis are not trying to inform us about this matter, despite Bishop Ushaw's famous chronology (taking us back to a creation that happened only six thousand years ago) based on the genealogies of this book. But what would Enns says about a historical Adam, a historical fall, and the like? Conveniently, he does not tell us. The real issue in my judgment is not scientific claims. The real issue is historical claims, and they are being made in abundance in Genesis and elsewhere in the OT and NT.

If all that Enns wanted to claim is that God enters our world and speaks in ways that the immediate audience of some revelation can (usually) understand, that would be one thing. The question, however, is whether "accommodation" also includes adopting errant ways of speaking. Again, if all that Enns wanted to claim is that all history writing is interpretive, this would be unobjectionable. But in fact, in the process of recognizing diversity (say between parallel accounts in 1-2 Samuel and 1-2 Chronicles), the question then becomes when does diversity become distortion or even contradiction? Or are we asking the wrong question if both sets of texts are interpretive, and at the historical level they are only intended to give us a general impression of the historical facts?

Enns is so busy demonstrating the diversity that he doesn't engage these kinds of questions. Sometimes, sadly, he even sounds like those who would simply baptize diversity and call it inherently good without raising the question of its relationship to unity. In fact, Enns at points pleads agnosticism. Listen to what he says: "So what did Nathan *actually* say [to David]? What 2 Samuel reports? What 1 Chronicles reports? Neither? A little of both? The answer is I don't know, and neither does anyone else. In fact I am beginning to suspect that this is not the primary question the Bible is set up to answer."[6] But even if it was a secondary question the Bible was set up to answer, it would still have to be assessed historically. What makes Enns's whole discussion so odd is that on the one hand he wants to argue for the historically conditioned nature of the whole Bible, yet on the other hand he wants to urge it isn't (or isn't mainly) set up to answer historical questions.

Perhaps he should have remembered the principle of subsequence. First and Second Samuel was written long before 1-2 Chronicles, and the latter text presupposes that the former is in play and widely known, which is precisely what allows the Chronicler to take some liberties in order to make his own theological and ethical points. He assumes a preexisting fixed text. The same applies to the use of the OT in the NT, on which Enns spends the most time in his book. A homiletical use of the OT presupposes that the text being applied is already known to many, including probably at least some in the audience. As such there is some freedom with which the text can be handled. It can be paraphrased, echoed, rephrased, and rearranged according to the rules for preaching and teaching in that era. The homiletical use need not look the same as detailed contextual exegesis of a text, especially when the preacher is reading these texts through christological glasses and for Christian purposes. What one cannot deduce from this sort of usage is that either the author isn't much concerned with general historical accuracy or with properly quoting preexisting sacred texts. That would be like accusing Eugene Peterson of bad translation in his well-received creative and rather interpretive paraphrase *The Message*. This approach ignores the purpose and character of the project, which always assumes there are more literal translations out there that one can compare.

E PLURIBUS UNUM?

Enns has a particular ax to grind with various sorts of harmonizing of the text, some of which is justified and some not. He is right, on the one hand, to say that one must be cautious about blending a bunch of texts together, such as proverbs in Proverbs, in order to generate a unified teaching on wealth.[7] He is equally right when he points out that Ecclesiastes has as one of its purposes to point out that life is full of contradictions, and so it is a true word about the vicissitudes of life. The "Bible reflects diversity because the human drama in which God participates is likewise diverse." He then adds, "But note that diversity in no way implies chaos and error."[8] This reassurance, while nice, is without substance. If we grant that we have diversity in the biblical text, which is true, then it is not sufficient either to just recognize or celebrate it. We must ask what sort of diversity we are encountering. And since this is God's word, we must ask the relationship of that diversity to the presumed unity of God's word as well. In particular we must ask what sort of truth claims such diverse literature is making. If we simply baptize the diversity and call it good, and yet we believe that all Scripture is God-breathed, then we must ask quite seriously, in what way can these things be true? How is this consistent not merely with the character of human beings and the human drama, but with the character of a truth-telling God and divine revelation?

Let us take, for instance, the example Enns cites of the differences in the fourth commandment between what we find in Exodus 20:8-10 and Deuteronomy 5:12-15. In particular, if we read these texts together, we note that the motives for the commandment in each of these texts differ. In Exodus the motive is rest on the seventh day, while in Deuteronomy there is concern to make sure Israelite servants get some rest just as their masters do. Enns then concludes, "God seems to be perfectly willing to allow his law to be adjusted over time."[9] Exactly so, but this adjustment is ostensibly one made by God, not caused by variant human readings or versions of the same commandment. Truth is contextualized in each case, without losing touch with the essence of the commandment. And here precisely is the point: unity of commandment but diversity of its application, motivation, and implications. The relationship of unity and diversity, of the one and the many, must be asked and answered, which Enns does not do. Thus, while it is right to insist "there is in the Bible a built-in dynamic quality that invites the faithful reader to consider the *situation* into which the Bible is applied,"[10] at the same time we cannot always know or accurately reconstruct the historical and social context. It is a moving target, whereas the text at least is a fixed one. Put another way, the relatively less-known context should not be taken as more clear and certain than the relatively more well-known text itself.

If all one really means to say is that "the Old Testament is not a flat book where all parts agree on a superficial level," but one then hastens to reassure that "there is coherence between the parts, but that coherence transcends the level of simple statements or propositions,"[11] then one has a duty to show wherein that coherence lies, or at least to provide some telling examples. To say that all this is a part of the ongoing saga of Israel and salvation history that climaxes in the story of Christ is not enough, nor is it enough to say that the general narrative arc is true. Particular truth claims about God, about human beings, and about their interrelationships among other subjects are being made along the way. One needs to ask what we should make of them and wherein lies the consistency, coherency, and unity of such material. It's not enough, even for evangelicals, to say that we should not read the text in a flat or literalistic way. This is true, but by now it is a well-known and shopworn truth.

Let's take an illustration of how Enns fails to pass the test of asking how a particular portion of the Bible can be the truthful word of God. In his discussion of the psalms, Enns rightly points to various texts that speak of Yahweh using the language of henotheism—the idea that there is a highest or most supreme God in the pantheon of deities. So, for example, we hear in Psalm 86:8, "Among the gods, there is none like you, O Lord" (cf. Pss 95:3; 96:4; 97:9; 135:5; 136:2). Is the author affirming or teaching henotheism rather than classic monotheism? Notice that the psalm texts in question are indeed making positive theological assertions about Yahweh. Enns then warns us, lest "we succumb to the temptation to interpret these psalms in a way that is compatible with what we 'know' to be true. Rather we must let all of Scripture have its say and be willing to compose as diverse a portrait of God as the biblical data demand."[12]

I suppose that Enns would be prepared to make the same remark about what Paul says in 1 Corinthians 8:5-6: "For even if there are so-called gods, whether in heaven or on earth (as indeed there are many 'gods' and many 'lords') yet for us there is but one God, the Father . . . and there is but one Lord, Jesus Christ." The problem is that in 1 Corinthians 8:5 Paul has in fact recited the principle that "there is no God but One." He is in fact revisiting and rewriting the Shema in this text, engaging in a christological reformulation of the credo. The net result of looking at this material in context shows that he is a convinced monotheist who thinks these other so-called gods, are not nothings; rather they are demons! This brings us back to the psalm texts. If we read the psalms just in the larger context of these particular psalms in one of the latter books of the Psalter, what do we learn? That the author(s) and the final editor are absolutely not affirming henotheism. They are saying that the one true God is greater than all the other pretenders and contenders, the so-called gods, or as we might call them the powers and principalities out there. Furthermore, the psalmist is speaking poetically and figuratively and perhaps even apologetically since some of these are exilic psalms written in a polytheistic setting.

The problem with Enns's analysis is it is too atomistic. So badly does he want each text to be allowed to have its own say, which in itself is a good instinct, that he fails to allow the larger literary and theological context, even just of the psalms, or even just this particular set of psalms, to help him recognize that using the notion of henotheism is not one of the creative ways the psalmist is revealing the truth about a complex God. The psalmist just means that the one true God puts all other so-called gods in the shade. It is like suggesting that we should not step back and look at the larger canvas of the portrait of God in the psalms and then evaluate how we should analyze the particulars of this corner of the portrait found in Psalms 95–136. But in fact, when the Psalter was edited and put together, someone did precisely that, arranging the materials according to certain categories, themes, and theological motifs. Should we not follow the cues of the original compiler of the psalms in these matters? Should we not think both globally and particularly about individual texts, in this case, psalms? In my view, the answer is yes. We should and must.

IS UNITY IN CHRIST THE UNITY OF THE BIBLE?

Enns then appeals to what could be called a christological unity of Scripture. There is no superficial or in some cases obvious unity to Scripture; indeed there are tensions in Scripture, which Enns says exist because God accommodates himself and his word to where we are and our condition.[13] He goes on to argue:

> The Bible is God's word in written form: Christ is God's word in
> human form. . . . The written word bears witness to the incarnate
> word, Christ. And what gives the written word its unity is not simply
> the words on the page, but the incarnate word who is more than

simply the sum of the biblical parts. He is the one through whom heaven and earth—including the Bible itself—were created, and he is the one in whom Israel's story reaches its climax. The Bible bears witness to Christ by Christ's design. He is over the Bible, beyond it separate from it, even though the Bible is *his* word and thus bears witness to him. . . . The tensions of the Old Testament should be seen within the context of the Christian Bible as a whole, where Christ—his life, death, and resurrection, and ascension—is given the focus it deserves. . . . If as Christians say, Christ is the focus of Scripture, we should allow that focus to come into play in how we understand Scripture.[14]

There are several things to commend about this statement, and several troubling aspects to it. In the first place, the OT was God's word for Israel long before it became God's word for the followers of Jesus. Indeed, one can say that God intended it this way. The books of the OT have a message, meaning, and truth quite apart from any christological use of the OT text. In fact, they still serve this function for practicing Jews today, as they should until the Lord returns. Second, there was no Christian NT when the writers of the NT spoke and wrote what they said in documents that we now call the NT. The only Bible they had was the OT, which they considered God-breathed, and they believed that the living word of God was still speaking to and through them orally in their own day. Third, the christological interpretation of the OT is, as Enns recognizes, only one of the hermeneutical moves made by the writers of NT documents. The OT has a straightforward moral use, an allegorical use, a typological use, and an ecclesiological use, and not all of these are christologically engendered or focused. Indeed, Enns himself recognizes the wide variety and creativity of the handling of the OT in the NT, but he fails to notice that these variations on a theme presume a basically stable text that serves as the baseline for all such variation.

THE USE OF THE OLD TESTAMENT
IN THE NEW TESTAMENT

Peter Enns is right that the NT writers do think that in broad strokes the OT both prepares for and bears witness to Christ. Christ is seen as the one in whom all the promises and prophecies of God—all the institutions of God's people including priest, temple, and sacrifice—find their climactic fulfillment. Thus, in the larger sense it is true to claim that the written word derives a sort of unity from the incarnate word to whom it points. This christological point, however, does not by any means allow us to gloss over the fact that the OT is also making any number of truth claims on its own and raises on its own the issue of what sort of truth, and what is the relationship of diversity and unity in the text itself.

Saying that the mere diversity in the text bears witness to the way God has chosen to reveal himself in historical particularity, however, is not enough. Not all diversity bears witness to incarnation. In particular, diversity to the point of division, distortion, self-contradiction, and various sorts of errors certainly would not bear witness to a God of truth. Revelation is about the unveiling of truth—coherent truth that has a unity to it, just as God has a unity—however many diverse ways that truth comes to be expressed.

In his detailed analysis of the way the OT is used in the NT, Enns draws three conclusions: (1) the NT writers were not engaging the OT in a effort to remain consistent with the original context and intention of the OT authors; (2) the NT writers were commenting on what the text meant; (3) the hermeneutical attitude they embodied should be embraced and followed by the church today.[15]

In regard to the first point, it is simply not possible to make this sort of sweeping statement about how the OT is used in the NT. Sometimes there is a rather clear effort at contextual exegesis, even to the point that the larger context of the OT quote is echoed or allowed to guide the NT author in his interpretation.[16] Second, it is also not the case that the NT writers were always and everywhere simply comment-

ing on what the text meant and perhaps its larger christological significance. This is often the case, but not always the case. For example, we
may assume that in Acts 8 the gist of what Philip is suggesting to the
Ethiopian eunuch is that Christ is the person referred to in Isaiah 53.
The author is trying to stress the ultimate referent of that text. In much
of the use of the ethics of the OT, both by Jesus and others (see, e.g.,
Matt 5–7), there is indeed often a focus on what the text says, and the
text is not interpreted always in some sort of christological or allegorical way. "No stealing" still means no stealing. "Honoring parents" still
means honoring parents, and so on. Simply examining the theological
use of the OT and not also the ethical and practical use of it in the NT
is a mistake.

Third, only in the broadest strokes can we follow the NT authors
in their creative and christological use of the OT.[17] The midrash/pesher
form of interpreting the OT, and the creative use of extrabiblical material and the like are not duplicatable on our part because we are not
early Jews, steeped in early Jewish methods of handling the OT. Besides,
the writers of the NT were inspired in ways and to degrees that we are
not. We should not pretend to be their equals. Even Bible scholars
today are closer to scribal interpreters of the text and proclaimers of
the text than they are to the inspired writers of the text itself. I do not
claim the ability to sense the sensus plenior of an OT text in a way that
an NT writer could do.

There may well be multiple layers of meaning in some OT texts, but
I would never have guessed that "do not muzzle the ox as it threshes
the grain" could indeed also be referred to ministers having a right to
benefit from their own hard work of ministry. Nor would I have the
audacity to turn the story of Sarah and Hagar into the sort of tour de
force, turn-things-on-its-head eschatological allegory that Paul does in
Galatians 4. I am afraid that there must be restraint in modern Christian interpretation and use of the OT for the very good reason that
we are not part of that original Jewish interpretive community that
produced the vast majority of the NT, though Luke–Acts was probably
written by a God-fearing Gentile.

AND SO?

Saying we are part of the church through all generations as though this were one continuous interpreting community is not enough. Which church, and with what hermeneutic, we would need to ask. I can talk about the fulfillment of Israel's story in the Christ story, and I can talk about Christians being children of Abraham because I have some guidance in the NT about doing so. But careful historical and contextual exegesis of the entire Bible is still the best guide, even for Christians, when it comes to learning what it says, what it means, and how we ought to use it today, lest we turn the Bible into another version of Bunyan's *Pilgrim's Progress*, or the parable of the Good Samaritan into an allegory about Christ and the church and the lost sinner, as Augustine did. This approach indeed would not be exegesis; it would be eisegesis—not merely a creative handling of the text, but a mishandling of it, reading into it things that violate the original meaning. Those who wish to handle a two-edged sword like God's living word need to be careful how they brandish the blade. Not only can one end up mutilating texts, one can end up mutilating lives as well.

If we take the study of Peter Enns as a cautionary word against ignoring or trying to explain away the diversity of the Scriptures, then he has done us a service. Taking him as offering a salutary warning against overly harmonistic ways of handling Scripture is also a fine approach. I too agree in principle that inspiration looks like what we have in the text, however diverse. If we take Enns to be reminding us that Christians should indeed see the climax of the story of God's people in Christ, then this too is helpful, and it reminds us that a christological use of the OT is a legitimate one, however carefully nuanced it needs to be.

But if we hear in Enns's book a plea to give up on trying to discern the relationship of unity and diversity in the canon, the relationship of truth to error, or a plea to become agnostic about the importance of the historical substance of the text, then I hope that we have misheard the author and would ignore such a subtext or plea. To claim that the Bible is God's word implies always and everywhere that it is making various sorts of truth claims—indeed, claims on us. And we do no service to the one who is the Way, the Truth, and the Life if we do not wrestle with the question "What is truth?" whenever we deal with the biblical text.

Chapter 4

TRUTH TELLING AS AN ART FORM

The first qualification for judging any piece of workmanship from a cork-screw to a cathedral is to know what it is—what it was intended to do and how it was meant to be used.

–C. S. Lewis

It was 1969, and the moon had become a front-burner topic because of Neil Armstrong's stroll across its dusty plains. A high school friend and I had borrowed my father's '55 Chevy (two-tone, column shift, classic) and were having a fun Saturday riding along the Blue Ridge Parkway in the mountains of North Carolina. We had all that we needed to have a big time, including a huge watermelon in the trunk. We were going to make the most of it. Unfortunately, stuff happens. We were riding along minding our own business when the clutch blew out. As the Bible says, "My countenance fell." There are no gas stations on the Blue Ridge Parkway. In fact, there are not even any signs directing you to gas stations, but we were lucky. A car came along and pushed us down an exit ramp and into a Texaco station. Once there we were stranded. We decided finally to hitchhike all the way back to High Point, where we lived. Unfortunately we forgot to take the watermelon out of the car, and it was a blazing hot July summer week. You can imagine how the car smelled a week later when we returned to the scene of the crime.

As luck would have it, we were soon picked up by a very elderly couple in an old black Plymouth. They were not very talkative at first, but then my friend Doug decided to strike up a conversation. His opening salvo was, "Well, what do you think about Neil Armstrong walking on the moon?" The man driving the car immediately replied, "Well, that's all fake. It's a Hollywood trick trying to make us believe the world is round and the moon revolves around it." I just sat there in stunned silence, thinking of what I had seen on TV. I began to realize I was in the car with flatlanders, people from the mountains who still believe the world is flat. My friend Doug, who is now a lawyer and who was already good at being contentious, decided to pursue the matter with some vigor. Obviously he did not recognize invincible ignorance when he saw it. I kept whispering to him, "Hush, Doug, we need this ride." It was of no avail. Doug asked the man, "Well, why do you believe the world is flat and the moon doesn't revolve around it?"

The man replied, "It says in the book of Revelations that the angels will stand on the four corners of the earth. Couldn't be round if it's got four corners, now, could it?" Now immediately I would say to be wary of anyone who begins a conversation with "It says in the book of Revelations." In the first place, that's not the name of the last book of the Bible; it's simply "Revelation." Second, this poor man had made an enormous genre mistake. He thought he could extract scientifically exact cosmology from an ancient prophet apocalyptic book—bless his heart. In fact, a lot of conservative Christians out there still think that way., and what is especially bad is that they think they are upholding a high view of the inspiration and authority of the Bible by doing so. In fact, what they've done is imposed a modern wooden hermeneutic on an ancient text and violated the way that text (in this case Rev 7:1) was meant to be used. They've assumed that the text was trying to convey one sort of information or truth, when in fact it was trying to convey a different sort of information—namely that God's messengers will be stationed and come from all points of the compass. In other words, even if you read the vision literally in its original historical context, it doesn't mean what our driver assumed it meant, which raises the important issue of genre.

GENRE: WHAT KIND OF LITERATURE ARE WE TALKING ABOUT?

One of the major keys to understanding the Bible at all is understanding the type or kind of literature we are reading. The term "genre" refers to the literary species a particular document exhibits. In the broadest terms, we are distinguishing between prose and poetry, between narrative and prophecy, between letters and sermons, to mention just a few categories. Each different type of literature sends its own signals as to how it ought to be interpreted, and each type requires a different approach. Even within the category of narrative, you simply can't approach a narrative parable in the same way you approach a historical narrative in the Gospels and Acts. At a minimum, if you don't read the New Testament with a certain degree of literary sensitivity—knowing what kind of literature you are dealing with, and what kind of information it is trying to convey—you are bound to make wrong assumptions and ask wrong questions.

A sort of facile assumption is often made that because the Bible is for everyone, then anyone could understand it just by picking it up and reading it. This assumption is false, and not because the Bible isn't pretty clear. Rather, our modern culture and cultural assumptions are in many cases so different from ancient assumptions. For example, in our day and age we expect precision when it comes to things like timing or dating, or reporting somebody's words. In an age before tape recorders, never mind camcorders and the like, ancient people had far less exacting standards when it came to things like telling time or telling a story in precise chronological order. We bring these sorts of modern assumptions to the text and just expect the text to conform to them, apparently on the basis of the theory that our vision of reality is not only correct, but is the same as ancient visions of reality.

Harold Lindsell once wrote a book entitled *The Battle for the Bible.* It was a big deal in the 1970s. In this famous text, he approached various historical questions as a modern historian would. He assumed that the Gospel accounts of Peter's denials of Christ must conform to modern notions of precision. He struggled to figure out the precise relationship between the denials by Peter, and when and where and how often the cock crowed. Wrestle mightily he did, and finally he came to the conclusion that Peter must have denied Christ six times, in order for him to fit the four different Gospel accounts together.

Now this conclusion is remarkable indeed, because absolutely none of the canonical Gospels suggest that Peter denied Christ any more or less than three times. This sort of false harmonizing of the texts does a disservice to the texts themselves and reflects a frantic and futile effort to explain away the differences between the accounts. Apparently it never occurred to Lindsell that perhaps the authors were simply giving a generalized account of this event and wanted the reader to know that Peter denied Christ three times, and that a cock crowed at some juncture in relationship to the event. He never seems to have realized that he was imposing a modern standard of precision that those Gospel writers were not using. Thus he became guilty of a major interpretive mistake: anachronism. Lindsell was a highly educated man, but he clearly did not know enough about the conventions of ancient biographical and historical works. Indeed, he made the very same mistake that the flatlander made: demanding that the text conform to certain modern conceptions of what is appropriate, real, or literally true.

So what types of literature do we find in the New Testament, and what are the ancient conventions that our New Testament writers sought to conform their books to, so they would be a word on target for their immediate audiences? We begin the New Testament with five narratives, with three of the Gospels reflecting the conventions of ancient biographies, and one of them, Luke–Acts, reflecting the conventions of ancient historical monographs. There was of course considerable overlap between the conventions used for ancient biographies and the conventions used for ancient historical monographs, and so not surprisingly Luke's Gospel does not look drastically different in form from Matthew's or Mark's. After the Gospels, we have a bunch of what appear on first blush to be letters, but in fact some of them are not. For example, Hebrews and 1 John are homilies or sermons, though Hebrews has an epistolary conclusion. Furthermore, in the oral culture of NT times, most of these letters were meant to be read aloud, and thus they conform more to the conventions of ancient speeches, acts of rhetorical persuasion, than they do to ancient letter conventions. I would argue that all of the letters and sermons we find in the NT, to one degree or another, are shaped by the oral conventions of rhetoric. They are documents that were meant to be read aloud and heard, and their oral and aural dimensions are crucial. In addition to these documents we have exactly one book of prophecy in the New Testament: Revelation. And it is not just any kind of prophecy, it is apocalyptic prophecy like that of Daniel, Ezekiel, and Zechariah. Revelation is actually a bit of a hybrid document since it also includes letters near its beginning, and epistolary elements at its end as well.

So there we have it. Ancient biographies, an ancient historical monograph in two volumes, discourses that since they couldn't be delivered in person were given epistolary frameworks and sent off to the remote audiences, sermons, and one book of mostly apocalyptic prophecy. Each of these types of literature has its own conventions, which, if we know them, will help us to understand what sort of questions we can ask these texts, and what sort of information and truth they are trying to convey. Let us take each in turn.

THE GOSPELS AS ANCIENT BIOGRAPHIES AND HISTORIES

One of the more obvious mistakes that is made in reading the gospels is assuming that they must surely be like modern biographies.[1] In a modern biography we have come to expect a womb-to-tomb account of a person's life, including discussion of his or her early childhood influences (and traumas). We expect a chronological account and a picture of the subject on the cover or the inside flap of the book. We expect precision of quotations, precision in regard to timing, and a balanced treatment of the life as a whole, including, if possible, the subject's own reflections. Finally we expect detailed research poring over many documents to ferret out the portrait that the biography will paint.

If these are our expectations, many moderns have not surprisingly been reluctant to see the Gospels as biographies. They look to most of us far more like Passion Narratives with long introductions. Even in the case of a life like that of John Fitzgerald Kennedy, who died a tragic and untimely death, modern biographers do not spend a third of their verbage on the last week of the subject's life, but the Gospel writers do exactly that. Yet on further review, Matthew, Mark, and John all conform quite nicely to the conventions of ancient biographies, which were quite different in scope and character than most modern biographies.

First, consider the limitations of length. While modern writers are sometimes put on a word count, they are not limited by the size of paper they have, unlike ancients. Ancient biographies were originally written on scrolls, and the maximum number of words you could get on a scroll, even by running them all together as they did in antiquity, is what we have in the Gospel of Luke. Ancient biographers and historians had to be able to squeeze all their material into a limited compass. Luke the historian couldn't manage it, so he filled up another entire scroll that we call Acts. Editing and condensing were the constant concern of ancient biographers and historians. They could not afford to be verbose, and they had to be selective. Not a single Gospel gives a physical description of Jesus, something that is de rigueur in a modern biography, especially if it does not include pictures. Apparently, ancients did not agree with those moderns who say "image is everything." Indeed they were more likely to sound like Martin Luther King Jr. in insisting that it was the content of one's character, not the color of a person's skin, that they were concerned to reveal.

A second distinguishing feature of ancient biographies is that the ancients were not much interested in or concerned about early child-hood development, for the very good reason that most ancients did not believe personality developed over time. They believed you were born with it and were stuck with it. It was simply revealed over time. They also had trouble believing people's character could change, and so the concept of conversion of whatever sort was viewed with suspicion. They tended to think that gender, geography (where you came from), and generation (who your father was) determined one's identity, in the ancient equivalent of the assertion that biology determines destiny.

Biographers in antiquity tended to focus on the adult life of the person in question, but typically with some mention of their birth and a good deal of focus on their death. How and to whom one was born, and how one died were thought to reveal the character of the individual, with death being especially revealing. Furthermore, dying in a shameful way was thought to cast a pall, indeed to reveal that one really was not a person of good character at all. Otherwise God—or in a pagan biography, the gods—would not have allowed one to die in such a cursed fashion. Here we can begin to see why the Gospel writers spend so very much of their limited scroll space on the death of Jesus. It required quite the argument to be able to suggest he was God's anointed one when he died in the most shameful way possible in antiquity: death by crucifixion.

Third, ancient biographies, unlike modern ones, did not tend to have a lot of editorial commenting by the author. They tended to portray a person by the indirect method—allowing the words and deeds of the person in question to speak for themselves, which is exactly what we find in Mark, Matthew, and John. What little editorial remarks we find are typically explanatory asides (for example, the comment about Jews' inhospitable relationships with Samaritans in John 4:9b).

What is especially important to note about ancient biographies is that they saw as their main goal an adequate and accurate unveiling of the character of the person in question. Whatever best served that end would be included in a biography, even if it involved matters of little historical consequence. So, for example, the story of the wedding feast at Cana hardly describes a historic occasion, but it is very revealing of the character of Jesus. Historians like Luke, not biographers, were concerned to relate events of historic significance.

Herein lies another difference between ancient biography and ancient historiography. While both sorts of writers were concerned about history, and were not conforming their narratives to ancient forms of fiction such as ancient novels or romances,[2] the historian had as his focus the crucial events, while the biographer addressed the crucial person. Thus Luke begins his Gospel by saying that he has observed, and intends to chronicle "the things that have happened amongst us." We would never guess from the beginning of Luke 1 that this was a story about Jesus. Genre signals in ancient documents were normally given at the beginning of a document, not at or near the end. Luke signals in 1:1-4 is that he will be writing an account of history, albeit salvation history, and that persons will be brought into the story insofar as they are relevant to the telling of that history, and then led quietly off the stage. For example, Luke shows no interest in the fate of Peter or Paul in his second volume. His concern is to show what events led to the Gospel spreading throughout the Holy Land and across the empire.

Ancient biographies not only did not pretend to be comprehensive, they tended to be highly selective, and the principle of arranging material, while broadly chronological, could involve a good deal of topical arrangement of material as well. Such biographers would not have expected complaints about their failure to offer exact chronological ordering of things. Nor were biographers much interested in historical causation (x led to y, which led to z). That was more the provenance of historians like Luke who even gives us synchronisms—the synching up of the micro history of Jesus or the early church with the macro history of the empire (see, e.g., Luke 3:1-2; Acts 18:2) insofar as the macro history helped explain the micro history.

Thus, when in Matthew we find five or six sections where Jesus does nothing but talk or teach (e.g., Matt 5-7) alternating with sections that are basically descriptions of actions, we realize immediately that Matthew is indulging in a kind of topical arrangement of teaching material. He is not suggesting that Jesus went whole days when he was nothing but a talking head, and other days where he did nothing but miracles. Within the broad chronological outline, Gospel biographers had considerable freedom in the way they could arrange their material, and they should never be faulted for not preserving exact chronology. They weren't attempting to offer such a thing. The same applies by and large to the issue of time references.

For example, in our earliest Gospel, Mark has a favorite adverb he uses dozens of times, especially in the first half of the book—*euthus*, usually translated "immediately." Translated this way, the term gives the narrative a sort of breathless feel, and one has an impression of Jesus racing around Galilee in a pell-mell fashion. But in fact, the term would perhaps better be translated "next." Another good example of this sort of phenomena is the phrase "after three days," which does not mean the same sort of thing as "on the third day." The former phrase is more general and means something like "after a while" or "after several days." A lot of the modern hand-wringing about whether a Gospel writer couldn't count and botched the chronology in regard to Jesus' death and resurrection could have been avoided had we recognized that "after three days" certainly did not need to mean after three twenty-four-hour days, whereas the phrase "on the third day" indicates that parts of three days were involved. Once again, modern notions about precision in chronology and timing are not helpful, apt, or accurate when one is reading first-century texts.

Two more items should be added at this juncture. First, biographies were the popular literature of the day and were not written for highbrow audiences, unlike histories, which tended to be written for a higher class of audience, and in Luke's case, probably for his patron Theophilus. Thus, to some degree, the historian would hold himself to a more exacting standard of reporting than a biographer might. Notice, for example, how Luke stresses in 1:1-4 that he has carefully done his homework, and intends to present Theophilus with an orderly account that will be clear and suit his historical purposes. In an age before tape recorders, long speeches would be summarized or the gist would be presented, unless one had some sort of written verbatim account at hand.

Second, if one studies the first five volumes of the New Testament in the context of ancient biographies and histories, one sees that our authors are seeking to make their documents comprehensible and clear for their own immediate audiences following the customs and conventions of writing in their own day, not ours. As such, we should see the Gospels as portraits of Jesus, interpretive portraits that do have a serious concern about getting the history right, but which have other concerns as well—theological, ethical, apologetical, evangelistic. Moreover, all written biographies and histories in any age are always facts plus interpretation, no less true today than then. Readers should see the Gospels as interpretive portraits rather than snapshots, and to treat them as works of historical art. We should not attempt to hold them to modern standards of either newspaper reporting or, for that matter, modern biographical and historical conventions. Thankfully we have four somewhat different portraits of Jesus in these documents, for he was a personality so large and his life was of such consequence that we would be much the poorer if all we had was the *Diatesseron*—the later harmonization blending all the Gospels together into one account, at the expense of some of the important differences that most reveal Jesus' character.

Now we must ask, how does this help us in regard to the question of seeing these documents as the word of God? What sort of canons of truth telling should we apply to such documents? Remember, inspiration looks like what we have in these documents, not what we would like to have. We have documents that conform to ancient standards of truth telling, historical reporting, and biographical writing. As such they stand up quite well when compared, say, to Plutarch's *Lives* of various famous persons, ranging from Julius Caesar to famous philosophers. Luke–Acts stands toe to toe with the very best ancient Hellenistic historiographical work of a Polybius or a Thucydides.

The more one reads such parallel ancient documents, the more one appreciates the character, integrity, and veraciousness of these gospel writers. One must judge a document on the basis of what it intends or attempts to accomplish, and within the contexts of the conventions it is observing. When one does that, it is not hard to say with a straight face that, yes, these books deserve to be considered words of God preserved in human words, written up according to existing standards and conventions so they would be a truthful and fruitful word on target for their original audiences. This is what inspiration looks like, and God in his wisdom did not choose to dispense the truth in the form of generic timeless remarks. Rather he used fully engaged Christian writers fully conversant with their age and audience, using their gifts and graces to their limits. Inspiration in their cases meant being inspired to do their very best, using all their abilities and knowledge, striving for excellence, and telling the truth in the most winsome ways they knew how. If we ask, were their portraits a good and true likeness of the historical Jesus, the answer is yes, and that's how they should be judged.

The same may be said of Luke's portrait of the life of the early church. Acts is not an exercise in gilding the lily, nor placing halos on saints who did not deserve it. It is not an exercise in hagiography. Rather, Acts is holy history, salvation history, history in which God intervenes repeatedly, but this does not distinguish Luke's historiography from, for example, Herodotus, the father of history, who likewise saw the divine hand in human affairs. Some moderns, though, have a hang-up with seeing God's work in the affairs of human beings.

Are there some texts in the first five books of the NT that causes moderns to pause and wrinkle our brows? Of course, and in a later chapter we deal with some samples of the so-called problem passages. Here, though, I can say that after thirty years of dealing with these texts as a historian and theologian and after writing commentaries on all these books, I still view these documents as veracious in the ways they intend to tell us the truth about historical, theological, and ethical matters, and thus they deserve to be included in Scripture and be considered part of the word of God.

POSTCARDS FROM THE EDGE: LETTERS, SERMONS, AND DISCOURSES

Evangelicals are far more comfortable in dealing with Paul's letters than they are in dealing with the gospels. They pose far fewer historical difficulties, and of course Protestants have mainly focused on Paul ever since the Reformation as a careful survey of the works of Luther, Calvin, Wesley, and their successors shows. In a sense Paul was seen as a more direct and quicker way to reach theological and ethical pay dirt, since he personally is addressing Christian people directly and dealing with issues in detail.

But therein lies the rub as well, because these are basically ad hoc documents, by which I mean they are even more clearly documents written to specific audiences for specific purposes at a specific time following specific conventions—in this case the conventions that applied to letter writing and rhetorical discourses. In other words, we have here even more historically particular documents, and as such they raise even more questions about how such documents can be the enduring word of God, since they are not addressed, at least apparently, to all persons in all times for the purpose of providing timeless spiritual McNuggets or everlasting truth capsules. How can Isaiah 40:8 apply to this material? Is it really the word of God that endures and speaks forever?

Interestingly enough, we have already seen that Paul for his own audience views his own proclamation and his own written documents as the word of God and not merely human words (see 1 Thess 2:13; 1 Cor 14:36-37). Equally audacious is Paul's hermeneutical move in 1 Corinthians 7 where he sets his own imperatives side by side with the teaching of Jesus and indicates that he sees them as just as binding on the audience. Notice that he distinguishes what the Lord said and says from what he is saying, but that he assumes both types of sayings carry the same clout and weight. By implication the church clearly continued to see Paul's letters as not only the ever-living and eternally relevant Word of God, but even as Scripture, not only by the fact that these documents all ended up in the canon, but also because by the end of the NT era, and long before there was a canon of the NT, some of these letters had been collected and were circulating in the church as Scripture. Second Peter 3:15, a part of what is perhaps our latest NT document, says, "So also our beloved brother Paul wrote to you according to the wisdom given him speaking of this as he does in *all his letters*. There are some things in them hard to understand, which the ignorant and unstable twist to their own destruction, *as they do the other Scriptures*." Notice two things: (1) these letters are now circulating well beyond their original recipients, and (2) they are ranked with "the other Scriptures" as sources of material that people can either use or abuse as foundational sacred writings. Clearly, others saw Paul's letters as the enduring word of God relevant to more than just their original audiences.

Perhaps this is a good place to say something about the difference between something being culturally relevant and being culturally relative. Paul's letters were doubtlessly culturally relevant—words on target for the first audience they addressed. This assessment, however, does not mean that they are culturally bound and only relevant to one particular time, setting, and audience. Frequently, scholars seem to make the mistake of assuming that because something is in an ad hoc document, it can only be relevant or binding on one particular audience.

Consider, for example, the case of other foundational documents—for example, the Constitution of the United States, the Bill of Rights, or the Declaration of Independence. Without question these documents reflect the language, thought patterns, and convictions of various persons in the eighteenth century, and they were written at a time when America was basically still just a collection of struggling colonies, emerging from the shadow of the mother country. Some things written in those documents are more time bound than others, but the most fundamental assumption about those documents, even today, is that they are still foundational and address present situations. Just ask the Supreme Court justices! They continue to refer to these documents to make authoritative rules about the law of the land, and rightly so. Just because a document is culturally conditioned and addresses a particular audience at a particular time, does not mean it is culturally bound and of no relevance or binding force on later audiences.

What do we need to know about these documents to help us avoid interpreting them in anachronistic manners, and reading into the text things that are not there? We are in danger of doing such things even with Paul's letters. For example, despite his brilliance, B. B. Warfield in discussing the Bible as God's word came to the conclusion that 1 Corinthians 13:10 ("but when the perfect/complete comes the partial comes to an end") refers to the closing of the NT canon (in the fourth century A.D.), at which juncture there would be no more legitimate prophesying and the like. He is not alone in this interpretation of this verse; indeed we find it in earlier church fathers, but he is certainly wrong, as the context will show. Paul is talking about when Jesus comes back and we see face-to-face the Truth Incarnate. This is perfectly clear from verse 13 of that same chapter. Thus verse 10 has an eschatological sense when it refers to a time "when we will know as we are known" and will no longer need prophecy.

Perhaps the most difficult concept to get across to modern readers of Paul's letters and the other NT documents that appear to be letters is that they are oral documents. I realize this sounds like an oxymoron, but they are quite literally surrogates for some face-to-face speech that the person wanted to give, but could not because he was elsewhere. These documents were therefore meant to be read aloud in Greek to their intended audience, and a good deal of their rhetorical effect is lost if the communication is not done in this way, for these documents are full of rhythm, rhyme, assonance, alliteration, and the like. In other words, they are geared for oral performance and meant to create an aural effect. And because they are basically speeches or sermons rather than pure texts, most of them follow the rules for ancient speeches, namely the rules of rhetoric.

Rhetoric was the ancient art of persuasion, not merely the art of speaking well or eloquently, and in an oral culture the rules for speaking had much more influence than the rules for writing letters. The early Greek church fathers, still in touch with the Greek of the NT period and recognizing the oral and aural nuances, insisted that Paul's letter needed to be analyzed following the rhetorical conventions of the day. If only we had continued to listen to Chrysostom and others when they told us this, we would have made far fewer mistakes in interpreting Paul than we do today. But alas, conservative Christians today are far more likely to treat Paul's letters as compendiums of theological nuggets, propositional truths, and ethical rules and regulations than they are to see this material as part of an ongoing dialogue, a conversation in context, that is being played out by the rules of rhetoric. These documents should be heard and appreciated like fine sermons or powerful discourses, not read as if they were texts written by Miss Manners.

Recognizing that these are rhetorical discourses prevents various sorts of elemental errors. For example, Romans is not a collection of Paul's greatest theological and ethical hits. It is simply not a sort of pithy summary of his main lines of thought. It is rather a very particular discourse meant to shore up the divisions between Gentile and Jewish Christians in Rome and prepare for Paul's appearance in that city. There are ever so many important Pauline discussions that are not included in Romans—for example, his discussion about resurrection or about the Lord's Supper—because this is an ad hoc document written for specific purposes at the time, just as all of his other letters are as well. Second, recognizing that Paul is speaking God's word into specific contexts in a rhetorical way means that we should recognize that what we have in Paul's letters is theologizing and ethicizing into these situations. None of these letters are theological or ethical textbooks done in the abstract or as a merely intellectual exercise. Paul is speaking a living word into an existing and ongoing situation.

A further key implication of recognizing the rhetorical nature of Paul's letters is that these are acts of persuasion. Paul is not trying to be objective; rather he is trying to convince, convict, and in some cases convert the audience to his points of view. Rhetoric is a culturally sensitive art, and what passes for good rhetoric in Paul's day might well look like sheer manipulation in our own day. Here again Paul was conforming to the conventions of his own day and what led to persuasion in his own time, not ours. Take, for example, the case of the little document we call Philemon.

In Philemon, Paul pulls out every rhetorical trick in his bag to get Philemon to manumit the slave Onesimus and send him back to Paul in Rome. For example, he flatters Philemon up front, calling him a dear friend and coworker who is generous and loving and kindhearted, and who has "refreshed the hearts of the saints" (vv. 1-6). Bear in mind that this letter is not a private letter to Philemon, but rather one that is to be read aloud before the entire church that meets in his house, and so the pressure will be on immediately to continue to manifest the character that Paul has praised. Then, using the techniques involved in an emotional appeal, stirring up pathos, Paul says he could command Philemon to do the right thing, yet he as an old man and now also a prisoner in Christ (can you hear the violins playing in the background?) would rather appeal to him in and out of love (vv. 8-9).

Finally he gets to the point of his appeal in verse 9. He refers to "my child Onesimus" making a claim on his life and saying that he has been converted through his time of being with Paul. Onesimus is a runaway slave, and as such subject to severe penalties from his master Philemon, which could even include execution. Remember, slaves were viewed as mobile property in the Roman Empire, not as persons in any legal sense. Using his oral skills Paul makes a play on the name of Onesimus, which is a nickname meaning "useful." In verse 11, Paul says he who was formerly "useless" has now indeed become "useful" to Paul and Philemon—that is, he has become a Christian—and Paul is sending him back to Philemon as such.

Then there is more emotional appeal. In verse 12, Paul says Onesimus is his very heart, and he is hoping that by sending him back to Philemon he will not stomp on Paul's heart, or break it. Clearly Paul is making Onesimus and what Philemon does with him a test of the friendship between the apostle and the slave owner. In verse 13, Paul implies that he wanted to keep Onesimus as he could have "served me in your place"—hinting that Philemon has not been serving him while he was in chains. Paul then adds that while he could have commanded, he "preferred to do nothing without your consent, in order that your good deed might be voluntary and not something forced. Perhaps this is why he was separated from you for a while, so that you might have him back forever, *no longer as a slave but more than a slave, a beloved brother . . .*" (vv. 14-16, italics added). The pressure is now being directly applied to Philemon to manumit or set free Onesimus once this letter is read out loud in the house church meeting. You can picture the other Christians looking at Philemon, and looking at Onesimus who has come with the letter from Paul, and wondering what the slave master would do. Then Paul speaks about Onesimus being "your brother both in the flesh and in the Lord," which seems to imply that Paul wants Philemon not only to set the slave free, but having made him a freedman, adopt him into his family as a full-fledged family member, entitled to inheritance. Notice how Paul gingerly spoke of Onesimus's running away as a divinely intended period of separation.

At verse 17, Paul then adds a further request. Not only should Philemon not punish Onesimus, but he should "welcome him as you would welcome me," with open arms. Notice the conditional remark "if you consider me your partner [in the Gospel]." Now Philemon's leadership status as a Christian coworker of Paul is on the line, depending on how he responds to the rhetorical pressure Paul is putting on him. Paul then says that if Onesimus owes Philemon anything (which he did—at a minimum he owed him the lost hours of work while he has been gone), then Philemon should charge it to Paul's account and he will pay the bill. But then not so subtly he adds, "I say nothing about your owing me your very [spiritual] life" (verse 19). In other words, it is Philemon who has the larger debt. And then Paul says directly, "Let me have this benefit [i.e., use—again punning on the slave's name] from you. Refresh my heart in Christ" (v. 20). Paul is asking for the slave to be sent back so he can continue to help Paul in the ministry.

The coup de grace comes in verses 21-22. Paul says he is confident of Philemon's "obedience." He may have earlier said he would prefer to request rather than command in this matter, but as the discourse closes it is clear that the desired response is not optional, even if it is somewhat voluntary (assuming this rhetoric achieves its persuasive goal). Then finally Paul says "Oh, one more thing. Prepare a guest room for me for I am hoping to be restored to you through your prayers." In other words, you'd better do what I ask, for I will be coming to make sure of the outcome. This sort of emotive arm-twisting would be seen as manipulative today, but in that passionate, rhetoric-saturated culture it was par for the course, a quite normal and acceptable practice.

How today, in a very different culture, might we use this as the word of God, especially if Paul's rhetorical salvo would be seen as too heavy-handed for our audiences? I suspect Paul's answer would be that we should preserve the principle he is arguing for—freedom and brotherhood in Christ, and forgiveness of sins—but package the request in a way that would be persuasive to our audience. The art of persuasion is still the essence of the nature of preaching and evangelism, but for it to be a word on target the rhetorical strategies and techniques must change with the culture.

Whatever else one says, I think here we see clearly the trajectory of Paul's thought about slavery. He is working to change the worldview on this subject within the community of Christ where he has authority and influence. He does not suggest leading a slave revolt, but rather appeals to Christians to work out the implications of the gospel of freedom and respect and brotherhood in their own contexts and to exhibit it in their own communities. Seen in this light, we then must assume that the household codes found in Colossians and Ephesians that deal with slavery are steps along the way to the dramatic conclusion we find in Philemon, with its call for manumission. In Colossians we have first-order discourse, where Paul must begin where the audience is; some of them are already slave owners, and Paul needs to Christianize the situation as much as he can until he can get them to the point where they hear the argument for manumission without simply rejecting it. Ephesians takes the argument a bit further in a Christian direction, reminding slave masters that they have a master in heaven, and God is impartial, and so they must answer to God and stop abusing and threatening their slaves. Indeed, they must serve them as they are being served by them (6:7-9).

Paul's statements are a subtle form of revolutionary rhetoric, but then the church always was a voluntary society. By voluntary society I mean that no one was obligated to be a member of a house church in that day. Paul knew this quite well, and so in a voluntary society, one cannot simply always command. Rather, one must first persuade so the commands will be heard and heeded in the context of voluntary compliance. Change in a society is necessarily slow when it happens with the consent of those who are being asked to change their behavior. Paul is putting the leaven of the gospel not into the dough of the world in general, but into the community of Christ, expecting them to change first whether the issue be slavery, or women in ministry, or other concerns.

When we make allowances for Paul's rhetorical techniques and devices, we then learn how to read his letters rightly. We understand that the whole letter, for example, is one discourse. We understand that the parts need to be seen in relationship to the whole, and not treated as sound bites and proof texts for our own modern agendas. Having listening patiently to the whole discourse, we then have a sense of how particular teachings and commandments could be used today as the word of God, and equally importantly how they ought not to be used.

We learn the differences between a problem-solving letter like, say, Philemon or 1 Corinthians—where pressing issues, both theological and ethical, must be dealt with—and a progress-oriented letter such as Philippians where Paul is basically saying to carry on in the direction you've been going. We also learn the difference between a letter that is essentially a sermon, rather than an ad hoc discourse—such as Ephesians, which is meant to circulate through various churches and is more generic in character—and a letter such as Colossians which is indeed an ad hoc document directed to specific problems in a specific church, even though it covers a good deal of the same ground as Ephesians. Knowing the difference between deliberative and epideictic rhetoric, which are respectively exhibited in Colossians and Ephesians, helps us understand the differing functions and purposes of these two documents—one meant to change behavior, the other (Ephesians) to reinforce existing values and virtues. Understanding the rhetorical character of a document is key to understanding how this or that particular word from God is meant to work and be used even now.

The question one has to ask about such documents is not just what do they say and mean as they attempt to convey a word of God for these Christians, but also why have they said these sorts of things in these sorts of situations for these sorts of people. As I like to say to my students, a text without a context is just a pretext for whatever you want it to mean. One of the most crucial contexts for our understanding is the rhetorical one, since these are speeches or sermons. One small example must illustrate this. At the end of 1 Corinthians 12, Paul engages in a series of rhetorical questions (vv. 29-31). Each of the questions begins in the Greek with *mē*, which means "not," and so the sentence begins with a negative and can only expect a negative response to each of these questions: "Not all are apostles are they? Not all are prophets are they? Not all are teachers are they? Not all do powerful deeds do they? Not all have the grace gift of healing do they? Not all speak in tongues do they? Not all interpret do they?" The only possible response to a rhetorical question which begins with "not" is no. We could have avoided a lot of modern conservative charismatic Christian squabbles if we had recognized that Paul is insisting that not all Christians speak or should speak in tongues any more than all are apostles or healers. Contextual exegesis, and knowing the rhetorical force of a rhetorical question, prevents anachronism and helps us to rightly use God's word as enunciated by Paul.

We could say much more along these lines. We could point out how James is a sermon in sapiential form, drawing on counter-order wisdom and conventional wisdom, some of it coming from his brother Jesus. If you do not understand the rhetoric of wisdom literature, you are not going to understand how this material served as God's word then and can still do so now. You could also make the mistake of thinking that James is correcting Paul's view of faith, works, and their interrelationship when in fact Paul would have quite agreed that faith without works is dead, is no living faith at all, and he too would be prepared to insist on commandments, imperatives, and the law of Christ for Christians as they exhibit the obedience that flows forth from genuine faith. In other words, understanding these texts in their original contexts makes clear that some of the supposed contradictions between one part of the Scripture and another are in fact moderns reading their own issues back into the text, and so problematizing the text itself. We have Luther to thank for leading us down this wrong road when it comes to pitting James over against Paul, faith over against works, grace over against law, and so on.

The issues between James and Paul had to do with whether Gentiles had to keep the entire Mosaic law in order to be in fellowship with Jewish Christians. In time, they both agreed that they did not. They agreed that Gentiles needed to simply renounce and avoid idolatry and immorality, the heart of the Ten Commandments, to become Christians. What they disagreed on was whether Jewish Christians were obligated to keep the Mosaic law or not: did they need to continue to be Torah-true Jews as followers of Jesus?

James seems to have thought the answer to this question was yes, Paul thought that while observing the law might be a good missionary strategy to win Jews (see 1 Cor 9), it was at most a blessed option and not a obligation for anyone who was a Christian, not even Jewish Christians. The issue between James and Paul then was a pragmatic one having to do with how Jewish Christians should live. Paul thought

Christ had fulfilled and was the goal and end of the Mosaic law, as did the author of Hebrews. James had not quite fully grasped or perhaps accepted the notion that new occasions teach new duties, and that all persons in Christ, even Jews, were under a new covenant.

What do we then make of the fact that both James and Paul wrote documents that made it into the canon? We can only assume that the church fathers realized that on some issues Christians could agree to disagree. They left the tension in the canon rather than editing it out on this pragmatic issue, just as they left the differences in Gospel accounts in the canon rather than settling for the *Diatesseron*. They saw this tension as not just a healthy compromise but an embracing of a scope of views which could be called faithful and true, and within the bounds of being called God's inspired Word. As I have said, inspiration looks like what we have in the canon, truth telling looks like what we have in the canon, and the word of God looks like what we actually have in the canon in all its particulars. Inspiration, truth telling, and the word of God do not necessarily conform to what we moderns might like them to look like to answer all our questions or clear up places where we think we have found contradictions (or at least apparent contradictions).

APOCALYPSE NOW: REVELATION AND OBFUSCATION

A good rule of thumb is to interpret the Bible starting with the clearer material and working to the more difficult and complex material. Starting with the book of Revelation is never a good idea, as the story that began this chapter demonstrates. As I write this we are coming out of the 2006 border war between Hezbollah and the Israelis, and of course the prognosticators have been making their lists and checking them twice and suggesting once more for the umpteenth time that we are on the verge of Armageddon. The numbers forty, seventy, and the like keep being debated and batted around on the Internet, where dispensational fervor and ferment on such issues know no bounds.

The sad part is that Jesus would say to those prognosticators, "You know neither the Scriptures nor the power of God." The New Testament is full of great expectations, but it doesn't degenerate into prognostication and calculating and date setting when the end will come. Indeed, to the contrary, Jesus warns in Mark 13:32 that no one, not even the Son himself during his ministry, knows the timing of the second coming of Jesus. Only God knows. One would have thought that this verse would have forestalled prognostication, but pious curiosity knows no limits when it comes to this sort of stuff. One thing, however, stands out about all such predictions of the timing of the second coming: in the last two thousand years, they have had a 100 percent failure rate. The remarkable apocalyptic prophecy in Revelation that ends the canon has been stripped of its historical context and rhetorical setting and has sadly become the special source document of those who fail altogether to bother studying the Bible in light of its original language, historical context, and rhetorical character. But if ever a book needed to be read in the light of the kind or genre of literature it is, it is the book of Revelation.

Only one book of prophecy appears in the NT, and it is no ordinary, garden-variety prophecy like we find in Amos or Micah or Obadiah. Rather, it is apocalyptic prophecy that can be traced back to Zechariah, Daniel, and Ezekiel—visionary prophecy by its very nature. We have already said a bit about the character of visionary prophecy, but here we will stress its analogical and metaphorical facets rather than literal descriptions of the reality it is discussing. Let me be clear: John does believe he is talking about a reality, present and in some cases future. But the sort of rhetoric he uses to describe it, rhetoric involving multiheaded beasts and the like, is clearly metaphorical and symbolic in character. Thus, if we ask, does he think Mr. 666 is a real person, the answer is probably yes. After all, he depicts him as being like a notorious figure of his own day, Nero who persecuted Christians. But he avoids naming the person and rather wants to give a character description of the kind of person he is or will be. Such character descriptions are generic enough that they could fit a Nero, or for that matter an Adolf Hitler or another tyrant in another age. This is the character of deliberately generic future prophecy—it is multivalent, and so can be seen to refer to various persons. The point to stress is that he is using a form of coded language that made sense to ancients, not moderns without considerable study of this type of ancient prophecy.

Our problem is that we do not live in the early Jewish world where this sort of prophecy was readily understood and made sense. Instead we must contend with the ridiculous ideas that this book was written especially for late-twentieth- and early-twenty-first-century Christians, and no one could possibly have understood the book before now, since it's all coming to pass right now. Plagues of bugs are subsequently assumed to refer to flights of helicopters, and Gog and Magog are assumed to be modern Iraq and Iran, and so on. What I want to know is, if this modern line of reasoning is correct, why isn't the rider on the white horse the Lone Ranger or maybe Clint Eastwood? That would be a decoding of the text that would make sense to my childhood interest in cowboy stories. But seriously, this whole way of interpreting the book of Revelation is so far out of bounds that it is hard to know where to start to correct it.

Let's try this. As Revelation 2–3 makes very clear, this book was written for first-century Christians in western Asia Minor. It was the word of God for them first, and it had a meaning for them. It is not just the word of God for late Western Christians who have far too much time on their hands and spend far too much money buying those sad *Left Behind* novels which should be left behind, being both bad literature and bad theology. It is a fundamental mistake of inter-pretation to assume that only we—the enlightened ones, assumed to be living now on the cusp of the eschaton—could understand this book. At least interpreters like Calvin and Wesley basically said they did not understand this kind of complex literature and so they did not write huge tomes on it. But now fools rush in where Protestant luminaries feared to tread.

One of the most important conclusions that one needs to draw from the fact that Revelation was written to first-century Christians, in a language and form of prophecy they could understand, is this: whatever the text could not possibly have meant for them back then and there, it cannot possibly mean now. If, for example, no first-century Christian could have understood a coded reference to a particular late Western bad guy named Osama bin Laden in the reference to Mr. 666, neither should we. What the text meant in the first century it still means today. Its meaning has not changed, though the application of the text may change. To suggest that the original audiences of this document who lived in that culture, spoke Greek, and read apocalyptic prophecy, couldn't possibly have made sense of this material, but modern persons with no historical, linguistic, or rhetorical training or knowledge can, is the height of arrogance. Talk about solipsism.

Second, apocalyptic prophecy is intentionally multivalent or generic in character. It uses universal symbols of good and evil that can be applied to the wicked or the saints in any age of church history. Of course, our author sees history climaxing with a final cataclysm but since he, like every other NT writer, believes they are already living in the eschatological age, he believes that the sort of things he is writing about are already happening and will continue to happen right up to the point when Jesus returns. Dates like 1948 mean nothing to our author, as if they triggered the end times. To the contrary, the end times began when Jesus began to bring God's divine saving reign on earth, and since every age of history has had earthquakes, plagues, wars, false prophets, and false messianic figures, the book of Revelation has been seen to be relevant in all those ages, including our own. Generic symbols work that way. They speak about regular human crises and normal cosmic events.

What the book of Revelation does not speak of is a pretribulation rapture of the faithful. To the contrary, it tells the audience to be prepared to suffer, and even endure martyrdom—quite the opposite of providing them with an escape clause when the big tribulation comes.

It is not an accident that the martyrs under the altar in heaven are featured in Revelation 6:9-11 and again they appear as ruling with Christ in Revelation 20. This book does not tell the audience to get ready to rumble in Iraq, but rather to be prepared to be a martyr for the faith. This point is especially clear in the letters to the churches, where "the one who conquers" is the one who maintains the faith unto death with martyrdom without compromising the faith. This behavior is seen as the means of overcoming the enemy. For example, hear Revelation 2:10: "Be faithful even to the point of death, and I will give you the crown of life. . . . Those who overcome will not be hurt at all by the second [i.e., eternal] death." So much for Revelation being an incitement for Christians to engage in a Middle East war.

But even more tragic about much of the modern dispensational interpretation of this book is that Revelation is theocratic in character. It tells Christians that God in the person of Christ will sort out the issues of injustice and evil when he returns. And when one reads Revelation 19–21 carefully, one discovers there will be no great Armageddon battle between human armies. On the contrary, we are told that when the final crisis comes after the millennium, fire will come down from heaven itself and consume the evil armies and Satan will be thrown into the lake of fire (Rev 20:7-10). In other words, rather than a final battle, heaven will sort out the issue directly by judging these armies directly. It has nothing to do with current struggles between different human groups in the Middle East.

Equally misguided is the whole notion that the Jerusalem temple will be and must be rebuilt before the end can come. This claim is just the opposite of what John of Patmos tells us in Revelation 21. Far from predicting a rebuilding of the temple anywhere in the book of Revelation, he says that when the new heaven and new earth show up, there will be no temple at all (Rev 21:22). God and the Lamb become the sanctuary for God's people in the end, when God dwells with them forever upon the earth. Sadly, so many misinterpretations of the book of Revelation are available these days that one wonders if this is what John warned against at the end when he told his audience not to add to or subtract anything from this book (Rev 22:18-19) on pain of divine judgment.

But we must return for a moment to that pretribulation rapture idea that has fueled so much modern escapist evangelical thinking, even leading to some saying that we should not try to be peacemakers in the Middle East, as we are just impeding progress in the march to the rapture and the millennium! I have shown in another study that this idea did not really exist in Christian history before about 1820 when a teenage girl in Glasgow claimed to have a vision of a rapture, which a minister named Darby took too seriously.[3] It is a recent idea that has become a linchpin in the theological system of modern dispensationalism. Unfortunately, the idea is unbiblical, one foisted on several NT texts rather than found in them.

Consider the two texts in Revelation usually thought to refer to this phenomena: Revelation 4:1-2: "After this I looked and a door was open in heaven. And the voice I had first heard speaking to me like a trumpet said: 'Come up here and I will show you what must take place after this,' And at once I was in the Spirit, and there before me was a throne." Is this a description of John's personal and private trip to heaven courtesy of Spirit Air? Actually it is not. He is describing having an apocalyptic vision. John's feet are still firmly on terra firma, but "in the Spirit" he has a vision of heaven and what is happening in that celestial place. The language here is typical of visionary language. Notice the similar language in Revelation 1:10: "on the Lord's Day, I was in the Spirit, and I heard behind me a loud voice like a trumpet." Or again we could refer to Revelation 17:3 when an angel comes to John and offers to show him the great punishment of the harlot, and then in verse 3 we hear, "Then the angel carried me away into the desert. There I saw a woman." John doesn't really make a trip to the Sahara. He is still on Patmos, but in the Spirit through a visionary experience he sees these things.

But what about texts like Matthew 24:36-43, which speaks of two standing in a field and one is taken and the other is left, or two standing at a handmill and one is taken and one is left? Here again, interpreting prophecy in its proper context is key. In Matthew 24:37 our evangelist says that as it was in the days of Noah, so it will be when the Son of Man returns. What happened in the days of Noah? The ones who were taken, indeed swept away by God's judgment in the form of the flood, were the wicked. The ones left behind, floating on top of the sea of judgment, were Noah's family. To be taken then is shorthand for being taken in judgment or taken away for judgment. It has nothing to do with a pretribulation rapture. The ones who are left behind after judgment comes are fortunate and are wiping their brows.

Last is 1 Thessalonians 4:16-18, a description of the second coming in terms of the imagery of when a king comes and visits a city. Clearly enough the text speaks of Christ and his entourage coming down out of heaven, and also of the dead in Christ rising from the graves and the living Christians joining them in meeting Christ in the air. They are depicted as being like the greeting committee that goes out of the walled city and meets the dignitary out where he is on the road to show him proper hospitality and roll out the red carpet. But in this imagery the place where this gathering goes thereafter is not back where the king came from, but rather into the place from whence the greeting committee came. Not only is the meeting of Christ and the saints not in heaven but rather, as the text says, in the air, but what happens thereafter, as described elsewhere in Paul's letters, would have been clear enough to the Thessalonians used to seeing greeting parties go outside of the city and welcome into town visiting dignitaries. Context is everything, and knowing the function of the use of the analogy with "appearings" or "visitations" of royal figures is crucial to interpreting such a passage.

Unless one wants to call the greeting of Christ in the air and the return with him immediately to earth for the final historical events a rapture, there is no such rapture theology anywhere in the NT, or in the OT for that matter. The consistent witness of the NT is that Christians will continue to be martyrs throughout every church age, including during the last troubles and trials of the end of human history that pre-

cede the Parousia. This is why in Revelation 12 the woman, who represents God's persecuted and pursued people, flees not into heaven, but
into the desert where God provides protection for her on earth, not in
heaven, from old Mr. Dragon Breath. The gates of Hades, the land of
the dead, will not prevail against his people. The community of Christ
will not vanish from the earth, though it will lose its share of martyrs
along the way. Revelation is a call to faithfulness, even if necessary
unto death. It is not a call to arms or Armageddon.

In this chapter we have attempted to unpack the whole issue of the
genre or literary types and kinds of material we find in the NT, whether
biographies or histories or rhetorical discourses in the form of letters,
or sermons or apocalypses. None of this literature can be rightly understood unless one picks up and faithfully reads the genre signals. Misinterpretation by moderns is inevitable if one is oblivious to such things
and simply brings modern assumptions to the text.

I have tried to show how recognizing and interpreting these texts
in the way they were originally intended to be heard and read prevents
us from making numerous mistakes—not only the mistakes from the
right of dispensational fundamentalists, but also the mistakes from
the left, which assumes that the Bible is riddled with errors and can't
be understood to be God's truthful word. Neither of these positions is
correct, nor are they helpful in getting at the truth. But both of these
positions have one thing in common: they both assume that we know
better today what is the truth about these matters than the very persons who wrote and received these documents. Karl Donfried is right
to complain about the assumptions and misuse of the Bible by both
the religious right and the religious left.[4]

I make no such assumptions. I assume that these ancient inspired
writers knew what they were talking about, understood these various
kinds of literature in detail, were persons of integrity operating in good
faith, and were trying to convey some truth, some word of God, to
their audiences, and so secondarily to us as well. The more I have
learned about the particularity and actual character of these books,

the more I have become convinced that they do indeed believe they are conveying God's word, God's truth, to their audiences, but we must ask what sort of truths they are trying to teach us.

The answer is: truths about God, about ourselves, about the inter-relationship of the two, about human history and its meaning, about God's redemptive work, and about proper human belief and behavior. We should not look for instructions about the age or shape of the earth, for while we have cosmological assumptions made in these texts, the only cosmology the Bible teaches is that there is a material universe created by God, and there is a spiritual realm which came to be seen as involving both heaven and hell. We should not expect the Bible to be a scientific textbook in a prescientific age. The original audiences would have not understood such a textbook if it had been given to them anyway. We should not look for specific detailed prophe-cies about the events leading to the return of Christ when in fact we have only been given general warnings about the *kind* of events that will happen, which for the most part have happened in every age of human history. I believe there is a reason for this approach: God has revealed enough about the future which he holds in his hands to give us hope, but not so much that we do not have to have and exercise faith. Prognostication is the abandonment of faith and proper expecta-tion in order to engage in fruitless calculations, which in the past have all been wrong.

One more thing. Sometimes I am asked, why should I have to do all this study to understand the Bible? There is the assumption that since one has the Holy Spirit in one's life as a believer, that all you need is a brain, true faith, and a good translation of the Bible. Perhaps this could be said to be adequate for the most basic of truths, as for instance who is the savior of the world, but it is certainly not adequate for understanding the intricacies of the most challenging and exciting book ever written. You need to give the Holy Spirit more to work with, is the way I like to put it. On one level it is strange that thinking Chris-tians would even ask such a question. After all, we go to specialists to help us understand law, medicine, politics, and any other complex subject. Why should we think it would be different with the Bible?

Again I would stress that the basic issue for us is not "Is the Bible clear?" but rather is our considerable cultural distance from the book and the literary conventions used to compose it. In our next chapter, we study some particular texts, certain core samples that are often thought to be problematic for the view that the NT could be the word of God. We shall see that rumors of the NT being riddled with errors are greatly exaggerated. Indeed, when all is properly taken into consideration, we are hard pressed to find any real or significant errors at all.

Chapter 5

CAN THESE THINGS BE TRUE?

The primary purpose of Scripture is for the church to eat and drink its contents in order to understand better who God is, what he has done, and what it means to be his people, redeemed in the crucified and risen God.

—Peter Enns

BETWEEN THE SURFACE AND THE SUBSTANCE OF THE TEXT

In the last chapter we discussed at some length the broader perspective of genre as a window into knowing what kinds of information and truth we could hope to garner from the NT documents. I stressed toward the end of the chapter that the authors are making certain historical, theological, ethical, and rhetorical claims in the main. Claims are not being made on a whole host of other subjects, such as scientific cosmology, chemistry, or physics, and so we must be able to distinguish between what truths an author is attempting to teach and matters that are perhaps mentioned in passing but no truth claims are being made about them. This is not unlike the distinction one would make between the awkward and sometimes errant Greek grammar we find in the NT and the content itself of the text, which is in no way compromised by the recognition of these infelicities of speech.

A good example of the incidental nature of some things mentioned in Scripture is the practice of baptism for the dead mentioned in passing in 1 Corinthians 15:29. Paul neither endorses nor prohibits the practice, nor the theology that is behind it, so the most we can assume is that he does not think the practice aberrant or bad enough to be worth banning at that juncture. Instead, he uses the existing Corinthian practice as an ad hoc argument furthering his case for resurrection. A lot of this sort of material in the Scripture is mentioned in passing or to serve a rhetorical purpose and does not deserve to be scrutinized too long or hard because the author is not intending to teach us anything about the matter. Any good preacher will pick up common material from his day that helps make his case, but about which the author is not trying to claim anything profound.

A further implication of the previous chapter is that all of the NT literature is tendentious, by which I mean it is argued from and for a particular point of view, namely a Christian one. The issue in regard to the five narratives in the NT is not whether they involve Christian interpretations but whether those interpretations illumine or obscure, reveal or conceal, delineate or distort the truths and ideas the author wants to unveil.

Furthermore, different sorts of truth claim, must be evaluated differently. If, for example, an author is making a claim about history (e.g., Jesus died on the cross), that is one sort of claim. If, however, he is in addition making a theological truth claim (Jesus died on a cross *for our sins*), that is something more and in some respects different. Moreover, if the author is making a claim about ethics or practice (e.g., women should be allowed to pray and prophesy in the church if they will wear signs of authority on their heads), that is still another matter. Or if an author uses a particular rhetorical device like dramatic hyperbole (e.g., "all Cretans are liars") to make a point, the truthful quality must be evaluated in light of the author's intent and the rhetorical device being used. These are the right sort of distinctions to make, and they lead to asking the right questions about such texts. It is not possible to simply read the New Testament as if all of its statements were meant to be taken in a literal sense. All the material must be taken seriously, but in fact in each case we must let the genre signals dictate how we approach it.

Truth can be conveyed just as well by fiction as by historical narrative, and we have both in the NT (e.g., parables are fiction and the narratives in the book of Acts are not), but each example and its truth claims must be evaluated on the basis of the kind of literature it is. To claim that an author made a mistake about the theory of gravity, for example, is neither helpful nor fair when he was not trying to teach us anything about that sort of subject. It is equally unhelpful to say that the world must be flat since Revelation 7 in an apocalyptic vision mentions its corners! But it is not just naiveté and modern anachronistic thinking that leads us to misunderstand what the NT is and isn't saying and claiming. A further problem falls under the rubric of skepticism—historical, theological, ethical, and other sorts of skepticism, and unfortunately this very sort of attitude permeates the work of some of the real Bible experts in the scholarly world.

JUSTIFICATION BY DOUBT: A SCHOLARLY MALAISE

Scholars are a funny lot. I ought to know; I'm one of them. Some are eccentric, some are eclectic, some are extraordinary. But when you participate in the rarified air of biblical scholarship, a particular sort of historical scholarship, it seems that this discipline especially brings the peculiar out of the woodwork. Biblical scholarship becomes a ripe field where the odd try to get even. I guess this is to be expected since the Bible is Western culture's number-one all-time bestseller, its number-one artifact and icon.

But there is a particular trait of some biblical scholars, indeed many of them, that I would like to comment on, because it drives too much of what passes for critical biblical scholarship: the tendency I call justification by doubt. A scholar tries to demonstrate scholarly acumen by showing not merely great learning or good critical thinking, but how much he or she can explain away, dismiss, discredit, or otherwise douse with cold water. This activity in itself is sometimes mistakenly called "critical scholarship," apparently in contradistinction to uncritical or precritical scholarship. And having once trotted out this label, it is then assumed that any real scholar worth her or his salt will want to be a skeptic so they can then be revered as a critical scholar. Otherwise they are not really being scholarly.

Here is where I call the bluff of those who think this way. I was recently reading a very fine manuscript by a friend and fellow NT scholar, Craig Evans. He says in this manuscript that sometimes skepticism is mistaken for critical thinking. Some scholars think the more skeptical they are, the more scholarly they are being. He adds that adopting an unwarranted and unreasonably skeptical posture is no more justified when it comes to the Bible than adopting a gullible one that accepts anything and everything that comes down the pike masquerading as real scholarship. He is so right about this. Let it be said that the Bible has over the last several millennia survived the critical scrutiny of many of the greatest minds that ever existed. We shouldn't think that it is now in danger of being explained away or set aside or shown to be irrelevant. To paraphrase Charles Spurgeon, "Defend the Bible? It needs about as much defense as a lion!"

My main point is this. Skepticism is itself a faith posture, a presupposition that affects and infects how one reads biblical texts, just as ardent faith is also a faith posture. Any historical scholar needs to recognize this and take into account what his or her faith posture, inclinations, or predispositions are before approaching the biblical text. But here's the rub. Some scholars, mistaking skepticism for critical thinking, assume that they are being objective, approaching the text in a value-free way with no axes to grind, while persons of faith approach the text in a subjective manner that is tendentious and necessarily predetermines the outcome of the interpretation. Neither approach is valid.

No purely objective, value-free scholarship is out there to be read. Some do a better job than others do of admitting this and owning up to their presuppositions and inclinations, and some do a better job than others of being objective. Those who are aware of their own commitments and take them into account and even correct for them are the persons who really ought to be called "critical scholars," whether they are persons of no apparent faith, agnostic, or of one or another sort of ardent faith. A critical scholar is one who is capable of being self-critical and self-corrective, as well as being able to cast a discerning eye on this or that biblical text.

It is also not good scholarship to have as a beginning point a posture of distrust toward the subject of one's historical study. One ought to begin with a posture of trust when approaching a certain historical subject, not with a hermeneutic of suspicion, for the very good reason that proving, or even just showing a reasonably strong case for, a positive after you have assumed a strong negative is virtually impossible. It is like trying to prove you didn't do something. Ancient texts deserve the same respect and benefit of the doubt and willingness to trust and listen to, at least initially, that biblical scholars want their colleagues to exhibit when evaluating their own modern works.

In the end, justification by doubt is not a good starting point for critical scholarship. You haven't necessarily explained something just because you think you have explained it away, any more than you have proved something just because you have demonstrated that the Bible claims this or that. Historical enquiry requires data to be analyzed, not lightly dismissed or simply received. Skepticism is no more scholarly than gullibility, but they both have one thing in common: they are both faith postures, not critical stances. In regard to the posture of this scholar, it seems to me that I should approach the NT authors with respect, and not assume that I know more than they do about what actually happened in antiquity. I also think that one must start, at least, by giving an ancient author the benefit of the doubt. If we then proceed to find good reasons to doubt that this person is a careful writer, or to doubt he is veracious, then well and good. A more reserved point of view is warranted. But it is a good thing as a starting point to extend the same courtesy to ancient authors as we do to modern ones—namely, that we assume that their truth claims are innocent and correct until proven guilty. After all, even skeptical scholars hope their audiences will make this assumption about their work.

PROBLEMS OF A HISTORICAL NATURE

Bart's Smoking Gun

In his recent book *Misquoting Jesus*,[1] Bart Ehrman sadly but quite honestly chronicles his descent into agnosticism from a previous position of fundamentalism. There were times in reading his story that I really wanted to say to him, "But Bart, fundamentalism with its wooden hermeneutic and its view of what must be the case about the truth claims of the Bible is by no means the only possible orthodox point of view. It's not necessary to throw the baby out with the bath water, especially when we are talking about the baby Jesus!" The truth is that the NT writers could make incidental errors of fact and interpretation about various things and still be absolutely right about Jesus, his life, death, resurrection, and so on. People have found various errors in respected classic history volumes, for example, Shelby Foote's wonderful three-volume series on the Civil War. Yet most reviewers would quickly add that in the vast majority of the cases, he gets things exactly right. The truth claims of each text should be evaluated on a case-by-case basis.

Bart's problem is that he could not regard the Bible as the Word of God if he found even one clear error in it. For him, finding that error set off the line of dominos that led to a good deal of skepticism about the truth claims of the NT texts. Bart's approach is more than mildly ironic since his mentor, Bruce Metzger, who I also studied with, knew those same problems and difficulties and was wont to say to whoever asked, "Have you never considered the possibility of inspired errors?" By this he meant there might be incidental mistakes in the NT, honest mistakes made in matters that did not touch the real subject or heart of the matter that the author was trying to address. This is certainly a more mediating position between fundamentalism and rank skepticism. While I have some issues with this point of view, I think it is a possible one, and Metzger I think would even add that maybe God designed the Bible that way so human beings would not commit the sin of bibliolatry—the turning of the Bible into a golden calf, mistaking the means for the end, and even exalting the word written over the Word Incarnate.

But returning to Ehrman's dilemma, what text was the smoking gun for him, the clear proof that the NT makes some claims that are clearly false? As it turns out, it was Mark 2:25-26, where it appears to be claimed that Abiathar was the high priest on the occasion that David entered the house of God and ate the shewbread. It is no help—one might say it is the last refuge of a scoundrel—to claim that Mark is accurately reporting exactly what Jesus said, but Jesus made a mistake. That simply removes the problem one step further back from the veracity of the Bible to the veracity of Jesus himself. While a biblical writer may truthfully report an error or a lie (e.g., compare Acts 5:7-10), this does not seem to be the case here in Mark. Mark would not likely want to portray Jesus making a mistake about the Bible. How then do we deal with this text?

In order to sort out the issues, several points need to be made. First, the relevant OT text is 1 Samuel 21, but anyone who has ever done text criticism on the OT knows that large portions of 1 Samuel are textually uncertain. Indeed 1 Samuel presents us with more textual problems in the Hebrew than perhaps the vast majority of other OT books. Nevertheless, with the text as we now have it, it appears that 1 Samuel 21 indicates that the father of Abiathar, whose name was Abimelech, was the priest when this incident in the life of David took place. But not only are there issues from the Hebrew end of the text, there is also the further issue of the Greek text of Mark. We need to bear in mind the following facts:

- Abiathar was a far more important figure than his father, and one could argue, as Aramaic specialist Maurice Casey has done, that his presence on this occasion in the holy place can be reasonably deduced from the context of 1 Samuel 21. Casey's view is that Mark is translating from an Aramaic original that perhaps goes back to Peter. He suggests that since Jesus was speaking in Aramaic, not Greek, that the Aramaic was "in the day of Abiathar the high priest."[2] If this is what Jesus said, then there is not a problem, at least at the level of Jesus' comment.

- There is an issue with the Greek itself. Much depends on how one takes the preposition *epi* with the genitive form of the noun here. If we take it to mean "at the time when Abiathar was high priest," then Mark seems to have made a mistake here. He will have rendered the Aramaic in an inadequate or misleading manner. However, another grammatical option is possible. This construction could mean "under Abiathar the high priest." This construction is understandable if in fact Abiathar was the main high priest during that entire period of time, especially when it seems clear that sometimes the son would already function in the role, being mentored by the father, though technically the father was still high priest (consider the example of Annas and Caiphas in the NT).

- We have various Greek manuscripts, including some good though mostly Western ones (D, W, it, and some Syriac ones) that do not have the Abiathar phrase at all. These witnesses, however, are not our earliest and best, and we may suspect they reflect later attempts to solve the dilemma. What we can say, ignoring these later textual variants, is that there are various quite legitimate ways of viewing these verses in Mark that do not result in either Jesus or Mark having failed their Bible quiz on 1 Samuel 21. Since Mark gets it right in various other places in his Gospel, we should give his elliptical and sometimes Semitized Greek a break here. Certainly, perfectly good scholars of great faith, little faith, and no Christian faith have been prepared to say that it is not clear that Mark makes an error here due to the various possibilities of the Hebrew, the Greek, and the possible Aramaic of Jesus' own speech.

Dueling Birth Narratives?

When I was filming the Christmas special *The Mystery of Jesus* for CBS, I kept being asked, why are the Matthean and Lukan birth narratives so different, and aren't some of these differences actually disagreements? For example, does one birth narrative portray Bethlehem as Jesus' and his family's hometown while the other one says Nazareth? These two accounts do indeed differ in various particulars, but differences and disagreements are not the same! We should not assume that differences automatically indicate dueling or contradictory accounts. I especially stress this approach when we realize that while Matthew is writing a biography of Jesus, Luke on the other hand is approaching the matter as a good Hellenistic historian would, and his main focus is on events of salvation history that are crucial. These two different ways of approaching the stories about Jesus' birth have to be taken into account if we are going to fairly assess what is going on in Matthew 1–2 and Luke 1–2.

Let us also note from the outset that despite having different purposes in writing, and also different audiences to convince, it is remarkable that both accounts stress that Jesus came into this world by means of an unexpected and miraculous virginal conception (which is certainly nothing like the ancient tales of mythological gods mating with human women and producing prodigies like Alexander the Great or Julius Caesar). Also, both accounts stress that Jesus was born in Bethlehem despite the fact that they both know that Jesus was called "Jesus of Nazareth" and that his family lived there after his birth.

In other words, when one gets to the real miraculous heart of the story, both Gospel writers affirm the same astounding miracle, despite the historical issues it created. That is, a skeptical person then (and now) is bound to suggest that Jesus must have been illegitimate. And when one realizes that no one in early Judaism interpreted the Hebrew text of Isaiah 7:14 to refer to a virginal conception like that recorded in the Gospels, it appears clear that it was the event in the life of Mary that caused reinterpretation of the text of Isaiah 7:14. Messianic exegesis of that text of Isaiah is not the source of the story of the virginal conception, as if it were prophecy historicized in a fictitious kind of way. The inclusion of the story of the virginal conception by both evangelists, who recognize the problems the story will create for an evangelistic religion in a culture not expecting a virginally conceived messiah, speaks well for the seriousness of purpose and concern for historical accuracy of these authors. And if they were concerned to be fair to the historical evidence about so controversial a matter, it would seem likely that they may be trusted on more minor points as well. But let us consider some particulars of the two texts by asking some questions.

Question 1: Does Luke tell us that Jesus' family lived in Nazareth but visited Bethlehem at the time of his birth, while Matthew's account indicates that the holy family first lived in Bethlehem, then went to Egypt and finally to Nazareth? Well, no, this is not quite accurate. Matthew's Gospel does not give us the prequel. It does not tell us where the holy family resided before Jesus was born. In fact Matthew 1 does not indicate the locale of the events described in that chapter at all, including the story of Joseph's learning of Mary's pregnancy, his resolve to divorce her quietly, and the subsequent vision given to Joseph.

Question 2: Does Luke tell us Jesus was born in a barn, being cast out by the innkeeper, while Matthew suggests Jesus was born at home?

In the case of Luke 2:7, we have a problem of mistranslation. The Greek word *katalumati* here should not be rendered "inn," but rather "guest room," which is what it means elsewhere in Luke, for example in his story of Jesus' partaking of the Passover in Jerusalem. When Luke wants to refer to a roadside inn, he uses a different word altogether, *pandochion* (Luke 10:34). In any case, Bethlehem was a tiny town on a small road and was unlikely to have a wayside inn. The long and short of all this is that Luke is telling us that Jesus was born in a manger, rather than in a guest room, presumably in their relatives' home in Bethlehem. But where would that manger have been? Normally in that culture it would be in the back of a person's house where one kept one's precious beast of burden. In some cases, some of these houses were built out from caves, with the animals in the back of the cave, and the house including both the cave and then the structure built out from the cave. In short, nothing in Luke's account suggests Jesus was born in a barn and away from kith and kin. Matthew 2:11 tells us that Mary, Joseph, and the baby are found in a house in Bethlehem. This does not contradict what Luke's account suggests, though clearly they are quite different—one stressing attendant shepherds, the other suggesting that sages visited later. These differences do not amount to contradictions.

Question 3: Matthew speaks of a flight into Egypt, while Luke does not mention such an occurrence. Is there a contradiction here? First of all, it is always dangerous to make too much of the silences of a text, either in a positive or a negative way. What Luke 2:24-52 does is recount several trips to Jerusalem the holy family made for various religious purposes, trips that in each case involved Jesus. The text does not say where the holy family set out from to make these religious pilgrimages, simply that they went to Jerusalem (cf. vv. 22 and 41) from somewhere. Also, judging from Matthew 2, the flight into Egypt seems to have transpired at a considerable period of time after the birth of Jesus.

Luke tells us nothing about what happened with the holy family from the time of the rite of purification shortly after the birth in

Jerusalem until they go up to Jerusalem again when Jesus is twelve—a huge gap in the narrative. Luke, it must be noted as well, is writing to a Gentile, and he is quite cautious in the way he presents Gentile rulers and their client kings such as Herod. Therefore, that we do not have the story about the slaughtering of the innocents in Luke's historical account is not a surprise. Luke is doing some apologetics for the new Christian movement, among his other purposes. We certainly cannot say that Luke's account contradicts Matthew's in regard to the flight into Egypt.

Question 4: Is the slaughter of the innocents really historically plausible? Wouldn't we have found a record of it in some other Gospel than just Matthew's if a grisly event like that actually happened? Various sorts of historical assumptions are behind these kinds of questions. And here we must stress again that Bethlehem was a two-stoplight town—only a small village in Jesus' day, as the archaeological evidence indicates. If there was indeed a slaughter of the innocents, in such a small village it surely wouldn't have involved more than a handful of infants who were two and under. And what we know about Herod the Great's character from Josephus the Jewish historian and other sources suggests that such an action would be completely in character with the man, an individual who was so paranoid about threats to his throne that he killed various of his own wives and offspring. Jesus seems to have been born only a few years before the death of Herod the Great, perhaps in the period 6-4 BC. There is nothing at all historically implausible about this event transpiring, Nor is it surprising that if he knew of it Luke did not recount it, for the apologetical reasons mentioned above.

I have dealt with these sorts of problems in the birth narratives because one frequently hears that the birth narratives are more historically problematic than other parts of the gospels, but I do not really think this is the case. The rest of the gospels are just as miraculous as the birth narratives, so they do not differ in that respect, and furthermore the birth narratives do not represent a different literary kind or caliber of historical or biographical writing than we find elsewhere in these gospels.

Common Census? The Quirinius Question

Some scholars have suggested that Luke 2:1-4 is the most historically problematic passage in all of Luke–Acts (which makes up a third of the NT)—perhaps in the entire NT. It is argued that Luke has jumbled up when the famous census of Quirinius took place, the one that prompted the rebellion of Judas the Galilean well after the time of Herod's death. It is also argued that a census as described in Luke 2:1-4 is highly improbable, with families having to go to ancestral hometowns to register for the census. Furthermore, Quirinius was sent to be governor of the province of Syria (and so at that time of Judea) in AD 6, not somewhere between 6 and 4 BC. After AD 6 he did indeed take a famous census of the region and even did a survey tour himself of the property in the region. Josephus the Jewish historian is perfectly clear about this (*Ant.* 18.1-2), and no evidence states that he was governor in the region twice. Has Luke really made a chronological blunder this big?

In the first place, Acts 5:37 shows quite clearly that Luke knew that the famous census of Quirinius took place well after the time of Jesus' birth, and precipitated the major revolt led by Judas the Galilean in AD 6–7. Second, we do know that the Emperor Augustus set out to get tax revenues from all his provinces, and the precursor to that would be a census. Since the enrollment of the empire had already begun before the time of Jesus' birth, what Luke 2:1 might well mean is that Caesar decreed that all *the rest* of the empire be enrolled, some of the work having already been completed. Roman historians are clear that the reign of Augustus was the first time that a tax assessment of the whole Roman Empire was accomplished.[3] Luke could very well be referring in a more general way to this ongoing process.

In addition, the Greek of Luke 2:2 is peculiar. It could read, "This was the first or former census which happened during when Quirinius was ruler of Syria," or one can even take the word *prōtē* here to mean "prior to" or "before," so the sentence would read, "This enrollment was before when Quirinius was ruler of Syria." Thus, either Luke is alluding to a census before the famous one of Quirinius, or perhaps we should take note of the historical fact that toward the close of the rule of Herod the Great, Quirinius had already been made consul in the region (as of 12 BC), and he might have imposed a taxation of Herod's territory in the process of downgrading his authority and control over the territory.

Finally, as for the journey to ancestral homes for registration, we have evidence from Egypt for such a practice, and it may well be that the Romans, being aware of the tribal and clan nature of Israel, used the same practice in the Holy Land. In other words, there are certainly plausible explanations for even the apparently most intractable of historical difficulties. If problems like those reviewed above are not without some possible explanation, then we should give these ancient biographers and historians the benefit of the doubt in other cases. We have only been able to deal with a core sampling of these difficulties, but they suffice to show how answers are not lacking to such issues.[4]

TEXT CRITICISM AND THE "ORTHODOX CORRUPTION OF SCRIPTURE"

Text criticism is something of a misnomer. When scholars talk about "text criticism," they are not actually busily criticizing biblical texts in the modern negative sense of the word "criticize." Instead they are talking about the task of reconstructing the original Greek text of the NT from the extant copies that we have, comparing and contrasting them and figuring out the earliest readings. We do not have the original copies of any of the Greek NT documents, bur rather fragments and whole manuscripts that date from the second century right up through the Middle Ages and beyond. A few of these fragments even date to the first half of the second century A.D., and since over four thousand part or whole manuscripts of the Greek NT have been discovered in the last 150 years, we may hope to find even earlier fragments and draw even closer to the original texts. In fact, one could argue that the further we have gotten away from the time of the NT era, providentially the more discoveries of importance have been made to help us overcome the time and manuscript gap.

In his recent study *Misquoting Jesus*, Bart Ehrman does a good job of summarizing the practice of text criticism, his area of doctoral expertise. He then goes on to cite some examples of textual corruption in which later scribes added things to the text, or altered the text to suit certain orthodox theological (and ethical) agendas. Yes, there were some unscrupulous Christian scribes just as there were unscrupulous Jewish and Greco-Roman scribes in that era. Bart, for example, makes a great deal out of the fact that in a text like 1 John 5:7-8 we have the addition in some late manuscripts of the Vulgate such that the text reads, "For there are three that testify [in heaven, the Father, the Word, and the Holy Spirit and these three are one. And there are three that testify on earth] the Spirit, the water and the blood: and the three are in agreement." The earlier and better Greek evidence of what these verses say does not include the material in brackets above. In fact, no Greek manuscript that dates before the sixteenth century has this addition, and scholars are in perfect agreement that this later insertion has no chance of reflecting what the original text said. Our earliest and best Greek witnesses rule this out, and I have no dispute with the conclusion that this was added to bolster the doctrine of the Trinity and give it a firmer basis in the text of the NT.

But what follows from this sort of very late evidence? Actually nothing much. Plenty of places in the NT that are not in any real textual dispute speak of God in a Trinitarian way. We may think of the baptismal formula in Matthew 28:19, or the benediction at the end of 2 Corinthians (13:14), or the use of the words "God," "the Son," and "the Spirit" "says" to introduce OT quotes in the book of Hebrews. In other words, the raw stuff of Trinitarian ideas and formulae are found in various NT texts that are not in dispute in regard to whether they were originally part of these documents. While the full-blown later creedal doctrine of the Trinity in an elaborated form cannot be found in the NT, nevertheless we do have the evidence that orthodox Christians were already thinking this way at the beginnings of church history.

The Trinity is not a later idea foisted on early Christian theology, but rather one found in a nodal state already in the NT text. This should hardly surprise us since the earliest Jewish Christians were already worshiping Jesus as Lord and praying to him to return, and monotheistic Jews certainly did not worship mere rabbis or prophets, or pray to them to return from heaven (cf., for example, the worship of Jesus in Rev 5 and the prayer in 1 Cor 16:22). Proto-orthodoxy already existed in the NT era and continued to develop over the course of the following centuries in a trajectory that was well grounded in the foundational documents. Thus, it is quite impossible to argue on the basis of late textual variants either (1) that there are no Trinitarian texts in the NT, (2) that the idea of the Trinity only arises after the NT era, or (3) that there was no such thing as orthodoxy in the earliest decades of the church.[5]

Whether one favors christological and Trinitarian orthodoxy or disagrees with it, it will not do to say from a historical point of view that it only arose after the councils of Nicea in 325 or Chalcedon in 450 or later. This is simply false. Furthermore, no first-century textual evidence exists whatsoever for alternative Christianities that did not proclaim Jesus was the crucified and risen Lord, nor is there such evidence for first-century Gnostic variants of early Christianity as I have shown at length elsewhere.[6]

The historical evidence is perfectly clear: orthodoxy begins in the first century and continues to be refined thereafter. Later Gnostic or Marcionite or Ebionite ideas and Christologies are just that: later second- to fourth-century offshoots from the original tree that did not begin to bud, bloom, or flower before the second century, and could not be said to exist as movements before the second century A.D.

It's also time to stop talking about lost Christianities. They are not lost, as we have known about them for a very long time, and it is doubtful we should really call them forms of Christianity because they conflict with our earliest and best evidence of what that movement believed and looked like at so many important points. Rather than call them "lost Christianities," we should call them "laid-aside heresies," which is exactly what the earliest church fathers, who were in a position to actually know the real character of these movements, called them. The evidence and arguments of persons like Tertullian, Hippolytus, and Irenaeus should not be lightly dismissed or laid aside. There was already an orthodoxy in the second century that they were defending long before the creedal meetings. These church fathers rightly rejected such aberrations as inconsistent with the earlier apostolic witness about Jesus and the gospel and indeed inconsistent with the Jewish teachings and human life of Jesus the Christ himself.

Finally, in his recent sociological analysis of Gnosticism, Rodney Stark makes clear that even in its heyday, Gnosticism was not seen as either very appealing to many nor as very Christian. Thus he concludes:

> These heretics did not pose any real threat to the Christian church, if for no other reason than that their doctrines were so bizarre and the religious practices advocated by most of them . . . were so extreme as to appeal only to a few. As doctrines define behavioral prohibitions, they can matter a lot! Even if their friends and relatives do join, most people will not embrace a life of austere denial—a loveless, sexless, childless, meatless, bathless existence—especially if it offers no greater or more plausible posthumous rewards . . . than does a faith that is far less restrictive. For most Greco-Romans, it was far more attractive to be a conventional Christian or indeed to remain a pagan.[7]

ETHICAL DILEMMAS: THE HOUSEHOLD CODE IN COLOSSIANS

Sometimes the NT, like the OT, is criticized on ethical grounds. The argument goes something like this. At least certain parts of the NT can't possibly be the enduring and living word of God because they promote reprehensible ethical practices like slavery or the subjugation of women. These major issues should not be lumped together under one heading. They each deserve a full treatment, which we can't offer with the amount of space we have here. What we can do, however, is spend some time talking about the NT household codes found in Colossians 3:18-4:21 and Ephesians 5:21-6:9 since they have drawn the most ire from various modern commentators. In fact, these texts have created such a furor in the modern discussion of Paul's letters and their authority as word of God for Christian praxis today that the reader must be patient as we go into more detail on this subject than we needed to on the previous ones discussed in this chapter.

A few preliminary remarks are in order. First, I would argue that these texts, rightly understood, are not promoting either slavery or the unilateral submission of women to men. The culture into which the NT was written was a highly patriarchal one, and indeed a huge percentage of the economy of the Roman Empire was dependent on slave labor. These are simply facts, and it is in no way surprising that some NT authors felt the need to comment on these existing institutions or even to try and help Christians enmeshed in such a fallen world live a more Christian life and lifestyle. I would suggest that is exactly what we find going on in the NT, attempts to limit the damaging effects on Christians of these existing ubiquitous and iniquitous social institutions, not license their ethically objectionable practices and dimensions.

The issues of submission and obedience are often discussed in the NT in regard to all persons in relationship to God, and various different groups of believers in relationship to each other, including the instruction in Ephesians 5:21, which urges all Christians to submit to and serve all other Christians out of reverence for Christ. If one has a problem with all forms of submission and obedience that involve intrapersonal relationships between Christians, then indeed one has a problem with the NT itself. I would not call this an ethical problem in the NT, however; I would call it one kind of modern attitude that even our American culture itself—whether we think of the business world, or the world of education, or the military—would overwhelmingly reject, and rightly so. I don't hear much hew and cry against the importance of children obeying their parents, or objections to soldiers obeying their commanding officers on the battlefield, and if one doesn't object to these things, then in fact one is not objecting to submission and obedience in general or in principle when it comes to intrapersonal human relationships.

Some scholars have suspected that this Colossian code and the one in Ephesians and perhaps also the one in 1 Peter were constructed either to counter a revolutionary spirit among Hellenistic Christians, particularly slaves and women, or that it was apologetical in character countering the notion that Christians were social radicals. The problem with both of these suggestions is that they do not really account for the exhortations to parents and children, nor for the fact that the Colossian code is directed to those who are already Christians in Colossae, and directed to the whole household. Equally unconvincing is the suggestion that there is nothing profoundly Christian or especially radical about these household codes; as if they just baptize the status quo and call it good. To the contrary, when one compares this material to either the ancient discussion of household management in Aristotle and other sources, or the Stoic or Greco-Roman codes, one is profoundly struck not just by the Christian elements but also the social engineering that is being undertaken here to limit the abuse of power by the head of the household, using Christian rationales to equalize and personalize as well as Christianize the relationship between that head and the rest of the family.

The fact is that we do not really find in most of the parallel literature the exhortation to the head of the household to love their wives, or not to break the spirit of their children, or to treat their slaves with some equity and justice.[8] Thus while what we find here may not be totally unique (most of it is found in bits and pieces elsewhere), it is certainly distinctive of a Christian approach to these interrelationships: the attempt to embed the Christian faith and its ethical values in the social structures that already exist. Tom Wright puts the matter well: "It is . . . extremely unlikely that Paul, having warned the young Christians *against* conforming their lives to the present world, would now require just that of them after all. Nor does he. The Stoics (who provide some of the closest parallels to these household lists) based their teaching on the law of nature: this is the way the world is, so this is how you must live in harmony with it. Paul bases his on the law of the *new* nature: Christ releases you to be truly human, and you must now learn to express your true self according to the divine pattern, not in self-assertion but in self-giving."[9] The attempt to see this code as an effort to stabilize the Pauline community in the post-Pauline situation and demonstrate that it was a supporter of the conventional cultural household codes and traditional virtues ignores the profound Christianizing of this material and the way it goes *against* the flow of the culture. It also goes against various aspects of traditional Jewish wisdom, which did seek to repristinize patriarchy (compare the attitude toward women's roles in Sirach and Josephus, *Against Apion* 2.24-30).

At this juncture we should also address the question of why we find this sort of advice given to slaves and masters if in fact we are correct in deducing that Paul was arguing for the manumission of a slave in Philemon, and indeed arguing on the basis of the principle that those who are brothers or sisters should not be or be treated as slaves. To strengthen the point even more, 1 Corinthians 7 quite clearly not only says that Christians should not become slaves, but also that they should avail themselves of the opportunity for freedom if it is presented to them. Why then is Colossians different? There are at least six factors of importance here.

1. Paul is here addressing an existing situation of Christian households that have slaves, and clearly he is trying to minimize the possibility for abusive or un-Christian behavior by either master or slave (or others). He is regulating an existing condition, not endorsing the institution of slavery. Limiting rather than licensing the situation is the ethical move Paul is trying to make here. The same applies to his comments about the patriarchal family structure.

2. One must take into consideration that Paul is not addressing
   a personal convert or close friend here. Indeed, he is addressing a group of Christians who are not his converts and who,
   so far as we know, he has never addressed in a letter before.
   Levels of moral discourse are possible, depending on the audience one is addressing. If the goal is damage control, as it is
   here, which is believed to be all that can be accomplished on
   this first occasion of discourse, Paul understandably does not
   fire all of his guns on this occasion when it comes to the institutions of slavery or patriarchy. This is Paul's opening gambit
   with the Colossians on these subjects, not his last word with
   them. It must be judged in that light.

3. Even in the form in which this household code appears here,
   it is already a matter of swimming upstream as we shall see,
   going against the flow of much of the cultural assumptions
   about slavery and patriarchy.

4. The household code must not be abstracted from its present
   literary context and analyzed on its own, as is so often done,
   if the goal is to see what Paul is driving at in the use of this
   material. Not only must we take into consideration the larger
   social context in evaluating this material but also the immediate literary or exegetical context as well. When what comes
   immediately before the code is taken into account, it becomes
   perfectly obvious that Paul expects all household members to
   behave in ways that are in accord with Christian virtues and
   not continue or go back to old patterns of behavior in their
   family relationships. The general ethic enunciated in 3:5-17
   prepares for and undergirds the advice given in 3:18-4:1. If
   the ruling principles guiding conduct are love, peace, forgiveness, respect, and a recognition that in Christ even social
   relationships like slave and master or husband and wife have
   been relativized and transformed (3:11), then a reforming and
   refashioning of household relationships is not only possible

but required. Paul is not offering up suggestions in the form of a household code; rather he is exhorting by means of imperatives. Notice too how each exhortation is tied to the person in question's relationship with the Lord. Even the household ethic and its living out is Christocentric.

5. The trajectory of the remarks in this household code is as important as the advice actually given. This becomes clearer when we get to the parallel household code in Ephesians 5–6, where Paul has put even more Christian leaven into the dough of household relationships.

6. Understanding this material and judging it fairly is a matter of asking the right questions. The questions one needs to ask about this material is threefold: How does it compare to the standard advice given in the culture about household relationships? Where is this advice heading? What would the social situation look like if all the ethical advice given in and around these codes was followed faithfully?

In terms of the social provenance of the Colossian household code, this code may well reflect a situation where there were considerable expectations on the part of women and slaves that their treatment in the home would be different if the situation was Christian. But then is this code trying to dampen their enthusiasm for more freedom and less restrictions? Probably not, as what Paul actually says is not an attempt to put women or slaves or even children in their place, but rather to make sure that they behave like Christians in the social roles they are already and always have been playing. There is no evidence of a feminist or slave revolution in play in the church in Colossae that Paul is trying to stifle. Quite the contrary, Paul is trying to Christianize a difficult and possibly abusive situation on his *first* occasion of addressing the Colossians and so help the subordinate members of the household not merely survive but have a more Christian environment in which to operate. What most distinguishes this household code from those in the pagan or Jewish world in general is that Paul is giving strong limiting exhortations to the superordinate person in the family: the husband, father, master. In non-Christian household codes it is almost always only the subordinate members of the household who get such exhortations. What is new about the code here is the Christian limitations placed on the head of household, which is what would stand out to an ancient person hearing Paul's discourse for the first time.

Several structural elements in this household code should be kept in mind:

- The subordinate member of a given relationship is addressed first (wives, children, slaves), but always in tandem with the head of the household being exhorted. In fact, the head of the household gets three sets of exhortations, whereas everyone else only gets one.

- Each exhortation consists of an address, an admonition, and in some cases a motive or reason for the exhortation, sometimes a specifically Christian one.

- The groups are arranged from most to least intimate relationships (wife/husband; children/parents; slaves/masters). The writer is thus attempting comprehensiveness here. The head of the household must play three roles and therefore is given three sets of exhortations with limitations.[10]

Women are addressed first in verse 18, and here the term *gunaikes* surely means "wives." Paul is not attempting to address the general issue of the relationship of all Christian women to all Christian men here. Nor is there any reason to think he is merely commenting on behavior in Christian worship. What is said to the wife applies only in her relationship to her husband. Nothing is said about how she should relate to her father, her brother, her cousins, her friends, male leaders in the congregations, or men in general. This code focuses on a specific narrow social context. Here and throughout this code, all the members of the family are addressed as morally responsible individuals capable of hearing and heeding on their own the exhortation that is being given. Furthermore, here, unlike in 1 Corinthians 7, Paul does not seem to be addressing religiously mixed marriage situations. He is addressing homes where all the members of the family are assumed to be Christians and therefore can all be exhorted by Paul.

The verb *hypotassō* is critical in this section. We find it in the present tense, middle voice, which can then be translated, "wives submit yourselves . . ." Paul does not tell the husbands to subordinate their wives or even to exhort their wives to be subordinate. The exhortation goes directly to the wife, who must subordinate herself. This verb was not widely used in other Greek literature dealing with marriage, though Plutarch a little after the time of Paul does use it (*Advice to Bride and Groom* 142E in *Moralia* 2.322-33). Since this verb is also used of Christ's relationship to God the Father (1 Cor 15:28), and of believers to each other (Eph 5:21) it surely does not imply the ontological inferiority of the submitter to the one submitted to. Rather *hypotass* has to do with the nature of a relationship between two persons, and perhaps more to do with following the example of Christ who humbled himself and took a lower place. In other words, in a Christian context the verb has to do with humility and service as modeled by Christ, who even served the lost as well as believers. Notice too that we are not told in practical terms how this submission to husband actually is to be manifested. Paul assumes his audience knows what is implied.

The parallel exhortation to the husband in verse 19 involves the characteristic Christian virtue of *agapê*. This verb is not used in the discussion of the household duties of the husband in Hellenistic literature, and so by no means is a conventional exhortation being repeated here. It is not, however, a uniquely Christian word either, though it is a term that most often characterizes the Christian ethic. Wives are never exhorted to love their husbands in these Christian household codes in the NT. It is fair to assume that Paul thinks that these husbands especially need this exhortation.

This reference to *agapê* is followed by a negative corollary to the positive exhortation which shows clearly that Paul is trying to limit bad behavior by the head of household. The phrase could either be translated "don't be sharp with them" or "do not be embittered against them." The husband's action and his anger must be limited by love. As a Christian he is not free to do as he pleases with his wife. Contrast what Ben Sira says on this subject (who always takes the side of the husband and father in these matters; cf. Sir 25–26; 30:1-13; 42:9-14), with the views of Paul. Such a comparison reveals that while Ben Sira is trying to reinforce a patriarchal authority structure, Paul is not. Rather, Paul is trying to ameliorate the harm such an existing structure does and can do. Chrysostom grasped the spirit of what Paul was trying to accomplish in these exhortations to husband and wife: "Observe again that Paul has exhorted husbands and wives to reciprocity. . . . From being loved, the wife too becomes loving; and from her being submissive, the husband learns to yield" (*Hom. Col.*).

By far the longest single exhortation in this code comes in verses 22-25 in the direct address to slaves who, like the children, are also treated as responsible members of the congregation. In light of Colossians 3:11 they are seen as equal members, persons of equal sacred worth in the church. These verses should be read in light of that earlier text. Like the exhortation to children, the imperatives here begin with the command to obey in everything. The assumption must be, especially in light of 4:1, that the Christian master will be treating the slave fairly and properly. Masters are called "lords according to the flesh," with the implicit distinction from the Lord. The slave is exhorted to wholehearted labor and not just when he or she is being watched, in order to curry favor by appearing to be diligent. Paul is apparently dealing with a trait that was assumed to be commonplace, namely laziness when there was no supervision. While the clause at the end of verse 22 could refer to the slave's "lord according to the flesh," it is more likely another example of the Christianizing of this material with the implication that a Christian slave should always work with the recognition that the Lord is always watching, and so it should be done "in the fear of the Lord," being concerned about the Lord's evaluation of his conduct, rather than in fear of reprisals from the master. Verse 23 certainly further supports this interpretation. All work should be done from the heart and "as to the Lord, not as to human beings." This is interesting because it removes the usual motivation for human behavior and places the conduct strictly on the basis of Christian motivation. The approval one should seek is not human approval, but that of God, and the evaluation one should be concerned about is that of the Lord, not lords. The real reason and encouragement for such advice is given in verse 24.

Since Paul is addressing Christian slaves, he is clearly not referring to initial salvation as a reward. Rather it is the same sort of reward Jesus promises to believers for good conduct during their believing lives. This line of thinking certainly indicates, however, that Paul believes there will be rewards (lesser and greater) in the eschatological state based on one's behavior in this life (cf. 1 Cor 3:10-15). This is followed by the intriguing remark that in fact the slave belongs to or is enslaved to the Lord Christ. The reference to Christ leads into verse 25, where the reference is not clear. Is this a promise that Christ, who does not play favorites, will deal with unfair masters in due course and so Christian slaves should not misbehave if mistreated? This is certainly possible in light of 4:1. On the other hand, the sense could be that the slave is being warned against unrighteous conduct being repaid in the eschatological age, just as righteous conduct will be rewarded. Might the reason for this extended exhortation to the slave be the Onesimus situation, attempting to head off further illegal behavior by slaves in Colossae? This is certainly possible. The net effect of this advice is to place the conduct of the slave clearly under the light of divine scrutiny and to help the slave think this way about it, with a special stress on the slave working hard and wholeheartedly at what he or she does, knowing that their real lord to whom they are bound and even "enslaved" is Jesus, who died for them and set them free already from their sins and bad behavior. Note that traditional discussions of household management do not address slaves directly, but here they are addressed directly as both members of the household and as members of the house church. This section involving slaves and masters includes some five references to Christ as Lord to make very clear the thorough overhaul of the way that relationship should be envisioned and what motivates proper behavior when both parties are Christians. This approach contrasts drastically with the usual ways slaves were motivated to work hard (e.g., holding out rewards such as praise, food, better clothing: see Xenophon, *Oec.* 13.9-12). Finally we may note that the verb in 3:24b could be taken as imperative: "Be slaves of the Lord Jesus Christ."

Colossians 4:1 concludes the argument with a word for the masters. The stress is on Christian "lords" also having a Lord in heaven to whom they are answerable for their conduct. Conduct again is to be guided or modified because of the watchful eye of Christ:

> This notion that the masters of the household have a master over themselves is quite different from other discussions of the household in antiquity. . . . The writer does not say that in the slave/master relationship the master represents Christ, but the relationship within the ancient household that demonstrates both the possession of all believers by their Lord and their obligation to this Lord is that of slaves to their master. For this reason, it is the one that receives the most attention as a paradigm for the motivation that should inform all members of the household and that is summed up in the command of 3.24b: "Serve the Lord Christ."[11]

This last clause of the code clearly relativizes the position and power of the master within the Christian community.

Masters are not to cheat their slaves, but rather to provide them with what is right and fair. This is diametrically opposed to what Aristotle says when he remarks that the issue of justice is not raised in regard to slaves: there can be no injustice involved in the way one treats mere property (*Eth. Nic.* 5.1134b). Compared to Aristotle, what Paul is saying here is revolutionary. As Tom Wright says, this way of discussing things would have sounded odd, for what it suggests is "slaves too are human beings with rights. To talk of 'justice' and 'equality' in relation to slaves would sound extraordinary to most slave-owners of the ancient world."[12] Thus even if to our ears this advice sounds rather conventional or even conservative and commonplace, the truth is it was *not* in that day. Paul has already, on the first occasion of addressing the Colossians, been pushing the envelope of their thinking so that they will consider all subordinate members of the household, even slaves, as persons, with rights including the right to fair and equal treatment. Even more to the point, they are to be recognized as Christian persons, and the head of the household as a Christian must alter conduct in his relationship with all three sets of persons (the wife, the children, the slaves) so that the Lord will be pleased with his conduct. This curtailing and Christianizing of the head of the household's rights, privileges, and roles especially stands out in these exhortations as Paul, even in his first address to the Colossians, attempts to transform the character of Christian household relationships by ameliorating the harsh edges of the existing institutions of slavery and patriarchy.

So then, should we see this material as ethically reprehensible and in no way in character with what the word of God should look like if it reflects the character of a God of justice and equity? Not at all. Indeed, we should see it as a way station along the way to having Christian family structures that would free the subordinate members of the oppression they faced all too often in the Greco-Roman world. If one pays attention not only to the context of these remarks and how they go against the flow of the fallen culture, and also the trajectory of change in these remarks as Paul tries to reform the world by reforming first the extant Christian relationships in a church he did not found, then we will understand that even in the household codes, Paul has not baptized the existing structures of society and simply called them good. To the contrary, he has called them to account, with the head of the household coming in for a whole slew of restrictions and limitations in all of his roles. Indeed we can see where this entire argument is leading if we turn to Ephesians 5:21 where Paul says bluntly that all Christians should submit to and serve all other Christians out of reverence for Christ. The manifesto for more egalitarian change is on the tip of his tongue in Colossians, but he will wait until his second salvo, which was also probably sent to the Colossians as well as the Ephesians since the latter is a document meant to circulate throughout several of the Pauline churches. Even Paul must be exegeted in the larger context of what he says elsewhere and later.

In this chapter we have covered an enormous amount of ground in a few pages, and the NT raises many more questions and difficulties that for us that we cannot address here. If there are answers to the most strenuous of objections to seeing the texts we did study as God's living word, and so the truth that still speaks and guides us today, then we should expect there are also answers to less difficult problems as well, if we just diligently and carefully study the matters involved. In short, rightly understood and carefully handled, this material can and still should be taught and preached as God's word within the church today without either ignoring or explaining away what the text says. The rule that applies must be reiterated: one must consider as closely the original contexts and direction of a person's remarks as one does the content of a person's remarks if you are to understand the material correctly.

Chapter 6

DID THE CANON AND ITS TRANSLATORS MISFIRE?

To err is human, to forgive, divine.

—Alexander Pope

Human beings are error prone. There is no denying that fact. And sometimes it is very difficult indeed to determine what is and what is not an error, even in a field of discussion with which we are well familiar. Let me give you a historical illustration. I remember very well being taught about George Washington in elementary school, and I knew Mrs. McCallum to be a no-nonsense and careful kind of teacher. She taught us that George once cut down a cherry tree, and she had sources to prove that he had also said the famous line, "I cannot tell a lie, I did chop down the cherry tree," or words to that same effect. There were respected biographies written in the nineteenth century and afterward that argued for the historical truth of that event and subsequent confession. Turns out, however, it was yet another example of revisionist history written by someone overeager to polish the halo of our first president. We were snookered. Even Mrs. McCallum, as cautious as she was, was deceived.

But when we raise the question about errors in the Bible, we are raising the emotional temperature of the discussion many degrees above the debate about George Washington and the truth about him and that cherry tree. This book, after all, is supposed to be the word of God. Did the church really accept into the canon mistakes of various sorts? And what counts as an error anyway? While we are at it, is it true because it is in the canon of the NT and so in the Bible, or was it included in the canon of the NT because it was true in the first place? Inquiring minds want to know.

THE END OF AN ERROR?

In one sense we have been discussing the issue of errors and the word of God all along in this book. Now we just have to focus more clearly on some particulars. Perhaps we should list what does not count as an error and then say what does.

1. When an author intends to give a generalized report or the gist of something (a word or a deed of Jesus, for example) rather than a precise one, he should not be charged with an error unless we know with a high degree of probability that, in his generalizing, he has falsified the story or saying in some obvious way.

2. In ancient biographical and historical works of a high caliber in an age before tape recorders, a writer had the freedom to arrange, edit, and paraphrase what someone said. Most of the sort of minor differences we find between the parallel accounts of stories in the Gospels, or for example in the multiple accounts of Paul's conversion in Acts, can thus be explained in terms of editorial tendencies, differing uses of the same material, or deliberate rhetorical variation for the sake of amplification and the like. They do not represent errors. Indeed they are intentional changes—some stylistic, some substantive—that serve the larger purposes of truth telling that is

going on in a particular narrative. For example, as has often been noticed, the author of Matthew's Gospel has made more Jewish in character various phrases that he found and takes over from his Markan source. Thus, where the phrase "kingdom of God" shows up in Mark, in the same passage in Matthew it is frequently rendered "kingdom of heaven" (cf., e.g., Matt 13:11 and Mark 4:11). Mark, who is probably writing to a mostly Gentile Christian audience in the 60s, has somewhat Hellenized the account to help his audience understand the stories meanings. Matthew by contrast goes in the opposite direction and re-Judaizes this material because he is addressing a group of Jewish Christians probably in Galilee or perhaps Antioch. If we ask the question "What did Jesus originally say," the answer is that probably the Matthean account is closer to the original verbage of Jesus the Jew, even though it is in a later and derivative Gospel. This small illustration demonstrates that we simply can't judge errors in the NT on the basis of some modern criteria which says that unless it's verbatim, it is a mistake. Why not? Because that is to impose a standard of precision which these authors never intended to live up to, in some cases probably could not live up to, and in fact were not required to do so by even the highest canons of what counted as veracious literature in that day. We need to quit sweating the small stuff when these writers had the freedom, even as inspired writers, to do exactly what we see them doing in the NT. None of the original readers whom we know of became apoplectic over these things. These differences are not errors; they are intentional changes made to serve the larger truth claims that the authors want to make.

3. An event presented out of chronological order (e.g., the presentation of the cleansing of the temple in John 2) does not constitute a historical error, unless we can demonstrate that the author did not have other and larger reasons for

the arrangement of his material—say, for example, theological ordering of material. What we know about the Fourth Gospel is that it is highly schematized. It presents us with exactly seven sign miracles, seven "I am" sayings, and seven discourses. One of the themes of the first half of this Gospel is that Jesus replaces various of the institutions of Judaism with himself: he is the Lamb of God who takes away the world's sin; his body is the temple where God's living presence resides; he replaces Jewish purification water with the new wine of the Gospel, and so on. In other words, the cleansing of the temple is placed in John 2 for theological, not chronological reasons—perfectly good ones to convey a larger truth about Jesus.

4. Obviously the errors of translators made when rendering the original into another language cannot be predicated of the original inspired authors themselves. Finding an error in an English translation must lead to checking against the Greek original.

5. It is necessary to know the conventions that reveal how the OT was handled by early Jews, including those who wrote the NT books. When one knows such conventions, one then avoids making the mistake of accusing a biblical author of misrendering the OT text, when in fact they are often just paraphrasing or making a homiletical use without precise translation or literal interpretation of the text, just as we often do. For instance, we would never accuse Eugene Peterson of mistranslating the OT simply because he is offering a paraphrase in *The Message*. Mistakes, to be sure, he has made, but not because he decided to offer a paraphrase of the whole. The NT translator's intent must be taken into account.

6. What an error does and should look like is something that violates the principle of noncontradiction. That is, A and not-A cannot both be true at the same time, in the same way

ascribed to the same person. For example, if one Gospel actually said that Jesus was born in Nazareth, and another actually said he was born in Bethlehem, then of course they can both be wrong in their claim, but they can't both be right! Or if Jesus says, "Blessed are the peacemakers," in Matthew, but in Luke instead of finding a variant on this saying we find the claim that Jesus said, "Blessed are the warmongers," then somebody has to be wrong. Or if one Gospel claims that Jesus called himself "Son of Man" but another Gospel has a saying which claims, "And though Jesus never spoke of himself this way, others called Jesus the Son of Man," then there is an error here. If Paul claimed that the second coming was definitely going to happen in his lifetime, and then it didn't, then he made a considerable theological and chronological error. But in fact the most you can get out of Paul is that he thought it was possible that the thief in the night might show up sooner rather than later. His "thief in the night" metaphor says it all: Jesus will come at an unexpected and unpredictable time, whether sooner or later. He did not predict that within his lifetime or that generation Jesus would return from heaven.[1]

Taking into account all contextual issues and all conventions that I know of that were operative in the day and time of the NT writers, I have yet to find a single example of a clear violation of the principle of noncontradiction anywhere in the NT. There are dozens of differences in various parallel accounts, but we do not have dueling banjos in the Greek NT. I may be missing something, and I may be blind to some obvious blemishes in these texts. But in fact, the NT authors appear to me to be truthful and trustworthy in the various nuanced ways they wanted to present the truth on a variety of subjects, taking into account their intents, limitations, and freedoms. Their truthfulness was certainly one of the criteria used to help decide the issue of which early Christian documents should be considered Scripture.

BUT DID THE CANON MISFIRE?

Understandably, there is no debate that the Bible is the church's book, in various senses of that phrase. All living, breathing church members recognized the canon of twenty-seven books of the NT. This fact has sometimes led to the erroneous conclusion that interpretation of the Bible should be seen as an in-house matter (its true meaning comes to light only in close reading in community), and correct interpretation can only be accomplished by the Christian community. In a sense this argument is rather like the old Latin dictum, *nulla salvatus ex cathedra* (there is no salvation outside the church), only now the dictum reads, *nulla interpretum ex cathedra*. In some respects this is a reaction to those who would say that the canon is an artificial boundary and we should stop privileging these particular twenty-seven texts. The problem with this approach is that God's Spirit can and does reveal truth, even the truth about the Bible, to those outside the circle of the body of Christ. Furthermore these documents are the literary residue of a missionary movement which believed that God loved and had now revealed himself to the world, and that Christians were supposed to take this message to the streets throughout the empire, not study it in conventicles.

If all truth is God's truth, then the church does not have a corner on the market. The light dawns in the darkness often in strange and nonecclesiastical places. I often think of my discussions about the NT with my good friend A. J. Levine, a Jewish female NT scholar at Vanderbilt. She often understands the text better than I do, and not because she is part of a Christian Bible study, but rather because God is good and sheds his light abroad in the world. This is hardly surprising if John 3:16 is true, that God loves the world and desires to save the world, not merely the church. For these reasons and others I do not think it is either historically or theologically true to say that the church chose and formed the canon, and that it is first and foremost the church's book. No, the church recognized that these books told the apostolic truth, they spoke the word of God, and so they wished to preserve them in a collection. The church, then and now, should not assume it has or can simply assume authority over the word; it should rather submit to God's word as the early church did again and again.

Sometimes as well, this whole discussion is bound up with the discussion of whether there is unity in the Bible or the NT, and of what sort. While I certainly agree there is a unity to the Bible, the unity does not come from the fact that it was collected into an anthology by human beings. These books are in the canon because they were believed to be true in various senses. It is nearer to the mark to say that because these books are a revelation from God and were recognized to be the word of God written, they reflect a natural and not an artificial unity. All the writers of the NT were convinced Christians who shared a whole battery of beliefs about God and God's capacity to reveal the divine nature and save people in and through Jesus Christ. But even more importantly, the one revealer God is both the central character in the narrative, which in itself gives the story unity, and is also the author, the one who inspired the writing of these books in the first place.[2] Thus, while these books were written by convinced Christians, and most of them were written primarily for Christians (one exception might be Luke–Acts, which may be doing apologetics for an interested patron who is on the verge of Christian faith), this does not mean that these books should only and can only be properly studied and understood by Christians. In this respect the Bible is very different than Gnostic literature, which clearly presupposed you needed to be part of the insider group, the elect, to understand it. The NT writers understood the more universal character and scope of the truth, the word of God, the good news for all people, that they proclaimed.

In our earlier discussion of 2 Timothy 3:16, we pointed out what a very high view of the nature of the entire OT Paul had. He saw it all as God-breathed, which is why it has such authority. I thus find it more than a little puzzling when Luke Timothy Johnson, in an otherwise first-rate commentary on 1 and 2 Timothy, attempts to argue that the authority of the Bible doesn't rest on its inspiration, but on its canonicity.[3] This is surely not what Paul thinks about the OT as even the OT canon was not yet closed when 2 Timothy was written. Surely Paul believes these words have authority because they are God's words spoken in human words and through human beings, but they also reflect God's character and so are truthful and trustworthy.

If one studies the ancient concept of inspiration, whether in relationship to biblical or other prophets, prophetic words, inspired by God, had authority because of the source, character, and truthfulness of the one inspiring the prophet to speak. Indeed sometimes it was even believed that the deity in question took over the prophet and simply spoke through him or her.

The holy writings were not seen as merely revelatory of God's word; they were seen as a written form of God's word, such that God said what the Scriptures said, or when it was not an oracle, the text spoke truthfully about some subject. Whatever one's feelings about the fundamentalist/modernist discussion about the Bible and its authority, they should not be allowed to skew what one says about what is being asserted in 2 Timothy 3:16 and about ancient views of inspiration.

Johnson goes on to add that the Bible does not function as an exclusive deposit of revelation but as an essential and normative resource for discerning and measuring the divine self-disclosure. This is nearer the mark, but the discussion has been skewed by suggesting that canonization conveys authority on the text rather than canonization being the process of recognizing authority and truth in the text. But can we say more about the NT canon?

The formation of the NT canon, as we mentioned earlier, was a process that had already begun in the NT era, as 2 Peter 3:16 suggests. Paul Achtemeier stresses that "the formation of the canon represented the working out of forces that were already present in the primitive Christian community and that would have made some form of canon virtually inevitable."[4] It was not a matter of fourth-century politics, or a matter of a group of old men sitting down in the fourth century AD and deciding these issues. Nor was it a matter of ruling out a bunch of books that had previously been on somebody's canon list.[5]

There was never any positive buzz for inclusion of any of the Gnostic texts in the NT canon, indeed there was only negative press all along about those books. They were seen as heresy in their own day, and long afterward as well. And you can't be said to exclude something that was never included on anyone's sacred text list in the first place. Not even the earliest of the Gnostic texts, the Gospel of Thomas, was ever on a canon list or seriously considered for inclusion as a sacred text for Christians, suitable for study and to be read in worship.

Often lost in the discussion of NT canonization is the fact that the early church had to also decide what form of the OT it would accept as Scripture—the Hebrew text or the LXX in some form. The Greek LXX seems to have become the church's de facto OT for the most part in the second century AD.[6] In other words, they thought *a translation of the Bible could be viewed as the Scripture, the word of God,* which is good news for all those who are monolingual and whose spoken language does not include any of the biblical ones. The church fathers, however, were uncertain whether to include all the material found in the LXX or only the books found in the Hebrew Bible, and the question of order in regard to the last collection in the OT, the Writings, was an issue since the Hebrew OT does not end with Malachi.

Eusebius, the father of church history, informs us that it was actually some of the books that *did* make it into the NT canon which were debated and sometimes disputed—books like Hebrews, because it was anonymous, or the more obviously Jewish documents like the letters and sermons of James or Jude, or the only prophetic book that made the cut, Revelation. No debate ensued about whether to include any of the four earliest Gospels, Matthew, Mark, Luke, and John, nor was there a debate about the Pauline corpus, with the exception of Hebrews.

Before the late fourth century when these matters were mostly settled, there had also been some debate about other orthodox books including the Shepherd of Hermas or *1 Clement*, or *Barnabas*, and even a Jewish book like Wisdom of Solomon, which was greatly loved by many early Christians, and indeed had influenced Jesus himself. But there was no consensus on such books. There seems in fact to have been some suspicion that Hermas tried to correct the author of Hebrews in

Hebrews 6 who was (wrongly) understood by some to argue that sins committed after baptism were not to be forgiven and the person could not be restored. But orthodoxy was not deemed enough to recognize a book as Scripture; it needed to be an early witness, a first-century witness, one that went back directly or indirectly to the original eyewitnesses, apostles, and their coworkers or an early prophet like John of Patmos. In other words, a combination of historical and theological factors led to books being recognized as part of the canon. They were the word of God before they were accepted as canonical, and they had to be recognized as such.

The criteria discussed then by the early church fathers involved things like apostolicity in some sense (either from an apostle or one of his cohorts writing in the apostolic tradition), orthodoxy, truth telling, profitability of the document for training in Christian righteousness, and the like. Recognizing these criteria, it then becomes interesting and remarkable that the Eastern part of the church represented by Athanasius (in his festal letter in AD 367), the African part of the church in 397 which listed only these twenty-seven books, and then the Western part of the church represented by the pope, with the help of figures like Jerome, concluded that these twenty-seven books should be recognized as the Christian Scriptures. No one gathering of all the church fathers took place in one time or place to settle this issue, by Constantine or anyone else. Rather the process of discernment and discrimination was going on throughout the second through fourth centuries, and a settled agreement on the twenty-seven books was in place by the end of the fourth century. But this precise collection minus some of the Catholic Epistles (see below) was already suggested in the form of the Muratorian canon list by the end of the second century AD or the beginning of the third. Many if not most of the Gnostic documents were written after that canon list appeared. Again, no canon list, not even the heretic Marcion's list, included any Gnostic texts.

So then, properly speaking from a historical point of view, a book had to be widely recognized as true and orthodox and even apostolic in some sense before it could ever be recognized as Scripture, not the other way around. Canonizing a book didn't make it true or the word of God, though it gave added clout or authority after the fact. As we saw earlier, the word of God was a much larger category than the written Scriptures, and even referred to oral proclamation in its Christian form before there ever were any written Christian Scriptures. Once the canon was in place, though, it became the main litmus test of truth or error thereafter.

Positive and negative historical developments led toward canonization. For example, the dying off of the apostles and eyewitnesses and therefore the need to have things not only written down but collected and placed in safe places became crucial already in the second century AD. Then there was the wake-up call when you have figures like Marcion who came to Rome in about AD 144 and suggested a very truncated canon list—Luke's Gospel and Paul's letters minus the Pastorals. He entirely rejected the OT as proclaiming a vengeful God. Against this limited canon list, the church continued to say no; there was a wider corpus of writings, including more Gospels and more letters, that the church would use as its sacred texts as well as the OT. Justin Martyr said that the fourfold Gospel collection, which already circulated in a single codex in the second century, plus a collection of OT books were the Christian Scriptures. The earliest fuller canon list is the Muratorian canon list which probably dates to the end of the second century and included Matthew, Mark, Luke, John, Acts, the letters of Paul including the Pastorals, 1 and 2 John, Jude, and Revelation. Only James, Hebrews, 1–2 Peter, and 3 John are missing.

Another interesting criterion arises when we study this part of the story of canonization. As Luke Johnson says, it becomes clear when it is decided that the Shepherd of Hermas will not be included—and the instructions are given that it is fine to read privately, but ought not to be read in public worship—that a "key factor for canonization is not whether documents can be read or used by individuals but whether they are to be read publicly in worship."[7] When we get to Eusebius of Caesarea (AD 320–330), he enunciates three criteria for acceptance of such writings: use in the church, apostolic origins, and theological consistency with the clearly apostolic documents (*Hist. eccl.* 3.25.1-7). What he seems to be focusing on here is the criteria to be used to make decisions about the books still being disputed—James, Jude, 2 Peter, and 2-3 John—and whether they also can be included along with the universally recognized books: the four canonical Gospels, Acts, the letters of Paul, 1 John, 1 Peter, and Revelation.

Remarkably the various parts of the church, without political or ecclesiastical coercion, and under the guidance of the Holy Spirit, all came to the same conclusion about the twenty-seven books of the NT. It was not a matter of the church sitting down in a big meeting and forming the canon. Rather the church recognized the canon that had been forming since one of the first letters of Paul was written and spoke of the living word of God, oral, and then written, as something synonymous with the Christian message about Jesus. This is why Achtemeier is able to say:

> One can say then that the formation of the canon was coterminous with the life of the Christian community during its first three centuries of existence. It is not the case that some synod or council of bishops decided which books should be normative and thereafter required for Christians to accept. Rather the books that were finally included in the canon were included because over the centuries Christians had come to use them in their worship and instruction and to revere them for the power they displayed in engendering, enriching and correcting Christian faith. The canon thus represents the *collective experience of the Christian community during its formative centuries.*[8]

How then did we get from the fourth century until now with the huge proliferation of translations of the Bible? What happened in between?

THE BIBLE GOES GLOBAL IN LOCAL LANGUAGES

Sometimes missed in the discussion of the NT as Scripture and canon and the like is the fact that while the church was busy recognizing the Greek NT, it was also very busy translating it into numerous other languages. One of the earliest translations was the one into Coptic for Egyptians, which seems to date from as early as AD 270. Then, too, one must mention the translation into Ethiopic in at least as early as the fifth century AD.

Just to cite a few examples, we have found fragments of a Syriac version from about AD 300, not a surprise since one of the major early ethnic churches was the Syrian church.[9] Somewhere between AD 350 and 439, the Bible was translated into Armenian for those in the area of the Caucasus mountains and beyond, and for that same general vicinity a translation into Georgian took place about AD 450.

Latin was the official language of the Roman Empire, and so not surprisingly there was already a translation in old Latin of the Bible in North Africa perhaps as early as AD 195. This is not to be confused with the translation that became the classic and the standard: the so-called Latin Vulgate (*vulgatus* referring to the common tongue, from which we oddly enough get the word "vulgar") undertaken by Jerome. Jerome began his work sometime in about AD 390, finishing about 404, and what distinguished his work from others and earlier efforts is that he compared the LXX to a text of the Hebrew Scriptures in doing his Latin translation. This particular translation was to dominate the landscape through the Middle Ages, and unfortunately led in the Western part of the church to the neglect of the LXX, and even in many places the Greek NT itself. Not until the Renaissance and figures like Petrarch, who sparked a renewed interest in Greek and ancient Roman literature, did a renewed interest take place in having the Bible in the West in its original languages again.

Looking eastward, we know that the Bible was translated into Arabic from Coptic and Syriac versions at least as early as the sixth century AD. Sometime in the ninth century the Orthodox Church's missionary work going into the southern part of Russia led to a Slavonic translation of the Bible as well. Because of the dominance of Latin as the continued language of the church, even after the Roman Empire was long gone, it is not until the twelfth century AD that translations into the vernacular took place for French-, Italian-, and Spanish-speaking persons. Not surprisingly the Roman Catholic Church prohibited the use of these versions other than as aids to persons who could not read the Latin, and so as a supplement to the Latin Bible, which impeded progress on the translation front.

It took the invention of the printing press in the mid-fifteenth century (the first book was the Latin Vulgate rendering of the Bible, printed by Johannes Gutenberg); the rise of Luther, who provided his own translation into German (1522); the Reformation in general; and figures like Erasmus who produced a Greek New Testament (1516) to move things along more rapidly toward the proliferation of translations that would take into account the Greek and Hebrew texts, as Luther had done, using Erasmus's text and not just be based on the Vulgate. The important point is that the vernacular versions that began to appear after Gutenberg would increasingly go back and consult the original-language texts of the Bible.

Before we begin to talk about the English Bible, which requires a longer discussion, we should note four things about the translation of the Bible into all these languages:

1. It was a function of and reflected that Christianity was an evangelistic religion throughout this period, and the assumption was that people could not be saved unless they heard the Bible message in their own languages (see Acts 2).

2. This whole process happened in fits and starts, and not under some central authority's efforts. It happened for the most part because the need arose for all these translations as the missions went forward.

3. It was assumed that a translation of the Bible could be called Scripture or the word of God for this or that language group, yet . . .

4. Thank goodness some figures, such as Jerome, and much later Erasmus and Luther, realized that these vernacular transla-

tions needed to be in touch with the original Hebrew and Greek texts of the Bible. Since Erasmus's day we have not turned back from that principle when it comes to translation, and look where it has led. Today the whole Bible is available in more than 340 languages, and the NT in over 800 languages, and furthermore, at least one book of the Bible has been translated into more than 2,000 languages as of 1995. No other book of comparable antiquity or even from the modern age can make this claim.

THE RISE OF THE ENGLISH BIBLE: WYCLIFFE, TYNDALE, COVERDALE, AND KING JAMES

Without question, after the Latin Vulgate, no vernacular translation of the Bible has had more impact on Christian life and culture in general than the King James Version. What is seldom noted when the King James Version is busy being praised to the skies for its various qualities is that it was a translation that owed an enormous amount of its diction and memorable phrasing to its English predecessor versions, especially the partial OT and the entire NT that William Tyndale finished. Furthermore, at the other end of the equation, many are oblivious to the fact that the KJV went through various revised editions. But the story must begin with Wycliffe.

One of the key principles of the Reformation was that the Bible should be placed in the hands of ordinary persons, not kept in the scholar's study or chained to a pulpit in some church. This revolution was made possible by the rise of the printing press, which reduced enormously the laborious process of hand copying the Bible that had gone on since the first century AD, and well before then, counting the various books of the OT.

Yet our discussion in this section must start with John Wycliffe (1330–1384) who argued at length, and in both Latin and English no less, for an English translation of the Bible. There was great fear by the church hierarchy that placing the Bible into the hands of the laity might cause the breakdown of authority or even have a social leveling effect on society. The clerics' monopoly over the church might suffer as well.

When Wycliffe did his translation from the Latin Vulgate, or at least aided and abetted those who made the translation for him, he was roundly criticized. A certain Henry Knighton put it this way: "Wycliffe translated it from Latin into the English—not the anglic!—language. As a result, what was previously known only by learned clerics and those of good understanding has become common, and available to the laity—in fact, even to women who can read. As a result, the pearls of the Gospel have been scattered before swine."[10] Wycliffe's efforts opened the proverbial Pandora's box, and the response was not only swift in his day but consistent thereafter. The archbishop of Canterbury in 1407, Thomas Arundel, banned anyone from translating the Bible on their own initiative and authority into English! He also took the second step to ban the reading in private or public of any such English translation. Clearly enough he was worried that things were getting out of hand. The issue was sensitive well into the sixteenth century; John Colet, dean of St. Paul's cathedral in London, was suspended from his post in 1513 for translating the Lord's Prayer into English. Just when the clerics thought they were getting things under control, along came Martin Luther who published his German translation in 1522, and he had English admirers, notably William Tyndale (1496–1536).

Tyndale was no ordinary layperson. He had studied at Magdalen College at Oxford. Tyndale was later to complain that the Oxford dons would not allow him to study the Scriptures until after he had had many years of studying the Greek and Latin pagan classics. But there was a rise at both Oxford and Cambridge of interest in, and scholars competent in, both Greek and Hebrew during the course of the fifteenth and sixteenth centuries. This was a good thing too, since they would be needed on the translation committee for the King James Version in the early seventeenth century.

This rise in the interest in biblical languages happened in spite of the scholarly prejudice that only Latin was really worth knowing as the language of academia. Just how much and how long this Latin influence continued to be true can be seen from the fact that even in the first half of the eighteenth century we have the story from John Wesley that when he wanted to have conversations with the Moravian Peter Böhler, since Böhler's spoken English was poor, and the same could be said for Wesley's German, they spoke to each other in the language they were both fluent in—Latin, even though the subject matter was Protestant theology! If we need further testimony to the enduring impact of Latin and the Vulgate, we need only mention that Catholic services were still being done mostly in Latin when I was born in 1951. Vaticans I and II changed all that.

Tyndale was smart enough to realize that England was too volatile a place for him to translate the Bible into English, and so the poor man moved to Cologne in Germany and translated the NT during the period 1524–25. After some difficulties the first edition finally came out in book form in 1526 in Worms.

The high degree of Luther's influence on Tyndale can be seen from the table of contents of his NT, for, as Luther had done with his translation, he listed Hebrews, James, Jude, and Revelation as being of dubious authenticity, and they were placed at the end of the book and were not even numbered like the other books. The 1526 edition of Tyndale's translation was smuggled into England, an event that produced irreversible pressure for an English Bible to be produced and controlled in England. Despite the fact that Tyndale's name never appeared on a copy of his translation, he paid a heavy price for his efforts; he was hung and then burned at the stake on October 6, 1536, having been betrayed by those who opposed his efforts. His fate earned him a place in Foxe's *Book of Martyrs*.

Bishop Tunstall of London had gone on something of a personal crusade against Tyndale and his translation (both sad and ironic since Tyndale first came to Tunstall to ask if he would patronize the translation effort). One of the most amazing parts of this story is that Tunstall went all the way to Antwerp to stop the printing of the Tyndale Translation in 1529. Through a merchant named Augustine Packington he was offered an opportunity to buy as many copies as he liked of the translation for a price. The bishop agreed. Unbeknownst to the bishop, Packington went straight to Tyndale and told him about the deal. Tyndale was thrilled because suddenly he would have a lot more money to produce more copies, even if Tunstall took all the ones he bought and burned them. The deal was struck, and unwittingly the bishop funded the continuing publication of Tyndale's translation.

Tyndale in fact had a very great and rare gift of being able not only to translate the Bible but to translate it into beautiful and memorable English prose. To him we owe phrases like "my brother's keeper" (Gen 4), "the salt of the earth" (Matt 5), "a law unto themselves" (Rom 2), and "the powers that be" (Rom 13). Tyndale came up with the hybrid term "Jehovah," combining two different Hebrew names for God. He invented the English word "Passover" for the Hebrew *pesach*. We also owe to Tyndale use of terms like "scapegoat" and "atonement" for Hebrew terms that had no good direct English equivalents.

Tyndale unfortunately had not finished his translation of the OT when he was executed. Only the Pentateuch had been really completed, so it was left to a far less skilled translator Miles Coverdale (1488–1569), who almost entirely took over Tyndale's work and incorporated it into his own, adding a fresh translation of the rest of the OT depending most on Luther's German translation, it would appear. Coverdale's work first went to print in 1535, shortly before Tyndale was executed in England. One could in fact call Coverdale really a compilation of earlier translations, mostly Tyndale's.

With the help of Thomas Cromwell, an entrepreneur named Richard Grafton printed yet another English Bible shortly there after called Matthew's Bible. The text was in fact edited by John Rogers, who had been a close associate of Tyndale. It not only followed the Tyndale translation very closely, but had the additional benefit of being printed in Antwerp where additional pages of Tyndale's OT translation had turned up that had never made it into Tyndale's own book.

In 1539, a good sixty-plus years before the KJV, the Great Bible came out, the first authorized English translation. The Great Bible was simply a revision of the Matthew's Bible done by none other than Miles Coverdale himself, but with a table of contents that did not reflect Luther's biases against various books, including Hebrews and James. The reason it was called the Great Bible was due to its size, because in addition to the OT and NT it included the OT apocryphal books as well. This translation is mostly a retread of Tyndale, with some Coverdale blended in, especially where there was no Tyndale text to follow.

The next translation of note and influence was the famous Geneva Bible, which was largely the work of William Whittingham (1524–1579). His NT version was printed first in 1557, and once more it was heavily indebted to Tyndale, the real progenitor of all these later English versions. Whittingham's one real innovation is that he changed the nomenclature of those books that Luther was largely unhappy with from the "Catholic Epistles" to the "General Epistles," which made Protestants feel much better. The Geneva Bible was widely read and accepted in the latter part of the sixteenth century, but when James of Scotland came to the throne of England upon Elizabeth's death in 1603, there still had not been a decision taken on what Bible might become the official Bible of the English realm. As it turned out, James had a passionate dislike of the Geneva Bible because its marginal notes did not support the notion that the Bible upholds the divine right of kings, a doctrine about which James was passionate.

In 1604 King James convened a conference held at Hampton Court Palace in which he proposed to listen to the laments and complaints of both Puritans and Anglicans about church life in that period. Some of the complaints had to do with the Prayer Book, which the Puritans wanted abolished, something James was not prepared to do. Could he make a concession on another matter, which he saw as less crucial, that would placate the Puritans? The answer turned out to be yes, and it led to the KJV.

John Reynolds, the leader of the Puritan delegation, proposed a new Bible translation. James saw this as the concession that would ease the religious tensions. The decree was made that "a translation be made of the whole Bible, *as consonant as can be to the original Hebrew and Greek;* and this to be set out and printed without any marginal notes, and only to be used in all churches in England in time of divine service."[11] It is not clear whether the king officially authorized the translation, as the records of the period 1600–1613 were lost in a fire. The translation was to be done by fifty-four scholars from both Oxford and Cambridge (the only two English universities at the time), and Lancelot Andrewes, Regius Professor of Greek and Hebrew of Oxford, was to lead the team, yet James's close ally Bishop Richard Bancroft is the person who laid down the translation rules for this English Bible.

Rule 1 read: "The ordinary Bible read in the Church, commonly called the Bishop's Bible, to be followed and as little altered as the Truth of the original will permit." Now the Bishop's Bible of 1568 was simply a smaller version of the Great Bible, meant to compete with the Geneva Bible, though it never eclipsed the latter. This rule makes clear that the scholars on the translation team were to do their best to follow an earlier English translation, and they are further instructed to stick with the most commonly used renderings in this and other earlier English versions. Their process was to compare these earlier translations to the Hebrew and Greek text, and do their best to follow the lead of the earlier English versions. Rule 14 adds that they should consult Tyndale's, Matthew's, Coverdale's, and Geneva's translations and follow them where they agree better with the original language text. The King James translators did not attempt, nor did they see it as their duty, to produce an entirely fresh translation based just on the Greek and Hebrew texts of the Bible. As Alister McGrath makes abundantly clear, they saw themselves as standing on the shoulders of giants like Tyndale. They were not trying to be innovators, but nor were they mere copiers of earlier versions, particularly in spots where there had been advances in original language study.[12] They were only as good as the original-language manuscripts they had would allow them to be.

Erasmus's Greek NT was based on five or six Greek manuscripts, none of which were any earlier than the tenth century AD. Nevertheless, this allowed Erasmus to make some corrections of errors found in the Latin Vulgate. The next edition of the Greek NT, the so-called Bezan text (compiled by Theodore Beza in Geneva), has the same liabilities of not having any really early Greek manuscripts to follow. The Bezan text of the Greek NT came to be called the Textus Receptus, but this was not because any church ever officially pronounced it to be the best Greek NT text. It was simply the best available to scholars at that time, and the KJV team used it in their translation work. One other more technical point needs to be made. The Textus Receptus is not simply identical with the so-called Byzantine text that became so important in the eastern part of the Roman Empire from the fourth century onward, although they are close at many points. The vast majority of scholars today do not think that either the Textus Receptus or the Byzantine Greek text reflects our earliest and best text of the Greek NT. This in turn means that translations largely based on the Textus Receptus, such as the KJV, are today not considered by the vast majority of NT scholars as the best rendering of what the original text of the Greek NT said.

Not surprisingly, considering where the universities were in England, and taking into account Tyndale's own Oxford pedigree, the English that we find in the King James is basically the English of southeastern England, not the English of the northern part of the country (much less the King's English, as he was a Scot!). It took from 1604 to 1610 for the six different teams of scholars to finish their work. From the start, strong consideration was given to the aural dimension to the text, as the KJV was primarily a translation to be used in public services. The teams undoubtedly read their translations aloud and tried them out on each other, something we could use more of with modern translations. In the original preface to the KJV, the translators state plainly, "Truly (Good Christian Reader) we never thought from the beginning, that we should need to make a new Translation, nor yet to make of a bad one a good one, . . . but to make a good one better, or out of many good ones, one principal good one . . . that hath been our endeavor."[13]

Miles Smith, one of the translators of the KJV, made the following comments about the authority and inspiration of the Bible: "The original thereof being from God, not man; the inditer, the holy spirit, not the wit of Apostles or Prophets; the Penmen such as were sanctified from the womb, and endued with a principle portion of God's spirit; the matter, verity, piety, purity, uprightness; the form, God's word, God's testimony, God's oracle, the word of truth, the word of salvation."[14] Notice that he is not referring to his and his colleagues' translation work, he is referring to "the original thereof." On the scale of the aforementioned taxonomy of views of what Scripture is, this can be characterized as either view 1 or view 2.[15]

There is no evidence that the KJV translators ever saw themselves as uniquely inspired to do what they did. Instead, they saw themselves as those who followed in the human footsteps of their predecessors wherever possible, making changes cautiously. They were under no delusions that they had created a perfect translation but they thought it to be the best yet available in English, and so it was. They also freely admitted that there were many words, especially in the Hebrew text— for instance, names of birds—that they were unsure how to render into English. The preface is commendably modest about the difficulties and imperfections of all translations including this one. The translators realized that there is great difficulty in managing a balance between faithfulness and elegance.

Smith was both passionate and eloquent about how important it was for the translators to do their best to render the Bible into good common English, and he adds in that first preface, "Translation it is that openeth the window to let the light in; that breaketh the shell, that we may eat the kernel; that putteth aside the curtain, that we might look into the Most Holy place, that removeth the cover of the well, that we might come by the water. . . . Indeed without translation into the vulgar tongue, the unlearned are but like children at Jacob's well (which is deep) . . . without a bucket or something to draw with."[16]

Unfortunately, there were many printer's errors in the first edition of 1611, which led to a second edition only shortly thereafter in 1613 where most of the errors were corrected. Bishop Bancroft's decision that the original editions of the KJV would include the translation of the Apocrypha caused some chagrin, and not surprisingly in due course the Puritans lobbied to have it removed in later editions. Not surprisingly as well, various Puritans, when they moved to America, did not bring a KJV with them. Their Bible of choice was the Geneva Bible.

We have in a short span here gone on a long odyssey taking us from the process that led up to the canonization of the NT, to the historical process that led to its translations into many languages, most importantly of all into English. The story has many twists and turns, but at every step of the way two things are clear. Those involved in these many labors believed the written-down Bible was itself one expression of the word of God. They also believed that foreign-language translations that were careful and faithful also could reasonably approximate the original language texts and so deserve to be called the word of God in a secondary or derivative sense. But as Miles Smith pointed out, only the original thereof deserves that title in the full and complete sense.

Chapter 7

HOW TO PICK A TRANSLATION
WITHOUT LOSING YOUR RELIGION

We must wrestle with their use of words, syntax, and literary forms, which
express their ideas, and we must hear those ideas within both the author's
and reader's cultural contexts and presuppositions, if ever we are adequately
to understand what they intended by their words.

—Gordon Fee

"Something gets lost in translation." Most readers of the Bible, if they
have studied any language that is foreign to them, know the truth of
this cliché. No two languages are exactly identical. There are words,
phrases, idioms, and grammatical constructions in one language that
do not have exact equivalents in another. If I call up my friend Hans in
Germany, who knows no English, and I say the literal German equivalent of "I have an ax to grind," Hans is going think I have become a
lumberjack, not that I have an agenda. Idioms especially differ from
one language to another, and furthermore, idioms, slang, and normal
usage keep changing in any living language. Studying a dead language
like Latin and translating it is far easier. For example, in the 1950s the
term "hip" was used to refer to someone who was avant garde, really

"with it." It was replaced sometime in the 1960s with the term "cool," and of course neither uses of either word was a literal denotation of those words. Sometimes an author will use the denotated or dictionary meaning of a word, and sometimes the connotated meaning.

Understandably, then, picking an appropriate translation can become a bewildering and indeed frustrating process, especially with as many English translations of the Bible as are available. It was certainly easier to decide this issue in the seventeenth century when the KJV began to dominate the landscape. Why is it so complicated now, and why are there so many translations?

WHY SO MANY MODERN TRANSLATIONS OF GOD'S WORD?

Two major reasons explain the abundance of modern translations of the Bible, besides of course that Bible publishers want to make money. The first of these is that since the late nineteenth century, we have discovered literally thousands of manuscripts of various parts of the Bible that help us to get closer to the original text of both the OT and the NT. Most everyone is familiar with the Qumran or Dead Sea Scrolls that were discovered in the late 1940s and which have helped us to come much closer to the original Hebrew text of various parts of the OT, especially Isaiah. In fact, today we have about five thousand copies of parts or the whole of the NT in Greek, something the King James translators could only have dreamed of, bound as they were largely to one source, the Bezan text, and it not very ancient, only really reflecting the late Byzantine textual tradition. The earlier and earlier bits of NT or OT scrolls we find, the more revisions need to be made as we work our way back to the original texts.

But not only new discoveries prompt new translations. English is also a living language that keeps changing. Two illustrations can help us here. In Acts 26:14 in the original KJV the text read, "It hurts you to kick against the pricks." Today, understandably, since the word "prick" carries a very different connotation in our world than it did in 1611, it is more apt and less scandalous to translate, "It is hard for you to kick against the goad" (NIV). A goad is a cattle prod of sorts with spikes sticking out of it, and the saying actually means that "your actions are futile, indeed self-destructive, for it is futile to resist your destiny."

Or consider one of the most beloved verses in the OT—Psalm 23:1. The older English versions have "The Lord is my shepherd, I shall not want." This is problematic today for the very good reason that while the word "want," as in "be in want," in 1611 had the sense of "lacking" or "needing" something, today this sentence may well suggest that the psalmist doesn't want God, which is not at all the intended sense of the sentence. The sentence actually means "Since Yahweh is my shepherd I shall lack for nothing (essential)." Thus we see that the pressure for new translations comes both from archaeological discoveries and because English is a moving target—a living and developing language. How then does one sort out which Bible will be right for one's own situation and needs?

THE BIBLE SHOPPER'S GUIDE

When it comes to Bibles, one size (and type) does not fit all. Different translations are done for different purposes and different audiences. So a better first question than "Which Bible should I buy?" is "Who am I buying this for, and what do they already know when it comes to the Bible, the Jewish or Christian faith, and so on?" You also want to ask the question, "What age range was this translation written for?" Different Bibles target different audiences. You need to be aware of this before you walk into Billy Bob's Christian bookstore and plunk your money down on the counter. In other words, you need to come as an informed consumer—informed about the different Bibles, and informed about who the recipient is.

Bibles range in scope from very paraphrastic (e.g., the Message or the Living Bible), to somewhat periphrastic (the New Living Translation) to idiomatic translations (e.g., NRSV, TNIV, NEB, Jerusalem Bible, NKJV, TEV—in fact, most translations fall into this camp) to nearly literal translations (NASB, the NET Bible, and a few others). Here is not the place to debate the literal versus nonliteral issue of translation, but you should be aware that there is no such thing as an absolutely literal translation because: (1) English is a very different (and nongenderized) language than the biblical languages (i.e., we don't have masculine or feminine nouns and adjectives unlike Hebrew and Greek); (2) the structure of English sentences is often different from these biblical languages; (3) there are words in these languages which have no one word English equivalent; and (4) sometimes the language in the source is used figuratively and sometimes literally. We could keep giving many more reasons that there is no absolutely literal translation—and frankly you wouldn't want such a translation because you would have to keep unscrambling the word order, the syntax, and other difficulties. The bottom line is, you want a translation that conveys most accurately the *original meaning* of the biblical text. More often than not, this translation will tend to be idiomatic.

What do I mean by an idiomatic translation? This approach to translating, while following a word-for-word approach if it makes sense in English, tends to go for a meaning-for-meaning, concept-for-concept approach, being sensitive to idioms in both the biblical language and in our own. For example, the word "foot" was an idiom in Hebrew for the genitals, in particular the male genitals. When we read that Saul covered or uncovered his foot, we are talking about him relieving himself. How should the translator translate this, given that a literal translation will not convey the meaning? A rendering of the meaning rather than just what the text says might be preferable, given that not everyone is going to use an annotated Bible with notes. A good rule of thumb is that if the translation has to have umpteen notes to explain just the meaning of the words and phrases in the translation, it is probably either too literal or too paraphrastic.

Meaning occurs in contexts. Words do not really have meaning in isolation from their use and contexts. Take, for example, the English word "row." It could be a verb telling a person in a boat what to do. It could be a noun referring to a line of seats. It could refer to a fight and would be pronounced differently in that usage. Words only have meaning in contexts, which is as true of words in the original biblical languages as ours. It is not true that "in the beginning was the dictionary." Dictionaries are compilations derived from the study of how words are used in various real texts and contexts. Moral to the story: go for a Bible that best conveys the meaning of the original inspired text to the particular target audience you have in mind.

Let us suppose you are shopping for a children's Bible. The question then becomes what age of child? If you are dealing with really young children, you could go for the Living Bible, which was originally done as a paraphrase for children by Ken Taylor, or the Today's English Version (TEV—originally Good News for Modern Man) which is written with no words over an eighth-grade vocabulary. It contains none of what my granny used to call twenty-five-dollar words. If you are buying a young adult a Bible for graduation or confirmation, you need to take into account what sort of reader they are. If the goal is to get them to read the Bible stories at all, the Message is not a bad choice, but it is a paraphrase that tends to be far more interpretive rather than less, compared to an idiomatic translation.

When we are dealing with the idiomatic translations, which for the most part are the most widely used and most popular, a variety of factors should be kept in mind.

> Principle One: All other things being equal, a team translation will be much better than an individual translation. Why? Because no one person is an expert in the meaning of every verse of the Bible. Thus, Eugene Peterson's or Ken Taylor's paraphrase or J. B. Phillips's translation done all by himself, is less likely to be accurate at all points than a team translation.

> Principle Two: Not all teams are created equal. For example, the team led by Lancelot Andrewes who translated the KJV in 1611 was only as good as its skills in the biblical languages and in the English of Shakespeare's era. More to the point, they could only be as good

as the original language manuscripts that lay before them. The truth is, we have far better and earlier manuscripts of both the Hebrew and the Greek texts of the Bible today than they did back then, and so we can produce a translation much closer to the original wording than they could have done.

While we are dealing with the KJV, it is well to point out that we don't speak olde Englishe, yea verily, anymore. There is an issue of archaic English if you are a KJV-only person, and you discover that you have to end up retranslating the English of the Bible since English is a living language. I once had a young lady in Sunday school in Durham, England, ask me why the Psalm says, "God is an aweful God." I tried to explain that the word "aweful" in 1611 meant full of awe and wonder, whereas today it means "bbbbbbbad to the bone." In fact, the word is spelled differently: "awful." The interesting thing is that the KJV was even a bit archaic in its own day, following English usages from the previous century, and in particular following Tyndale as we saw in the last chapter. Elegance of language is an issue for some folks, which tends to mean the use of more formal and sometimes archaic English. Thus, the ESV strives for a bit less modern English, and it can be said to be adopting and adapting the RSV of several decades ago as a baseline. The ESV thus has a more traditional and formal feel because the English language has certainly become less formal and more filled with new words, including all sorts of new slang, due to the technological revolution and the rise of the Internet. The danger with such a translation is that it becomes a glorious anachronism that does not speak in the most up-to-date form of a living language.

Up-to-date translations are typically more useful now than archaic ones. The Bible is hard enough to understand without having to deal with archaic English. What about the NKJV? It overcomes the archaic language issue to a considerable extent, but alas, it doesn't do a better job with the text criticism. There are consequences to knowing that the Byzantine Text and the Textus Receptus do not represent the earliest and best text of numerous biblical verses. If you do a translation that pays too much homage to any of these later texts, then you are ignoring the evidence from second- and third- and fourth-century papyri and codexes that indicate that the original text did not have this word or that phrase, and so on. Unfortunately that is the story of the NKJV. Most experts on the text of the NT would not advise us to pick a translation that doesn't do justice to the earliest and best evidence we have about what the Greek text originally said.

The question you must ask is, do I want an English translation that does its very best to give me what the original inspired writer wrote plus nothing, or do I want to sing, "If it was good enough for Grandma, it's good enough for me"? In my view those who know something about the history of the English translation of the Bible (for instance, knowing how much of the KJV was cribbed from William Tyndale's translation) know that English translations are a work in progress. You cannot start acting as if a particular translation was dropped from the sky by God without error. There are no fully inspired or inerrant translations, only inspired original-language texts, which we are still in the process of recovering.

I personally would recommend for pulpit and pew use, and for Bible study for young adults or adults, one of the following Bibles: the TNIV (first choice, done by an excellent team of evangelical scholars), the Jerusalem Bible (particularly if you want a Catholic Bible that has the OT Apocrypha), or the NRSV (less preferable but still good, and done by a theologically broad group of translators). In some respects the NRSV is too tied down to the RSV as well, which was of course a revision of the KJV. The New Living Translation (not to be confused with the Living Bible) is a bit too paraphrastic for my taste, and the TEV is especially for congregations mainly composed of those without college degrees. If you are into using multiple decent translations of the Bible, *The Evangelical Parallel New Testament* published by Oxford is a very useful tool. Its parallel column presentation allows a comparison of the translations and reveals where there are difficult verses, and lets us know why any Bible study leader needs commentaries to make sense of the text especially with difficult verses.

Two translations to avoid are the New World Translation (the Jehovah's Witness translation, which makes a mess of the Greek in various places) and the Amplified Bible, which is not bad as a tool for Bible study, although not as useful for reading in church or to be used as a pew Bible; it's too confusing, frankly.

What about study Bibles? There are too many to mention. My rule of thumb is that one should go after a study Bible that is based on one of the better idiomatic translations. But you may well find that the notes in some study Bibles are either too easy on the one end of the spectrum or too technical at the other end of the spectrum. The decision depends on where you, or the person you are buying the Bible for, are on the educational pilgrimage toward better understanding of the Bible.

Another issue that is more difficult to adjudicate is that some study Bibles have a very specific sectarian orientation or bias. The classic example would be the Scofield Reference Bible, which was set up with notes and even headings in the text to support dispensational theology. This is not a good type of Bible with which to start an in-depth study. The American Bible Society has put out a study Bible with a wealth of resources called the Learning Bible, based on the Contemporary English Version. This Bible is good for college students especially. One may also want to consider the Net Bible, though it is a bit overwhelming for some first-timers. The NRSV and TNIV study Bibles are quite good as well.

Obviously the whole issue of picking an English Bible translation becomes an emotional issue and is especially problematized in evangelical churches because theological issues and issues such as the use of gender-inclusive language enter into the discussion of differing translations. The word "liberal" or "conservative" is bandied about, sadly enough, when in fact translators are notably cautious in their approach to things, usually being careful to follow good precedent in previous translations. This in fact has been a guiding principle of translation ever since the KJV itself was produced. The fact is, various good and useful translations are available that closely enough approximate the Greek NT to be called a faithful rendering of the text. My own preference at the moment is for the TNIV, though of course it may eventually be eclipsed by an even better translation.

THE BATTLE OVER GENDER-INCLUSIVE LANGUAGE

In regard to the issue of gender-inclusive language, the English language has largely moved on from the place where we ought to be comfortable called women "men" or using the term "mankind" rather than "humankind." Just in terms of normal English usage today, the use of "men" or "mankind" in a gender-inclusive sense is usually considered objectionable both inside and outside the church. Most women whom I have had contact with in the church, especially women under the age of fifty, including in conservative and evangelical churches, feel excluded by the constant use of such language. Excluding half your audience in the way you speak is not good, and there are plenty of texts in the NT where both women and men are part of the audience. In such cases one can just as easily render the term *adelphoi* (brothers) as "brothers and sisters" without losing the spiritual-family-language flavor of the address.

For some conservative Christians, this approach to language becomes a theological issue because of a strong belief in the subordination of women to men. Not surprisingly those promoting that kind of agenda are happier with a translation that supports their agenda to put women in their place, which they believe is as a subheading under men. But all Christians need to understand that the interpretive issues involved in when and when not to use gender-inclusive language are considerable. Let's take an example. The Greek word *anthrōpos* means "human being"; it does not mean "male." Thus, when Jesus is called in the Gospels "Son of *anthrōpos*," it would certainly be appropriate to translate the phrase "Son of Humanity," but in fact even gender-inclusive translations tend not to do this for the very good reason that Jesus was a male—a man.

But you see what complicates the issue is whether one thinks this phrase is being used in a technical sense or in a very generic sense, at least at times in the Gospels. For example, in Mark 2:27-28 we have a dilemma. Verse 27 clearly is referring to human beings in general, and it is said that the sabbath is made for them, not the other way around. But the very next verse is connected to the previous one and seems to say, "So the 'Son of Man' is Lord even over the sabbath." The question then becomes: is verse 28 a particular reference to Jesus alone being Lord over the sabbath, or is this continuation of verse 27 just a continuation of the thought of the previous verse about humans in general? If the latter is true, you could render it "the Son of Humanity is Lord over the sabbath," especially since the term *anthrōpos* is used in both these verses and since the discussion in that context is not about Jesus' behavior in particular, but rather that of his disciples. There are, however, far more instances in Mark when it seems clear that Jesus alone is meant by the phrase (e.g. Mark 2:10; 8:31; 9:31; 10:45; 14:62). And there is the further issue that when Jesus uses the phrase as a self-reference, he usually seems to be alluding to Daniel 7, and the Son of Man figure in that text. In these cases, the phrase becomes a rather technical one, "the aforementioned Son of Man" with a backward glance towards Daniel. This issue is truly complex.

I personally am not happy with the neutering of the genderized language when we are talking about the Christian family-of-faith language—brothers and sisters. The term "friends" or "folks" leaves the spiritual-family connotations out of the picture, which is not helpful. More problematic is with a phrase such as in Acts 2:14, where we literally have the vocative "men, Jews" or in 2:29 where the Greek literally reads "men, brothers." The problems here are legion. In that highly patriarchal culture, even the term *andres* could be used in a gender-inclusive way, so even the term "men" could mean "men and women." But this is confusing for most modern audiences. Second, there is the further question of what Peter means by "brothers" in 2:29. The term seems clearly not to be used in a Christian sense, but rather to mean fellow Jews, in which case it alludes to an ethnic and not a spiritual connection per se. The parallel between 2:14, where it says "men, Jews," and this text suggests this conclusion as well. The language then would not be the language of spiritual kinship or what is sometimes called fictive kinship, but rather of ethnicity. In all such cases the judgment call of when to depart from a literal reading which would only confuse a modern audience, and when to give a more literal rendering, has to be decided on a case-by-case basis, with the principle being what best conveys the actual intended meaning of the author, so far as we can tell.

Even inclusive translations like the NIV and TNIV do not generally mess with the Godhead language. For instance, God is still called "Father" in the Lord's Prayer in Matthew 5:9 in these translations, not least because Jesus himself seems to have insisted on calling God "Abba," when this was not a term used by early Jews as a way of addressing God in prayer before him.[1] Something would be lost in translation if such a usage was just rendered "Divine Parent," not least because Jesus related to God as "Abba," not as Mother (for he had a human mother, but not a human father), but also because the sense of intimacy conveyed by "Abba" would be lost by that more generic terminology.

A fact often lost in the Bible translation wars is that the Bible was originally translated already as early as the second century AD not as a blunt instrument by which Christians could bash one another, but as a tool of missionary work. A clear sign of the times is that most translations now are made for those who are already Christians, and for nurture purposes. Lost is the sense of "these things are written in order that you may believe Jesus is the Christ, the Son of God " (John 20:31). This fact has not been lost on the tireless Gideons, who have done no end of good in spreading Bibles into every nook and cranny of the world they could reach. But alas, they have so wed themselves to the KJV or in some cases the NKJV that they are not availing themselves of the best scholarly work on the shape of the original Greek text, and so on the translation that derives from it. With knowledge comes responsibility, and one can only hope that they will soon switch to a better, more accurate translation of the Bible which includes what ought to be in there, and leaves out later additions like John 7:53–8:11 and Mark 16:9-20, not to mention the later Western additions to the text of Acts such as we see in Acts 8:37. We NT scholars live in hope on these issues, but we realize how sensitive such issues are because devout Christians become attached to their English translations and have done so ever since 1611.

Let us close this brief discussion with a story. With regularity I teach in Moscow at an evangelical seminary training budding Russian ministers. I have been at this for a decade now. The alert reader of this book will remember that one of the first vernacular translations of the Bible in that part of the world was into Old Slavonic.[2] That translation is still the one being used all over Russia, even though it is hopelessly out of date, indeed over a millennium out of date (the translation being done in the 900s!). This is the sad state of affairs of vernacular translations in so very many places in the world, and the end result is that when I go to Moscow, usually my host Dr. Tsutserov has to translate the Bible text on the spot from the Greek or the English for the students. How can it be that we English-speaking Christians have so many translations to choose from, and many countries have only one, and it is in an archaic form of some indigenous language? The missionary spirit prompting translation of the Bible in the first place needs to revive, or perhaps better yet, the two-thirds world churches need to begin to do their own translations as they increasingly become the majority of the church itself.

One suspects, however, that now that English is the language of the Internet, and the Internet is a runaway success, this will further the cause of those who want the English Bible in some form to be the whole world's Bible, which brings up an issue that we can only broach in passing as we close: the issue of cultural imperialism, however subtle or unintended. Language has been and always will be the gateway, carrier, indeed the entrée of a culture, in this case English-speaking, largely Western culture. Issues of cultural sensitivity come into play when an English Bible becomes the Bible of choice in missionary work in a non-Western culture. These issues we have hardly begun to address in the conservative church in America; indeed in some quarters we are not even aware of the issues. I am fortunate enough to teach at a seminary that has a school of world mission. We deal with these issues with some regularity, and we must continue to do so.

The genius of the Gospel and the Christian faith is that it can be indigenized into any culture. The leaven of the Gospel can be placed into any lump. Indeed, the book of Acts is all about that sort of indigenizing efforts—for example, when Paul spoke to the Areopagus in Athens in Acts 17. If Jesus is the savior of the world and the Bible is the living word of God unto this day, then the Bible needs to be in the languages of every tribe and tongue and people and nation, and needs to be indigenized into their cultures and their lives without the loss of the substance of the faith. Indeed, we are told in Mark 13:10 that the Gospel must first be preached to all the nations before the end time or the second coming can happen.

We still have many dialects into which not even a portion of the NT has been translated. What are we waiting for? Wycliffe Translators would love to hear from us. Perhaps someone reading this book could become the William Tyndale for another whole people. What an exciting thought! May it happen in these times and in my lifetime. The Bible truly is God's living word for all generations of God's people, and we may trust that the prophet knew what he was saying when we are told that God's Word never returns to him void.

Chapter 8

RIGHTLY DIVIDING THE WORD OF TRUTH

The issue is whether one is wont to begin with a theological a priori and conform historical questions to that a priori (= telling the exegetes what God could or could not have done even before one looks at the date), or whether one starts with a historical investigation and expresses one's theological constructs in light of that investigation (= telling the theologian what God in light of historical probabilities seems to have done). . . . What the text means—that is—how it is a word for us—that is the crucial hermeneutical question."

—Gordon Fee

Misleading approaches to Scripture often fail to consider the entire canonical context of Christian Scripture as a narrational and theological whole centered in the Trinitarian God who has revealed himself definitively in the death and resurrection of Jesus Christ.

—Karl P. Donfried

"Hermeneutics" is the term applied to the science of the interpretation of any text, in this case the NT. In this chapter, we devote our attention to the issues of how to appropriately interpret these sacred texts, bearing in mind that we have been dealing with this issue already at various junctures in this book when we talked about the genre of the books and interpretive problems. We placed a premium from the outset on contextual interpretation of the word of God, which requires study and hard work to understand the various literary, historical, social, and rhetorical contexts of this first-century literature. We also cautioned against bringing our own modern assumptions and preconceptions into the reading of the NT. We stressed that a text without a context is just a pretext for our reading things into the text. We also stressed that what the text meant in the first century is still its meaning today, and whatever it could not possibly have meant back then, it can't mean today either. Last, we made a distinction between meaning and significance. A text can have a significance for us that is not part of its original meaning. In such cases some wish to talk about a surplus of meaning (a *sensus plenior*) but it would be better to talk about a variety of implications and applications. This part of our study offers a good juncture to consider some of the traditional rules of interpretation that go back at least to the Reformation, and in some cases before then.

THE RULES OF THE ROAD

Rule One: Sola Scriptura

One of the battle cries of the Reformation was to insist on *sola scriptura*, which meant that the final authority over the church was the Bible alone. What was not said in this slogan, but was understood, was the Bible alone, rightly interpreted. Protestants have continued to affirm this principle in one form or another ever since the Reformation. One of the things this principle implied was that no nonbiblical tradition itself was immune to revision or critique on the basis of the Bible, no matter how long-standing the tradition.

With the Bible seen as the court of last resort, and the litmus test of truth about matters that the word of God spoke to, this in itself set up a kind of suspicion about pneumatic claims. If someone said, "The Spirit told me . . . ," and what was said was seen as clearly at variance with what the Bible said on the selfsame subject, then this fresh "revelation" must be critiqued by the canonical one. Sometimes this approach went so far as to suggest that the Holy Spirit wasn't speaking independently of God's word anymore, but was simply leading believers into the truth that was in that word; sometimes as well, this means that while the Spirit could lead persons to say things that went beyond the clear teachings of the Bible, the Spirit that inspired the Scripture itself would never lead a person to claim something that contradicts or goes against the text of the Bible. This principle was especially to be put to the test whenever a more pneumatic, charismatic, or experientially oriented revival movement arose within post-Reformation church history.

This kind of tension between the word and what is thought to be the voice of the Spirit still arises today when some churches or their representatives claim, for example, that God's Spirit has shown that same-sex sexual relationships are not, or are no longer sinful. Sometimes this hermeneutical move involves arguing that the Bible doesn't say what it appears to have said, but more often, since this move cannot explain away all the biblical data on this matter, the claim is made that new revelation has superseded the old, just as the NT eclipsed various things in the OT. The living voice of prophecy is appealed to, to justify breaking with traditional exegesis of various biblical passages and ultimately with some parts of the Bible itself. Not surprisingly, evangelicals who have been well schooled in *sola scriptura* have largely taken a negative or dim view of these sort of pneumatic claims as they seem to compromise the authority of the Bible as the definitive revelation of God's will and truth. If Rule One really is *sola scriptura*, then evangelicals are right to take a dim view of pneumatic claims that go against the Bible's explicit teaching.

Rule Two: Scripture Is Its Own Best Interpreter

In this day and age, one hears a great deal about canonical criticism and canonical theology, which is indeed a manifestation of the old principle that the first and best interpreter of the Bible is the Bible itself. One was in the first case to compare and contrast various texts within the Bible to gain an understanding of its meaning. It was assumed that the text was perspicuous, and the reader was especially encouraged to interpret the more difficult or puzzling passages on the basis of the clearer ones. The underlying assumption was that there was a single coherent mind behind all the Bible, and therefore a consistent and coherent revelation within the Bible.

Part of the problem with this principle is that it sometimes leads to a rather flat view of the whole Bible such that Levitical laws, for example, were thought to be able to inform the proper interpretation of New Testament institutions, which led to such problematic notions as Sunday being the Sabbath, the Lord's Supper being seen as like the Levitical sacrifices, church buildings being seen as temples, and a clerical class being seen as priests. The problem is that while one can find all of these institutions in the OT, one is hard pressed to find them all imposed on Christians in the NT. Sometimes this way of interpreting the NT so heavily in light of the OT has led to the elimination of the whole notion that much new is even going on in the NT. The NT is seen rather as the fulfillment or completion or even the renewal and perfect expression of the old. This way of looking at things has especially characterized certain forms of Reformed covenantal theology, and still does today.

At risk in this sort of approach to the Bible was losing any sense not only of the newness of the new covenant, but of progressive revelation in the Bible. Statements, for example, by Jesus in Mark 10 about Mosaic legislation being given originally because of the hardness of human hearts, but now that the Dominion is breaking in, new rules apply, and the original creation intent of God before Moses is being reinstated are either ignored or misinterpreted in the service of preserving one's covenantal theological approach. This is chiefly a front-to-back approach, by which I mean you start from the front of the Bible and read to the back, and this in turn means that your hermeneutic is so heavily Old Testamental that by the time you get to the NT it can hardly be more than just a fulfillment or renewal of the OT. The problem with this approach is it is not the approach of various NT authors, who *begin* with the Christ event and reread the OT in light of the Christ event.

A flat approach to the Bible sometimes involves the "one covenant but just in various administrations" view, which was seen by some Protestants as putting the emphasis entirely too strongly on the OT being allowed to determine how the NT can and ought to be understood. Yet there was general agreement that texts like Hebrews, and especially Hebrews 1:1-4, established with clarity that Christ and the revelation of God in Christ were to be seen as the climax of the revelation of God's truth and word. And if one is thinking narratologically, then of course a story must be read in light of its climax, and this changes not only what comes thereafter but also how one views what came before the climax as well.[1]

There was and is enormous debate about how much of the OT was still binding on Christians. One hermeneutical move suggested that all of the OT was still directly binding on Christians except for the portions that were said in the NT to be fulfilled or abrogated or superseded. The other major hermeneutical move, which caused far less difficulty in terms of Christian practice, was the suggestion that only those portions of the OT law which are explicitly reaffirmed in the NT are binding on Christians. Thus, for example, since nowhere in the NT are Christians said to be required to observe the Sabbath—indeed, there are texts that warn against being trapped into such practices (see Col 2:16)—this is no longer an obligation for Christians. For the most part, some form of this second hermeneutical suggestion about the relationship of Christians to obeying OT principles has been accepted and practiced.

Rule Three: The Analogy of Faith

One of the more dominant principles of interpretation in Protestantism, even until today, is the idea that there is a central theme of Scripture: the great theme of God's divine saving activity. This theme is then viewed as a norm so powerful that it led to the suggestion that if there was a passage of Scripture which seemed at odds with this central theme, that someone was obviously misunderstanding the import and message of that problematic passage.

The phrase *analogia fidei* (analogy of faith) comes from the rendering into Latin of Romans 12:3, but in fact this probably involves a rather clear misinterpretation of the meaning of that verse, which should be compared to Romans 12:6. The proper translation should likely be "according to the measure of faith." Prophets should prophesy, teachers should teach, leaders should lead according to the measure of their current faith, and not beyond it.[2] In other words, this passage has to do with a limitation, but it is not an attempt to provide a hermeneutical rule by which one can measure the interpretation of difficult passages nor provide a central theme as a norm to guide one in the interpretation of such difficult texts. To the contrary it is about limiting other ministerial activities (Scripture interpretation is never mentioned here) according to the measure or quantity of one's faith, whether great or small. The Reformers naturally had a problem with this Pauline idea of degrees of faith since they saw all saved persons as having the same saving faith, but in fact both Jesus and Paul regularly talk about little or large, small or great faith. Thus, it is no surprise that Paul would see this as something that should limit or guide the degree to which one exercises one's gift; one should do it in proportion to one's faith. Notice he does not say in proportion to one's abilities!

Rule Four: Sensus Literalis vs. Sensus Plenior

This Latin distinction has to do with the difference between a literal sense of the text and its fuller sense, which is to say its deeper or even hidden meaning. This mode of interpreting the text became common in the Middle Ages and led to the allegorizing of the text, especially the parables. Augustine's interpretation of the Good Samaritan parable is notorious. In it he claimed that the Good Samaritan was Jesus, and that he was administering the sacraments to the man lying on the side of the road who was dead in sin, and that the church was the inn, with the innkeeper being the minister, and the coins paid penance money, and so on. All of this was justified on the basis of the principle of the "deeper sense" of the text, but the problem was that it was not a deeper meaning that either Jesus could have encoded into this parable or his original audience could have understood him to be discussing. There was no church or sacraments in that sense when Jesus taught this parable.

If, however, we ask the question, can an author say more than he or she realizes, the answer must be yes. In dealing with an inspired text, one can argue that God was speaking at a deeper level than the human author fully realized at the time—as in a prophetic text like Isaiah 53. Did the human author of Isaiah 53 realize he was talking about Jesus, or even an individual messianic figure? Perhaps not. Some prophetic and poetic texts may then have a fuller or deeper sense. If some texts, perhaps particularly prophetic texts and the psalms, were thought by the earliest Christians to have a fuller meaning, only to be discovered later, do we then look for fulfillment of the literal sense of those same texts, or only of their deeper sense, or both? Or should we stick with the notion that a text may have a fuller significance later, not a fuller meaning? Much depends on one's view of the roles of the human and divine authors. Sensus plenior thinking argues that when the text was originally written, God encoded a deeper sense or significance to it, which is very different than giving the reader permission to "find" a meaning in the text. With sensus plenior, unlike reader-response readings, one can assume that there is a deeper meaning in the text, and so one does not need to creatively read one into the text.[3]

This whole sort of approach to interpretation has quite naturally made Protestant exegetes nervous because there seems to be no limits to what one could claim was a hidden or deeper meaning in the text. There seemed to be no controls. And an example like Augustine's allegorizing of the text makes such exegetes all the more skeptical about the idea. Better to stick to the notion that an author can say more than he realizes under inspiration, but it still had to be consistent with the literal sense of the text, and had to be intelligible to its original audiences.

Rule Five: Prediction vs. Fulfillment

Prediction is when a biblical author prophesies certain coming events. This may be distinguished from the concept of fulfillment. Christ is said in the NT to be the fulfillment of all sorts of ideas and institutions in the OT that were not predictive prophecy (e.g., the temple or the sacrificial system). Fulfillment then is a much larger category than prediction. Note the use of the psalms in the NT, which are songs, not prophecies to speak of christological matters in the NT (cf., e.g., Mark 1:11).

Isaiah 40-55, which is poetic prophecy, and the psalms which are not prophecies, are the two most used portions of Scripture in the NT. Only a few of the psalms could be said to be royal or messianic in their original settings, looking forward to an ideal king—Psalm 2 being one of them. Nevertheless, many more of them are used in the NT to describe personal experiences, for example, Jesus on the cross quoting the beginning of Psalm 22. Here we are actually dealing with the principle of analogy, namely that believers' experiences are parallel in various eras of salvation history. Thus, while the psalmist's words were about himself, they certainly accurately described the experience of Jesus as well.

There is in fact a kind of principle of analogy that is found in the Bible itself: the principle of typology. Typology involves the notion that there is a historical type and an ante-type—for example, Jesus and Melchizedek in Hebrews—and the ante-type foreshadows the type and indeed sets up an anticipation of a greater and more fulfilling example of this sort of person later. The idea in this case has to do with God operating in a similar fashion in various eras of salvation history, preparing for the climax of revelation in its earlier stages by prefigurements. This whole notion presupposes the idea of progressive revelation, and as such is an idea that not only the author of Hebrews, but also Paul seems to operate with (cf. 1 Cor 10, where the exodus events are seen as analogous to some aspects of Corinthian experience). More could be said along these lines, but we need now to proceed to the issue of how to move from interpretation to application of God's word today.

The typological use of the OT in Hebrews and elsewhere reminds us once more that the earliest Christians all thought that the OT speaks to Christians even in their new situation after the Christ event. But how? I would suggest that we first must recognize: (1) we are not under the old covenant any more in any of its administrations, but (2) a good bit of the old covenant is renewed in the new, and (3) even in texts that are not ethically binding on Christians, if we will but ask the right questions of the text, we can certainly find a late word of God to preach or teach from that text to a Christian audience.

Here are some of the questions I would suggest we ask of OT texts that are not binding on Christians: What does the text tell us about God? What does the text tell us about God's people? What does the text tell us about the interaction between God and his people? These questions can be asked of any text, and much can be garnered and learned from the answers we discover. But there is one more way, an experiential way, that a text of Scripture will come to life, namely when God uses it to speak to us more directly in a crisis situation. Let me give a personal example.

My wife was in the hospital in Durham, England, in 1979, and we were expecting our first child. We were thousands of miles from home in the United States, and apart from any close friends or family. Unfortunately my wife's blood pressure had gotten out of control, and the doctors had placed her in the hospital some three weeks before our child was due. The blood pressure kept rising, and finally the doctor said that Ann would need to be induced. This upset her no end, as we had gone through all the Lamaze classes and my wife is a biologist anyway. She did not want the baby drugged as it was coming into the world. I well remember being at the hospital with her, and we had been reading through some of the doom-and-gloom chapters of Ezekiel, particularly Ezekiel 36. Suddenly in the midst of a passage of dire warnings there were these sort of words of reassurance: "And I will multiply your kindred, and I will keep you safe, and I will bring you home."

Those reassurances were meant for the exilic Jews in Babylon long before the twentieth century, but God used those words to reassure my wife and I as well, and I said to her—"Honey, I think the baby is on the way. We've gotten a word from on high." I went home that night and did not change out of my clothes but rather paced the floor. My neighbor, who had a car, knocked on my door at four-something in the morning to collect me, and was shocked to find me ready. He asked me how in the world I knew he was coming at that hour. I told him we had had a divine reminder to be ready. Sure enough, Christy Ann was on the way without Ann being induced and was born in the late morning of August 14, 1979. Turns out that God knows how to use his ancient word to speak to us in our very different situations, and he applies the text more effectively and directly than we could possibly manage to do. We, on the other hand, need some guidelines and rules for using the text.

Rule Six: A Quadrilateral of Authorities

One of the pressing questions for Protestants that arise from the rules cited above and from our personal experiences as well is, what is the relationship of Scripture, reason, tradition, and experience? I would suggest that if and when we are talking about a subject on which the Bible directly teaches us something (matters theological, ethical, historical, or involving Christian praxis), then there is a principle that must be stated about the interrelationship of these four things. We can say that reason, tradition, and experience can all be seen as windows into the Scripture or avenues out of the Scripture by which we may express the truth of Scripture, but in no case and on no occasion should reason, tradition, or experience be seen as a higher authority than Scripture by which Scripture could be trumped *on some issue that Scripture directly addresses* and about which it makes claims on God's people.

This further principle is really the only one involving these four things that does justice to the foundational principle of *sola scriptura*. Suggesting that reason, tradition, or experience has equal authority with the Bible in one matter or another, or even higher authority, is a recipe for trouble and for compromising some of the essential verities of the word. This is not in any way to deny that reason is a good thing, or experience is a good thing, or tradition is a good thing, but they all must be normed by the Scriptures.

A person can have a genuine experience, a genuine religious experience, without it being a good one. That something is genuine and real does not in itself tell us the ethical or spiritual quality of the experience, or whether in the end it is good or bad for the person. Without the final objective norm of Scripture, it becomes difficult if not impossible to tell the difference between a heart-warming experience brought about by the work of the Spirit, and some sort of emotive "spiritual" experience that is neither edifying for the person in question nor glorifying to God.

For example, not far from where I live is Shaker Village in Pleasant Hill, Kentucky. One of the founders of the sect, Mother Ann Lee, had experiences that led her to claim (and her disciples to claim about her) that she had *all* the perfections of God in her, in female form! This went far beyond what the Wesleys said about being perfected in love by God's holy presence such that God's love could cast out all fear in the believer and leave just the living sense of God's loving presence. And it certainly went beyond what Paul claimed in Philippians about not having yet obtained a beatific state. Mother Ann Lee may have had real spiritual experiences, but when compared to what the Scriptures say about such experiences she was probably rightly judged by most to have had experiences engendered by some spirit other than the Holy Spirit.

Similarly with traditions. Many churches have traditions, and many of them are good. But if they fail the litmus test of being consistent with, coherent with, and a legitimate extension of Scripture, then they should not be insisted on or made requirements. For example, some low-church Protestant groups have long had a tradition of no sacraments at all, including no Christian baptism, but this directly violates the command to baptize persons in the Great Commission in Matthew 28. Or to give a Catholic example, to insist on the perpetual virginity of Mary and her immaculate conception as essential Christian doctrines not only goes beyond what Scripture says about Mary, in some cases it goes against various Scriptures which suggest not only that Mary had more than one child (and some by the normal means), but also that she sinned at times, unlike her eldest Son.

With "reason" we also have to be careful. A person can be perfectly reasonable and logical but be thinking in too narrow and small a compass or circle of thought. For example, it was reasonable on the surface of things to suggest that Hebrews 6 had something to say about the issue of postbaptismal sins, a major issue in the early centuries of church history, until more careful and detailed exegesis of this text showed that the subject of conversation was not sins after baptism, but rather apostasy after conversion, a far bigger and graver matter.

ON MOVING FROM INTERPRETATION TO APPLICATION

Different kinds of literature function differently as they try to convey their message to an audience. Narratives accomplish this basically by showing what they want the audience to know about belief and behavior, whereas letters, laws, sermons, and prophecies (except for visionary prophecy) accomplish their tasks more by telling what they want or expect. We have all these sorts of literature in the NT, and generally speaking, fewer mistakes in application seem to be made with material that is obviously didactic and direct than with narrative.

Sometimes when application is the topic, the material of the NT is broken down into two categories: principles and practices. This sort of process of discernment or ferreting out of materials from the text is undertaken in recognition that the text was written at another time; in another language to other contexts than our own; and that there are sufficient differences between then and now, and that culture and ours, that in many cases it is not possible to directly apply the text without such a process. "The past is like a foreign country, for they do things differently there."[4]

One of the questions that has to be raised from the outset is, is there any such thing as a biblical culture, or should we urge that the biblical patterns of belief and behavior can be indigenized into any culture? Some Christian groups have thought there was such a thing as a biblical culture. A good example of this is the Amish, who have chosen seventeenth- to eighteenth-century German agrarian culture as somehow the epitome of what biblical culture amounts to and should look like. The problem is that when one freezes the cultural expression like that, not only does the world pass the group in the fast lane as it continues to change, but the Amish become glorious anachronisms, echoes of a bygone era that make the Bible look antique and of no real relevance to where the world is today.

Not surprisingly, most modern discussions on this issue have opted for the view that there is no particular biblical culture either to be found on the earth today, nor is there one required or enunciated by the Bible itself. When one requires certain kinds of patterns of belief and behavior across generations and centuries, some things will be identical between Christians then and now, and other things will be similar. All Christians have always believed that Jesus Christ is the crucified and risen Lord, and all Christians have always known that there was a high standard of ethical behavior and praxis required of them, which included things like truth telling and loving neighbor on the one hand, and worshiping God and sharing fellowship on the other.

What is noticeable in discussions in the NT, in places like Acts 10 or 1 Corinthians 9, is that the audiences are being told that there should be fewer barriers between ethnic groups of people. They are being told that God is impartial and the God of all nations. They are being told in effect that all are one in Christ even though Jews don't cease to be Jewish and Gentiles don't cease to be Gentiles. But the implication is that there is a far wider realm of things indifferent adiaphora than there had been before the Christ event. For example, in regard to dress, Christians are not told how to dress in the NT, except that they are told to dress decently or modestly, in a fashion that will not distract people as they are worshiping God (see 1 Tim 2). In regard to food, in various places (cf. Mark 7:15-19; Acts 10) Christians are told that no food is unclean anymore, though some eating venues, such as pagan temples, should be avoided. In regard to housing or modes of transportation and other such practical aspects of life, the NT does not mandate things. In fact, it does not mandate much about day-to-day life except that one's entire lifestyle should honor God and be a blessing and a help to others and self on the one hand, and that one should avoid sins, which destroy relationships with God or human beings and damage one's self as well.

There is, however, an enormous freedom of choice about mundane things in the NT, and the *absence* of ritual purity rules and other sorts of practices that could be said to be ethnocentric and nurture ethnocentricity stands out in the NT compared to the OT. All of this is probably the natural outworking of a religion that was ardently evangelistic and universalistic in outlook and that wanted to convert other ethnic groups to Christ, not to a particular form of cultural expression.

Because there are many commonalities between the experiences of God's people in many different eras, we find that by analogy there is a relevance and a pointedness to many ancient texts when it comes to our lives. The principle of analogy especially comes into play as we read these texts, and understandably so. From a Christian point of view, God is the same God, human nature is in the same fallen condition, and God's solution to the human dilemma is the same today as it was in the time of the NT. Sometimes this principle of analogy is stated in the form of preserving the principle of the original in some equivalent practice when one is dealing with an issue of praxis or polity.

As one moves from interpretation to application, one can take a series of careful steps to ensure that one is making an application that is consonant with the original text. These principles I learned from one of my mentors Gordon Fee:

1. Understand as much as possible about the original historical setting and context of the text, remembering that the true meaning of the text must be something the human author and/or God would have wanted to say or allude to, to that original author and audience (e.g., 1 Cor 13, when the perfect comes' refers to what happens at the eschaton). Failure to attend to this rule leads to numerous errors and especially to anachronistic misreadings of the NT.

2. Hear the word as it is addressed to that original situation (the context of the original audience is crucial here).

3. Hear the word as it addresses our situation (here again, careful attention to context and the way the Bible can speak is crucial).

4. Apply the original meaning to new situations that are analogous and appropriate.[5]

Nothing, however, is as easy as that little outline suggests. The principle of analogy recognizes that no two cultural situations are ever exactly alike, but one looks for enough continuity between the two so that the original sense of the text can meaningfully be applied today. For example, the household codes reveal houses with slaves, but we do not have such households today, so some of this material is not applicable or analogous.

The basic rule of thumb is that while principles remain the same, practices often do and should change with the differing cultural situations (e.g., appropriate clothing in church will differ from culture to culture). But various mandated practices in the NT are clear, such as baptism and the Lord's Supper, and this in turn means that the NT cannot be reduced to just a bunch of principles. Indeed, narratives especially resist such reductionism.

Especially important to consider is how narratives function normatively and with authority. Stories are not merely told in the NT for entertainment. They are told to inform, inspire, and motivate, and they have a pedagogical dimension in these ways and in others. Sometimes the implicit message is to go and do likewise—for example, when we hear about the evangelistic efforts of Peter or Paul. Sometimes the implicit message is to go and do otherwise—for example, when we read the story of Judas betraying Jesus or the story of Ananias and Sapphira and Acts 5. The question then becomes how to tell the former stories from the latter. My suggestion would be that one looks for positive repeated patterns in the text. The summaries in Acts 2:42-47 and 4:32-35 of how the early church worshiped and fellowshiped reveal a positive repeated pattern. If there is only one pattern (e.g., that Christian baptism was required for all disciples—see Matt 28), then we can be reasonably sure that the author wants to inculcate similar beliefs and practices in the audience. Repetition is the key clue.

But what if we find varied patterns? For example, in some places in Acts we find people being baptized with water before they receive the Holy Spirit (see Acts 8—the story of Samaria). In some places we see them receiving the Spirit before they are baptized (Acts 10—Cornelius and family). In some places the two seem to be part of one event (Acts 8—the Ethiopian eunuch). What should we conclude from this? We should conclude that there is no normative ordering principle being taught in these stories at least on this matter.[6]

Narrative parables function similarly to other sorts of narratives in this regard, and there can be little doubt that certain principles of belief and behavior are being inculcated by the parables (see, for example, the interpretation in Luke 18:1: "then Jesus told his disciples a parable to show them that they should always pray and not give up"). These parables are not just nice little sermon illustrations; they are Jesus' public teaching meant to instruct the audiences on important kingdom matters, not only in regard to what God is up to, but also in regard to what they ought to be up to. Parables often have unsavory characters in them, for example, the thieves in the Good Samaritan parable. Thus caution must be exercised before one jumps to the conclusion that Jesus wants us to go and be like this or that character in the story. Sometimes he wants just the opposite.

In his recent discussion of how narrative or story functions with authority or has authority, Bishop Tom Wright says this:

> There are various ways in which stories might be thought to possess authority. Sometimes a story is told so that the actions of its characters may be imitated. It was because they had that impression that some early Fathers, embarrassed by the possibilities inherent in reading the Old Testament that way, insisted upon allegorical exegesis. More subtly, a story can be told with a view to creating a generalized ethos which may then be perpetuated this way or that. The problem with such models, popular in fact though they are within Christian reading of scripture, is that they are far too vague: they constitute a hermeneutical grab-bag or lucky dip. Rather, I suggest that stories in general, and certainly the biblical story, have a shape and a goal that must be observed and to which appropriate response must be made.
>
> But what might this appropriate response look like? Let me offer you a possible model, which is not in fact simply an illustration but actually corresponds, as I shall argue, to some important features of the biblical story, which (as I have been suggesting) is that which God has given to his people as the means of his exercising his authority. Suppose there exists a Shakespeare play whose fifth act had been lost. The first four acts provide, let us suppose, such a wealth of characterization, such a crescendo of excitement within the plot, that it is generally agreed that the play ought to be staged. Nevertheless, it is felt inappropriate actually to write a fifth act once and for all: it would freeze the play into one form, and commit Shakespeare as it were to being prospectively responsible for work not in fact his own. Better, it might be felt, to give the key parts to highly trained,

sensitive and experienced Shakespearian actors, who would immerse themselves in the first four acts, and in the language and culture of Shakespeare and his time, *and who would then be told to work out a fifth act for themselves.*

Consider the result. The first four acts, existing as they did, would be the undoubted "authority" for the task in hand. That is, anyone could properly object to the new improvisation on the grounds that this or that character was now behaving inconsistently, or that this or that sub-plot or theme, adumbrated earlier, had not reached its proper resolution. This "authority" of the first four acts would not consist in an implicit command that the actors should repeat the earlier parts of the play over and over again. It would consist in the fact of an as yet unfinished drama, which contained its own impetus, its own forward movement, which demanded to be concluded in the proper manner but which required of the actors a responsible entering into the story as it stood, in order first to understand how the threads could appropriately be drawn together, and then to put that understanding into effect by speaking and acting with both *innovation* and *consistency.*

This model could and perhaps should be adapted further; it offers in fact quite a range of possibilities. Among the detailed moves available within this model, which I shall explore and pursue elsewhere, is the possibility of seeing the five acts as follows: (1) Creation; (2) Fall; (3) Israel; (4) Jesus. The New Testament would then form the first scene in the fifth act, giving hints as well (Rom 8; 1 Cor 15; parts of the Apocalypse) of how the play is supposed to end. The church would then live under the "authority" of the extant story, being required to offer something between an improvisation and an actual performance of the final act. Appeal could always be made to the inconsistency of what was being offered with a major theme or characterization in the earlier material. Such an appeal—and such an offering!—would of course require sensitivity of a high order to the whole nature of the story and to the ways in which it would be (of course) inappropriate simply to repeat verbatim passages from earlier sections. Such sensitivity (cashing out the model in terms of church life) is precisely what one would have expected to be required; did we ever imagine that the application of biblical authority ought to be something that could be done by a well-programmed computer?[7]

This suggestion is very intriguing, and there is much to commend in it. But once more this sort of approach helps answer the question how should we live or behave, but it doesn't do much for the question of what is true, and how timely truths are incarnated in differing cultural settings. What is especially unclear from this proposal is what role direct imperatives that exist in the NT are to play while we are busy improvising on the basis of the earlier story. Wright is trying to avoid the "timeless truth" model that involves the strip mining of stories and other sorts of texts in such a reductionistic way that all that is left is a pile of principles and practices. I am sympathetic with his concern about reductionism, but I do not think we can avoid the truth claims issues, or even the issue of timeless truths or principles.

There can also be the objection to the above suggestions of Wright that I have already stressed; sometimes the function of a narrative is to tell us that we should go and do otherwise, sometimes that we should go and do likewise, and even mostly positive characters in a narrative sometimes have feet of clay. Any history that involves human behavior is bound to be messy and ambiguous, and while I would argue that the storied world does provide us examples to emulate and avoid, and at least Acts gives us a sense of the ethos of the early church, the stories are told to inculcate certain beliefs and behaviors that are often more directly and clearly spoken of in the letters and sermons of the NT, and that involve truth claims.

The authority of all of these stories has to do with them being grounded in both God and God's revelatory truth for the world that focuses on God's Son, Jesus. There are timed truths (truths for only a specific time period, such as the Levitical sacrificial system), and timeless truths (both theological and ethical as found in various places in the NT), and all of the NT can be said in one sense or another to involve timely truths—words of God on target for the situations to which they are addressed. The issue is a truth one, for even in regard to stories one must ask whether and in what sense the stories being told are "true."

There is no quick shortcut or substitute for doing the hard work of exegesis before one gets to the point of application. But the interpretive task is no harder than the application of the text; indeed in many cases it may be easier, for the good reason that figuring out how to live out of the text faithfully today, especially in an increasingly less Christian culture, is often more difficult than understanding the text.

Just prior to his expulsion from Germany in 1935, Karl Barth had a chance to offer a formal farewell to his students as the Nazis moved to strengthen their grasp on the intellectual life of the country. He ended with these words: "So listen to my piece of advice: exegesis, exegesis, and yet more exegesis! Keep to the Word, to the Scripture that has been given us."[8] This is still the right advice, and perhaps the single most important key to making sure we do not misapply the text today. Application without exegesis is bound to lead to misapplied, however well-intentioned, Bible teaching. But exegesis without application falls short of the call to holiness of life and behavior, which must accompany the need for right thinking and true believing. Christian thinking and believing must be fleshed out in Christian living, or we are like barren trees with no fruit. Remember that what attracts a hungry world to a tree is its fruit, not its bark or leaves!

Chapter 9

THE ART OF READING SCRIPTURE
IN A POSTMODERN WORLD

Something's comin' on. Don't know what it is, but it's getting stronger.
—David Clayton Thomas, Blood, Sweat, and Tears

Today we are at a crossroads. One road leads to hopelessness and despair, the other, to total extinction. Let us pray we choose wisely.
—Woody Allen

Trying to define postmodernism is like trying to catch the wind or at least like experiencing a strong wind. You can feel it happening, and it's definitely blowing some things away, but you can't see it, and it's hard to pin down and hard to know what to make of it. One of the main clues that it is happening, and is not just a figment of someone's imagination, is that it affects scholars, sages, skeptics, saints, sinners, and even the simple alike in various ways. We see its influence on art, music, and all sorts of writing. But what exactly is postmodernism? Is it just a trend, a zeitgeist, a passing fad, or is it a serious shift in the intellectual and cultural life of the West? And how exactly has it affected our reading of Scripture, our view of truth, and our recognition of the authority of the word of God?

First, let's consider some pundits' comments about postmodernity. One of the leading philosophers who has been an advocate of postmodernism is Jean-Francois Lyotard. He has suggested that postmodernism involves an attitude of incredulity toward metanarratives. This may come as some surprise to those who associate postmodernism with narratology, narrative readings of the Bible, a great appreciation for fiction, and the like. Richard Bauckham helpfully sums up Lyotard's objection to metanarratives. "A metanarrative is a totalizing theory that aims to subsume all events, all perspectives, and all forms of knowledge in a comprehensive explanation."[1] He adds that Lyotard opposed the "modern project," by which is meant the presumption that reality, both nature and human history, is fundamentally comprehensible to human reason. "Lyotard's opposition to it involves a skeptical epistemology, which stresses the opacity of reality to reason, and a radical espousal of pluralism and heterogeneity against universality and unity. The contingency of events and the intractability of 'difference' resist any totalizing theory. Metanarratives are necessarily authoritarian and oppressive, since they can subsume difference only by suppressing it."[2] Note that Lyotard was rejecting the metanarrative of progress and of evolution among other metanarratives. He was an equal opportunity critiquer of all such grand stories, and would not have been happy with biblically constructed metanarratives either.

At the heart of postmodernity is a protest against the whole concept of truth, which has been at the heart of the present study on God's word. Bauckham puts it this way: "Disillusioned by the failure of the modern hope of the emancipatory power of reason, postmodernism has decided that, far from setting free, truth oppresses because it delegitimizes difference," to which Bauckham replies, "This claim must simply be contested. For a start, there is a relativist paradox: the need to insist that there is one truth—the truth that there is no truth—and one justice—the right of every voice to equal status. If the postmodern relativist claim is fully embraced, then the incommensurability of language games makes it impossible to persuade others of the need to respect difference."³ Exactly, and so postmodernity as an intellectual movement is no friend of Christianity and its truth claims. Postmodernity offers up a relativism that denies absolute truth, a pluralism that valorizes difference whether or not it is or produces good or ill, and a universalism which suggests all is lost and all of us are permanently lost (see the Woody Allen quote above). Postmodernism does not suggest a valorizing of the idea that all are inherently found or saved, a very different and more naïve sort of universalism. It is too rooted in methodological, epistemological, and philosophical skepticism for that.

At a philosophical level, then, postmodernism does often involve epistemological skepticism, by which I mean skepticism about rationality, the reliability of the human senses, and thus skepticism about our ability to know the world or reality outside our own heads. Chuck Colson on the one hand has said that the postmodern generation "raised on channel-surfing has lost the capacity for linear thinking and analytical reasoning," and Al Gore can complain that postmodernism involves a bad combination of nihilism and narcissism.⁴ I think to a great extent these complaints are warranted. At a more philosophical level, David Harvey describes postmodernism as follows: "Postmodernism swims, even wallows, in the fragmentary and the chaotic currents of change as if that is all there is."⁵ Change is good and is to be celebrated. There is nothing so permanent as change. There is nothing truly permanent, nothing timeless, nothing always true. If this sounds familiar to those who have studied Christian intellectual currents ranging from process theology to situation ethics to open theism (is God just part of the process and lacking in omniscience?), it is because actually all of this seems to be a further development of a French intellectual movement that began a century ago.

Postmodernism can be said to be a reaction to modernism, a disillusionment with the Enlightenment project to shed the light of science and rationality on everything in the world with the belief that this will lead to human and cultural progress of various sorts. The disillusionment especially has been applied to the metanarratives of our culture, such as the myth of progress or the assumption that the better educated we are, the more humane and wise we will be. Postmodernity accepts constant change as did modernity, but has decided that the notion of progress is not merely elusive; it is obsolete.

Naïve optimism about humankind's ability to understand reality and accurately describe it in one compelling overarching metanarrative has been replaced by skepticism that such is possible. Indeed, one regular feature of postmodernism is the belief that if there is an overarching truth, it is ultimately not fully or really knowable because no one can escape one's own subjective perspective on such a thing. Everyone has a point of view, an opinion, and all the things they learn are viewed and filtered through their own subjective lens.

Those who are advocates or even aficionados of postmodernism often talk about outmoded foundationalism, by which they mean things like the belief that certain fundamental truths can be adequately expressed in propositions, principles, and the like. Analytical reasoning, logic, the belief that past history is knowable and important, and that one can profit from such knowledge are called into question. Postmodernism as a philosophy seems to owe a very great deal to the French existentialism of Sartre and Camus, which exalted subjective experience at the expense of objectivity, rationality, empirical truth, and the like.

Naturally enough, such views are bound to affect the way we read the Bible, which on the surface seems precisely to be an attempt to provide a metanarrative by which one can understand all life and reality. The Bible seems also to be suggesting that God's revelation is able to penetrate the human cloud of unknowing, even penetrate a person's subjectivity. Indeed, the Bible seems to be making truth claims about a host of subjects, and more to the point making truth claims on and about us as well.

Those who have read thus far into this study now know that I do not share many of the convictions that undergird postmodern thinking, and for theological reasons. They are antithetical to many of the truth claims, and indeed the whole notion of perspicuous revelation from

God, which undergirds the presentation of salvation history and the good news in the Bible. If God cannot penetrate my cloud of unknowing, then I cannot have a meaningful relationship with God, nor know anything with assurance about God. And if that is the case, it is hard to see how the Bible is in any sense the living word of God that reveals the divine character, human character, and the nature of the divine reclamation project we call salvation or salvation history. If God cannot tell his own story without stuttering or tell us our story clearly and coherently such that we can receive, believe, and understand it, then there is good reason for skepticism about metanarratives of all sorts, including the ones in the Bible. Having said this, we will now sample some of the effects of postmodernism on both popular and scholarly Christian literature, and then draw some conclusions about how all this should affect the way we read the Bible in the twenty-first century.

BLUE LIKE ELVIS, VELVET LIKE JAZZ, SECRET LIKE JESUS

The essence of jazz is improvisation on a musical movement, a theme, a phrase, even a note. Often it does not resolve or return to the main theme, it just keeps doing variations until the performer quits. In his very popular book *Blue Like Jazz: Non-Religious Thoughts on Christian Spirituality*,[6] Donald Miller draws an extended comparison of sorts between jazz and God. I have to say from the outset that I love the arts, I am myself a musician, and I love jazz as well, especially Coltrane and Miles and Evans and the like. And I like the creativity of Donald Miller's work. He writes well. The fact that his writing is currently cool is fine by me. But the fact that it is cool doesn't make it postmodern, any more than the beat poetry of Lawrence Ferlinghetti was postmodern when it was just hip. In fact, Miller talks a lot about the deeper metanarrative of his life and of reality in general. He talks about how the biblical story of the fall best explains the human condition, our brokenness. He does it in clever and unconventional ways, but it's clear enough he believes there is a genuine metanarrative that is normative, and he believes there is a structure to reality that can be truly identified and even called "truth."

Miller is just tired of conventional conservative religiosity, and who can blame him? I am almighty tired of it myself. He's looking for another form of Christian spirituality that seems more genuine and life-giving for him, and obviously for others, to judge by the popularity of his book. Even the conservative students at Asbury College are reading it. I had lunch across from one of them who was reading it for the third time—and even reading passages out loud to her friend in the restaurant, so persuaded was she about its narrative.

What about Rob Bell and his equally popular book with the cool title *Velvet Elvis?* Well, he is a fine storyteller. Like Miller he's quite good a conveying a Christian message through the relating of his own story. And here's a sample of the kind of thing he says when he wants to draw an important conclusion. Talking about trying to live the way Jesus would have us live, he says, "You begin realizing the reason this is the best way to live is that *it is rooted in profound truths about how the world is. You find yourself living more and more in tune with ultimate reality.*"[7] No, this sounds nothing like Lyotard mentioned earlier.

Indeed we will discover that Miller, Bell, and Brian McLaren (whom we have yet to speak about) all speak coherently and compellingly, not chaotically; all believe in metanarratives, specifically biblical ones; and all are prepared to talk about truth and ultimate reality. They are not cynics, but people with considerable faith. They do, however, in some cases manifest something of an allergic reaction to conventional forms and formulations of piety, worship, creeds, dogma, and doctrine. Fair enough, these things are forms of human expression and abstractions of and from the truth, not the living word of God itself. But if these folks are what the emergent church is all about, it's about as postmodern as Martin Luther was. It may be cool, fresh, innovative, and creative, but frankly it's not postmodern if by postmodern we mean what the philosophers and scholarly commentators on the movement (such as Umberto Eco) say the movement is all about.

Now it is certainly true about all three of these writers that they want some flexibility in the way we conceive of our beliefs. Rob Bell draws an analogy between a trampoline and doctrine. It has a fixed boundary and a stable foundation on the ground but it has some flexibility, there's some bounce, some give, some spring to it. It's an interesting analogy, and Bell goes on to say that doctrine is a wonderful servant but a horrible master. I can understand this, but it does not make Bell postmodern in the least, or even make him a relativist or a pluralist for that matter. All three of these writers also want some mystery back in their religion, some excitement. They don't want freeze-dried worship, and they don't want doctrinaire doctrines. They also like to focus on experience. All this sounds tremendously familiar to me.

It sounds like John Wesley and the Methodist revival of the eighteenth century with slight revamping. The same sort of stress on the importance of Christian experience is made, and the same distinction between essentials and "opinions" about doctrines is made. But John Wesley was certainly far from postmodern. He was not a nihilist or a narcissist, nor was he in any way fond of chaos or incoherence, nor did he see change as an end in itself. Further, he did believe that since God is in the mix, change in history or in an individual life has a purpose, a direction, a movement, a story, and a climax to which it is leading.

And, like Wesley, none of these three writers we are considering wants to subscribe to the radical subjectivity theory when it comes to epistemology and our ability to know the real world or the real God. In short, they all sound more like Wesley than they do like Lyotard, and like Wesley they see themselves as part of an emerging movement. This may well be a real work of the Spirit, and so we won't have an intellectual emergency in the emergent church movement, let's drop the whole notion that it has much to do with postmodernity.

One of the interesting things about reading these authors is that they like the radical Jesus, not the more conventional images, and they don't like the word "religion," they much prefer the broader and culturally more acceptable "spirituality." Their reaction to "Christian religion" is rather like Luther's reaction to indulgences, or Wesley's reaction to "merely outward religion" and "the almost Christian." They want the real thing, no jive, and it's all about feelings—deep feelings of contact with and experiencing God in Christ. Listen to how Don Miller describes what happened when he became a Christian and began to read the Bible seriously: "The truths of the Bible were magic, like messages from heaven, like codes, enchanted codes that offered power over life, a sort of power that turned sorrow to joy, hardship to challenge, and trial to opportunity. Nothing in my life was mundane."[8] There is a sense of joy, awe, and wonder in all these writers, and they speak without hesitation about knowable truths, especially in connection with Jesus. He's the mother lode who peaks their interest and the object of their deepest devotion. These are not relativists, nor are they postmodern in the usual philosophical sense of the term.

Nor are Don Miller and Rob Bell like my friend Marcus Borg. They don't say things like the Bible contains the word of God, but there is also a lot of all too human theology and ethics in there as well that should be rejected. They accept that the Bible is true, although they are often puzzled about how some things in the Bible could be the word of God. Yet they take for granted that God's revelation is in the Bible. Here, for example, is what Rob Bell says: "The Bible is open-ended. It has to be interpreted. And if it isn't interpreted it can't be put into action. . . . It is not possible to simply do what the Bible says. We must first make decisions about what it means at this time, in this place, for these people."[9] Notice that he assumes the Bible is still relevant and applicable after interpretation. Notice he still believes there is knowable divine truth and that it needs to be applied. In fact, he says, the Bible is alive.

Brian McLaren, however, seems to be somewhat different from these other two writers. Clearly enough he doesn't much like the orthodox interpretation of the atonement, but it's hard to deny that both Paul and the author of Hebrews speak of a penal and substitutionary view of the atonement. And in regard to orthopraxy, McLaren has made some surprisingly unbiblical comments about what "generous orthopraxy" might amount to when it comes to the issue of gay and lesbian behavior.[10] It appears, though it is hard to tell, that McLaren takes a pick-and-choose approach to which parts of the NT have divine authority for him, rather like Marcus Borg. Yet to be fair he is not a relativist, nor is he a universalist either.[11] He is also certainly not like any of the secular postmodern writers, nor can he really be said to reflect much of their philosophy. In the end, I don't see much that is truly postmodern about the emergent church movement, nor much that suggests a truly postmodern approach to the Bible. All of them seem to clearly affirm that there is something called truth and that the Bible is God's word. I believe in a winsome orthodoxy, and the call to such a thing is not a bad thing at all. I do not believe in being obnoxious for Jesus. I am, however, reminded of a famous quote attributed to Hans Frei that generosity without orthodoxy is nothing, but orthodoxy without generosity is worse than nothing.[12]

I am in agreement with most of Don Carson's critiques of the emergent church movement and their interest in postmodernity. In his helpful study *Becoming Conversant with the Emerging Church*,[13] he especially aptly points out the biblical weaknesses of this movement, particularly when it comes to biblical interpretation. They are aptly summed up in Dr. Robert Kellerman's review of Carson's book:

> Carson focuses on whether or not the Emergent Church is seeking to reform the Modernist Church through the Word of God (as Luther and Calvin sought to reform the Medieval Church with the Word of God). Noting the complexity of the movement, Carson offers specific critiques including: the Emergent Church does not truly understand post-modernity, it does not assess modernism and the Modern Church accurately or fairly, it tends to cater to post-modernity rather than confront it, and it fails to capture a balanced fully-orbed biblical theology instead choosing proof-texting (a very modern method). Carson provides logical argument and biblical theology to support his assessments throughout each of these areas of critique.[14]

Carson is particularly critiquing McLaren and Steve Chalke, another leader and writer from the emergent church perspective. Carson finds these two writers frustrating in their handling of the truth question and their failure to deal with tough questions. He finds that too often they do not use Scripture as the ultimate norm to evaluate experience, reason, and tradition. The weakness in biblical theology and doctrine of Scripture in these writers leads Carson to a startling conclusion: "I have to say, as kindly but as forcefully as I can, that to my mind, if words mean anything, both McLaren and Chalke have largely abandoned the Gospel. . . . I cannot see how their own words constitute anything less than a drift toward abandoning the gospel itself."[15] While one could complain this is too strong a declaration, I think he is right about the trajectory or drift of their arguments when it comes to using the Bible as the final litmus test for how we ought to believe and behave.

I have said enough here to make clear that these writers are not really postmodernists in the normal philosophical sense of the phrase, though one could say that McLaren has some postmodern tendencies. These writers are not fundamentalists either. They realize that the Bible has to be interpreted, and that everyone comes at the Bible from their own point of view, but they all believe that despite these factors, truth is still there to be found. It can be known and put into practice affecting both belief and behavior, both heart and mind, both attitude and action. But what about the more scholarly discussion of postmodernism and the Bible? Here we turn to the various essays in *The Art of Reading Scripture*.

THE ART OF READING SCRIPTURE IN A CHRISTIAN WAY

A number of the writers we have discussed thus far in this chapter have a sense of being part of a new reformation movement in church life. The same can be said of the fifteen scholars and pastors who participated in the Princeton Scripture Project between 1998 and 2002, whose reflections are encapsulated in the volume edited by Ellen Davis and Richard Hays entitled *The Art of Reading Scripture*. Their work is more thoughtful when it comes to the issue of postmodernism and biblical interpretation, and more thought-provoking as well.

The reformational tone of the volume is clear from the start. Once we get past the introduction, we have a list of nine (thankfully not ninety-five!) theses which were distilled from the discussions after the fact, theses that apparently all the contributors would basically agree on. They are as follows:

1. Scripture truthfully tells the story of God's actions of creating, judging, and saving the world.

2. Scripture is rightly understood in light of the church's rule of faith as a coherent dramatic narrative, which is explicated to mean the story of the work of the Triune God.

3. Faithful interpretation of Scripture requires an engagement with the entire narrative: the New Testament cannot be rightly understood apart from the Old, nor can the Old be rightly understood apart from the New.

4. Texts of Scripture do not have a single meaning limited to the intent of the original author. In accord with Jewish and Christian traditions, we affirm that Scripture has multiple complex senses given by God, the author of the whole drama. The notes say that the medieval "fourfold sense" is a helpful reminder of Scripture's multivalence.

5. The four canonical Gospels narrate the truth about Jesus.

6. Faithful interpretation of Scripture invites and presupposes participation in the community brought into being by God's redemptive action—the church (which is explained to mean that scriptural interpretation is properly a ecclesial activity whose goal is to participate in the reality of which the text speaks by bending the knee to worship the God revealed in Jesus Christ).

7. The saints of the church provide guidance for how to interpret and perform Scripture.

8. Christians need to read the Bible in dialogue with diverse others outside the church (the notes say especially with Jews).

9. We live in the tension between the already and the not yet of the kingdom of God; consequently Scripture calls the church to ongoing discernment, to continually fresh readings of the text in light of the Holy Spirit's ongoing work in the world.[16]

On first blush, this does not sound very postmodern at all. In fact it sounds like a working out of a hermeneutic of Scripture based on the seminal work of Brevard Childs, who helped spawn the canonical criticism movement. There was and is both promise and problems with that whole approach to Scripture, not the least of which is that it treats the Bible primarily as story and only secondarily if at all as history or historical narrative. Dramatic narrative—indeed a huge metanarrative of creation, fall, and redemption—is the overarching and undergirding paradigm here, however loosely or tightly the story hugs to the historical particulars (e.g., how many of the contributors to this volume think the fall was a historical event involving real persons named Adam and Eve)? As we have seen, the love for narrative and metanarrative is not a trait of postmodernism, which actually is all about the deconstruction of metanarratives, especially one's from hoary antiquity, and most especially biblical ones. There is strong emphasis on truth in several places in these theses, and on the Bible being Scripture—indeed all of it from Genesis to Revelation being Scripture and all of it being the proper context in which to interpret any isolated part of it. Some would call this an ideological approach to the Bible. I would call it a theological approach to the Bible, but what often goes begging in this approach is not only the historical and critical study of the Bible, but indeed historical element in the text of the Bible itself.

But there are more problems from the outset with this whole approach. The thirty-nine books of the Christian Old Testament were not in the first place a part of a Christian canon. They were the Hebrew Scriptures of Jews first, *including Jews like Jesus and all the writers of the New Testament, with the exception perhaps of Luke who knows only the LXX.*

One cannot possibly ignore this fact and do justice to the Jewishness of the NT itself, and if one does not do justice to that, one is not doing Christian interpretation of the Bible in a way that is consonant with its earliest Christian interpreters, such as Paul, for instance. Paul and other early Christians interpreted the OT through a christological and eschatological lens, and of course they viewed the whole OT in those lights. Very seldom, however, did they even hint at a Trinitarian reading of the OT, and in this regard they were miles apart from medieval exegetes.

Then there is the problem immediately apparent with the assumed theory of meaning presupposed in these theses. We have had occasion already to talk about intentionality and the need to interpret the Bible in the first instance in its various original contexts.[17] The canon of the Christian Bible itself is not the original context in which the Christians who wrote the NT interpreted things. I cannot emphasize this historical point too strongly. While I would certainly agree with these authors that a divine author is involved with all the human authors in these biblical texts, and I would also agree that a human author can be guided by God's Spirit to say more than he fully grasps on some occasions, this does not give one carte blanche to suggest that the whole Bible is multivalent. Multivalence needs to be demonstrated, not assumed, and it is linked to particular kinds of literature—for example, apocalyptic prophecy.

It is also a mistake to privilege the ecclesial community as the proper circle of interpretation. The Bible is in the first instance God's book, not the church's book, and God had a people before there ever was a church. The Bible is a revelation of God, to the Jew first and also to the Gentile, just as Paul said about the good news itself. But the real problem with privileging ecclesial interpretation is that God intended this book ultimately to be for the world, to be used as a tool for mission and evangelism, not just to nurture the synagogue and the church. This is God's love letter to the world, not merely his love letter to various groups already designated as God's people.

And since the issue of truth is raised from the very outset of these theses, let it be said that the Bible is not a Gnostic document in any way. Its truths are not only for the elite and the elect. Indeed, we often need nonbelievers' insights to help us to understand these truths *for the very good reason that these are universal truths, truths that make claims on all human beings, not just on the church and the synagogue.* It is no accident that the so-called most theological of all the Gospels, the Fourth Gospel, tells us in its purpose statement that "these things are written in order that you might believe Jesus is the Christ the Son of God" (John 20:29). The NT was written by and for mission-minded people who believed they had a message of truth that was universally applicable across all ethnic, social, religious, political, geographical, and intellectual boundaries. This was not a book written for monks or scholars to cloister around and decide to privilege for their own communities. Truth isn't like that, not even theological truth. The reason biblical truth isn't like that is because the *theology and ethics are grounded and indeed based in real historical events in space and time.* A theological approach to the Bible that is not properly historical and incarnational in approach is docetic at best and Gnostic at worst.

In short, weariness with the vagaries of the historical-critical method is no excuse for trying to do interpretation without dealing with history, even if it is theological interpretation, even if it is canonical interpretation. And perhaps here at last I have found something about these interpreters and the more popular ones mentioned earlier that is indeed truly postmodern: if not antihistorical in approach they are often ahistorical in approach. They are not much interested in history, geography, archaeology, those sorts of things. This is a tendency of postmodernism, and in regard to this tendency I would remind that those who ignore the historical past are doomed to repeat its mistakes, to paraphrase a famous quote. I have no problems with a confessional or theological reading that is historically aware and concerned about the issue of historical context and meaning. I do have a problem with confessional readings that violate the historical givenness of the text.

One of the worrying tendencies of several of these essays is the failure to be able to distinguish between meaning and significance, sometimes coupled with the failure to distinguish between exegesis and a homiletical use of the OT. On the former front, a text can have a larger significance or different significance or application for an audience other than and later than the original one, but this does not change the meaning of the text, nor does it give us permission to suggest all biblical texts have a multiplicity of means—rather like ink blots into which we can read our own meanings. Equally troubling is the failure to see that even if we follow the example of how NT writers use the OT christologically and otherwise, we can never afford to lose sight of the fact that much of this usage is pastoral and homiletical in character, by which I mean that they are not trying to tell us what the text meant or means so much as show us how it can be used for Christian purposes. *They presuppose an already extant, relatively fixed sacred text accessible to their audience such that if they choose to do something creative with the text, this is not seen as supplanting but rather only supplementing the historical and contextual meaning of the text.* This has nothing to do with their belief in some sort of sensus plenior, a later concept in any case. Bearing these general critiques in mind, we must turn to analyze several of the essays in more depth.

Ellen Davis's opening essay is helpful in various ways.[18] It calls us to read the Bible with openness to repentance. I quite agree with this. This implies to read it with humility while standing under the authority of the word, letting it exegete us. She also calls us to read the OT with an understanding of its witness to Christ. I agree with this provided that what is being discussed is messianic prophecy, royal psalms, and the like. I do not agree with this if what is meant is allegorizing the OT and finding Jesus under every rock there. She also sees a confessional reading as a reading with primarily theological interest. I would say theological interest is one thing that should be primary; historical interest is another. It is not appropriate to privilege theology over history when it comes to historically founded and grounded religions like

Christianity and historically particular books like the Bible, especially not for postmodern Christians who already have an ahistorical bent.

Davis goes on to stress that the Bible has as its aim to reveal to us the character and will of God, and of course our own character and the need for relationship with God. She says it is about "human life in the presence of God."[19] Indeed, but all of those lives have a historical givenness, they all bring their own cultural assumptions to the text. She stresses that the Bible is all about confronting us with the universal facts of life—sin, forgiveness, love, the need for redemption, the big-ticket theological issues. What strikes me about all these matters is that a Christian vision of these subjects is grounded in the life, death, and resurrection of Jesus. It is grounded in historical particulars and must not neglect or ignore or slight them in the least. We don't know how to interpret these ideas apart from the historical events of the life of Jesus. The Bible is not just about doing theology or doing ethics for that matter. It is about doing those things in the context of history, in the context of real human lives then and now, real historical issues and problems then and now.

It is intriguing that under the heading "Reading with an Understanding of the Old Testament Witness to Christ," Davis in fact does not discuss this subject, except to say that she wishes to honor the historical givenness of the text, and so when God says in the Babel story, "Let us go down and confuse their languages," she rightly takes this not as a reference to the Trinity, but rather as the divine response to "let us build a tower up to heaven . . ." The "we" may well be viewed as the angelic entourage in heaven in the former case. This is just good historical thinking about the text. She also, however, talks a good deal about the force and function of poetic language, for instance in prophecy, and how it is open-ended. There is truth in this, but what that means of course is that poetry should be interpreted rather differently than prose—it leaves more to and prompts more from the imagination. It can be allusive and elusive. But it definitely has a meaning encoded in the words that we must ferret out, even if it also, with the benefit of hindsight, has a surplus of meaning or at least more than one referent (who was the Suffering Servant) that only later events could help us see. The important thing here is that the text can mean more than its original historical intent, but it cannot mean other than its original meaning, by which I mean it cannot mean something contrary or at odds with what the original author had in mind. "Blessed are the peacemakers" cannot suddenly mean "blessed are the warmongers."

But Davis also very helpfully says the following: "Yet the Old Testament clarifies the fact that the Bible as a whole is relentlessly *theocentric*. Its pervasive focus is not salvation either personal or corporate, but rather revelation of the nature and will of God. From a biblical perspective, salvation is a subcategory of revelation—or better, salvation is a consequence of revelation fully received."[20] Just so, the OT is theocentric in the proper sense of the term, and the focus is on Yahweh, not on the Trinity, nor on Christology, nor on pneumatology. Of course, there are messianic passages and others with messianic implications, and there are places where we hear about God's spirit, but mostly that simply means his presence in the OT, it's not a reference to a separate person called the Holy Spirit. But this insight that salvation is a subcategory of God's self-revelation is exactly right. Indeed we could say that the two key categories for understanding the OT are progressive revelation of the divine nature and salvation history as a part and consequence of that. The OT was not written by Christians or in the first instance for Christians, and so Davis quite rightly cautions about the church reading the OT alone and ignoring the potential anti-Semitism, and the failure to pay attention to Jewish interpretation of these texts.

Richard Bauckham's essay is entitled "Reading Scripture as a Coherent Story." He begins by suggesting that narrative from creation to new creation is the rubric that holds the entire canon together, with even the nonnarrative bits set within the framework and serving and aiding the ongoing narrative in some way. The narrative is said to be presupposed in places where we have law or prophecy. He is right to add that Proverbs, and in general the wisdom literature, don't fit as neatly into a narratological schema. Crucial is his observation that "the canon is distorted if biblical theology focuses on salvation history at the expense of the wisdom literature of the Old Testament or the significance of creation throughout the canon."[21]

Bauckham has some wise words about inspiration and the Scriptures as well. He points out that we should not expect the Bible to have the same sort of unity it would have if written by a single human author with a uniform style and consistent vocabulary and hopefully a rather singular and coherent train of thought. "God's inspiration has evidently not suppressed the diversity of the many human minds and circumstances that, at the human level, have made the Scriptures the collection of widely varied material that it is."[22] Just so, but what then binds the book together?

Bauckham proceeds to point out how in the OT we have two tellings of the whole cycle from creation to the exile in Genesis through 2 Kings on the one hand, and then in 1–2 Chronicles, which takes us beyond the exile in fact. These bind some of the other more disparate bits to the whole; for example, the three short stories, Esther, Ruth, and Jonah, are set within the context of the assumed telling of that larger story found twice over as mentioned above. Interestingly, Bauckham suggests the only NT book that rivals the scope of 1–2 Chronicles is the Gospel of John, which begins before creation and ends at the end of John 21 with reference to the Parousia, but one could point perhaps to Hebrews and to Revelation as doing something comparable.

Bauckham shows at length how certain summaries give unity to the narrative as well (Deut 6:20-24; 26:5-9; Josh 24:2-13; 1 Chr 16:8-36; Neh 9:6-37; Pss 78; 105; 106; 135:8-12; 136; Acts 7:2-50; 13:17-41). The story is recounted or repeatedly resung. We also have summaries of the story of Jesus in the speeches of Acts (see 10:36-43) and in the four Gospels as well. Bauckham points to Revelation as the climax of prophecy, which involves the story seen from its end and summed up. There is then precedent within the canon from various writers to see the Bible in terms of a continuous and cumulative story, and the way it is told in the NT adds new chapters and so the story gains momentum and all the other earlier stories are gathered up into the good news looking for their cumulative effect.

Helpful is the distinction made between narrative and story.[23] The former is a smaller category than the latter, and so a narrative need not tell all the parts of a story, and indeed the order of events in a narrative may differ from their order in the larger story. A good example of this is where we find the cleansing of the temple in John (John 2) and where we find it in the Synoptics. A coherent narrative may be guided by larger principles than just chronology (if one is dealing with history) or where the event fit in the larger story or scheme of things in reality.

Perhaps one of the most crucial historical caveats or warnings in Bauckham's essay is what he says about intertextuality approaches run riot: "Texts are constantly being reinterpreted. There is obvious truth in this, but if it is the whole truth, if there is nothing outside the text, the story risks being subject to the interests and designs—or mere intellectual playfulness—of its interpreters."[24] Exactly, and this is why ahistorical approaches to the Bible—approaches, for example, that treat the Gospels as if they were narrative fiction and without referentiality to things outside of the narrative itself—are in the end reductionistic. They do not do justice to history or to these texts that are talking about history. While history does not need to be the focus of every approach to the Scriptures, it must be given its essential due or else solipsism sets in.

Bauckham concludes his essay by reminding us that while the Bible suggests that there will one day be closure for us all and indeed closure to the human story, here and now we are in the middle of things. Things have not yet been permanently resolved. There is still a world to be won and battles to be fought. We hope for and expect closure, but as of yet the divine author has not stepped out on the stage of history one final time to bring the curtain down. Until then the biblical story and our story goes on, intersecting, intertwining, mutually interpreting.

In his philosophical essay "Reading the Scripture Faithfully in a Postmodern Age," William Stacy Johnson offers the clarion call to one and all to get beyond foundationalism, especially in the interpretation of the Bible.²⁵ He thinks postmodernity can help us accomplish this sort of more open-ended, multivalent focus so that we can see the Bible "not so much as truth claims to be defended by philosophical foundations but as witnesses to the transforming power that no truth claim itself can contain."²⁶ He calls the attempt to ground Christian belief in an infallible text, experience, or magisterium a loss of Christian nerve and faith. He reminds that theology responds to revelation but is a fallible human construct.

What's wrong with this picture? It is hard to know where to begin. First of all this approach rests on postmodern assumptions that are not merely antagonistic to but antithetical to what the Bible itself suggests about the nature of revelation, and the nature of the witness to it in the Bible. It rests on assumptions about God's inability to speak clearly and adequately convey the truth to his creatures. The Bible is all about and contains witnesses to the transforming power of God, but this is far from all. It bears witness about history, theology, and ethics, to name but three things, and makes truth claims about all three. These truth claims are not usually defended by appeal to philosophical foundations or rubrics, though there are places in the argumentation of God with Job or Paul with his converts where we can see such things happening. The issue, however, is not an appeal to philosophical foundations but rather to theological ones—for example, to the nature and character of the living Word of God in all three of its forms: spoken, written, and incarnated in the person of Jesus. The failure to come to grips with the fact that the Bible bears witness to both the transforming power and the truth of God and God's character and plan is a very serious shortcoming of Johnson's approach. It's not an either/or proposition, it's both/and. In the end, Johnson is simply one more example of a person who's drunk too deeply from postmodern waters, and it has caused an allergic reaction to truth claims and the Bible as a book that tells the truth about a host of subjects, many of which shake and challenge us to our own personal foundations.

In his provocative challenge to reading the Bible in purely human and humanistic ways, Richard Hays in his essay urges reading Scripture in light of the resurrection.[27] Though he does not say so, one of the more provocative things about this suggestion in a postmodern setting is that we must read the Bible in the light of a historical and historic event that lies outside the text itself. He does not merely say read the Bible in light of the end of the story or the resurrection narratives in the Gospel, but rather in the light of the resurrection itself. He puts it this way:

> God is the subject of the crucial verbs in the biblical story. When we read Scripture in light of the resurrection, we read it as a story about the power of God who gives life to the dead, and calls into existence the things that do not exist. It is not a story about self-help, not a story about human wisdom, not a story about shaping our own identity. It is story about God—a God who has revealed himself definitively through a mighty act beyond all human capacity, raising Jesus from the dead and transforming the cosmos. Therefore, anthropocentric readings are at best flatted and truncated accounts of the story.[28]

I quite agree with all of this. And I would add that if what he says is true, then it should be child's play for God to reveal the divine nature adequately and accurately through his human messengers with words which we find in the Bible. If God can make something out of nothing, he can certainly write straight using a crooked human stick or flawed human instrument. This quote from Hays means quite clearly that narcissistic and nihilistic postmodernism and its hermeneutic of suspicion just won't do as a means of reading the biblical text. The biblical text is premodern not postmodern, and it requires critical realism, not postmodern philosophy to help us understand and read it.

Hays's proposition is also interesting in that he is ascribing to resurrection what I would ascribe to the Holy Spirit. The sort of retrospective, in the light of the Christ event, figural, or even spiritual readings of the OT he wants to advocate are in fact prompted not so much by reflection on the Easter event but by the Holy Spirit who leads the faithful reader not only into imaginative christological and eschatological readings of the text but into all truth, according to the Johannine sage. Perhaps we could say it is some of both.

It is, after all, primarily the resurrection that led early Jewish Christians to believe that indeed the eschatological divine saving activity otherwise known as the kingdom of God was indeed breaking into space and time. He is right that Jesus himself taught his disciples to read the OT messianically as Luke 24 suggests—seeing in Christ the one who of necessity had to live out what Isaiah and others had said was necessary for the Suffering Servant to do. He is right as well that Jesus taught the Sadducees that literalism was insufficient when thinking about the God of Abraham, the God of the living. Here is where I point out that Jesus is saying that we need to read the OT not only in light of the resurrection but in light of God who has from the beginning brought something into existence which did not previously exist. This is the character of an Almighty God.

Scripture should be read in the light of the character of our life-giving God. Indeed it should be read as partaking of that quality of life; it is the living Word of God and it also gives life, true insight, and transformation to those who will read it with trusting and believing eyes, for believing under the guidance of the eschatological Spirit leads to seeing and understanding and even knowing God. Resurrection made possible the sending of the Spirit, and the sending of the Spirit made possible the conversion and stimulation of the imagination of believing readers. The readings they came up with often went beyond the literal meaning of the text, but not against it, for there were hints in the text pushing them in those directions. Figural reading does not replace or make obsolescent the literal one—it extends it. It should actually be seen as more an exercise in Christian homiletical use of the OT text rather than lame attempts at careful exegetical interpretations of the text. In other words, it should be judged as we would judge sermons, not as we judge commentaries.

AND SO? BEYOND POSTMODERNITY

Postmodernity is overrated, and postmodern philosophy is poorly understood by many Christian interpreters, scholarly or popular. Richard Bauckham pushes us in the right direction when he urges that the essential nihilistic claims of postmodernism must be contested and rejected, not in favor of the secular claims of the meta-narratives of modernity, but in favor of a consistently premodern biblical metanarrative. Postmodernism is no friend to such meta-narratives any more than it is a friend to actual or absolute truth claims of most any sort. The inherent absurdity of postmodernism is shown in the statement that (1) there is no absolute truth *except* (2) the absolute certainty that there is no absolute truth. Radical relativism, and thus postmodernism is inherently self-contradictory. As Don Carson has warned, it should not be embraced by any of us as in the end it is antithetical to orthodoxy, whether generous or otherwise. Postmodernism and its philosophy need deconstruction, not the Bible.

What we have learned in this chapter is that in a postmodern age which is also largely biblically illiterate, we must expect resistance to any sort of truth claims, any sort of suggestion that the Bible is the word of God and has definitive answers to the human dilemma, any sort of suggestion that a good God could actually adequately and truthfully reveal his character and plan for us all by means of something called revelation and inspiration of persons and texts.

Yet hear the good news. The postmodern age likes mystery, awe, wonder, and beauty, even if it does not know that these things are but vehicles and garments of God's revelation, God's truth. The general ignorance of the dead dogmas of the past or the exegetical missteps of previous generations of Bible interpreters is a good thing, not a bad one. And postmoderns love a good story, still preferring ones with happy endings, whatever trials and tribulations come along the way.

We have such a Story ready to hand, and like the best stories this one is true, so true that it ends up telling us what is true about ourselves as well. We do not merely get sucked in by the story, we get sucked into the story. It becomes a part of us and we become a part of it—witnessing to its power and transforming truths. My advice to those dabbling with postmodern hermeneutics or philosophy or ways of looking at the world is simply this: don't sell your birthright for a mess of pottage. Life's too short.

In fact, the old apostle adequately warned us about days like these: "Preach the Word; be ready in season and out of season. . . . For the time is coming when people will not put up with sound doctrine. Instead, to suit their own desires, they will gather around them a great many teachers to say what their itching ears want to hear. They will turn away from the truth and turn aside to myths" (2 Tim 4:2-4). Fortunately for us, the God of the Bible is not confined to its pages. Indeed, God is alive and coming to a theater near you in the person of the Incarnate Word, Jesus the risen Christ. Be ready.

Afterword

THE SACRIFICE OF THE INTELLECT?

Americans have a hard time with the idea of bowing before some higher authority, be it human or divine. It goes against the grain of what they think freedom and independence are all about. Often I hear the question: does recognizing the Bible as God's Word require you to check your brain at the door; does it require a sacrifice of the intellect? My answer to this question is straightforward: no, it does not. It requires the sanctification of the intellect, not the sacrifice of the intellect. One is not required to get a frontal lobotomy to believe the Bible is God's written word.

It is not the brain that is required to be sacrificed, it is the self. Romans 12:1-2 is reasonably clear. Christians are to present themselves to God as living sacrifices, holy and acceptable to God for *the renewing of the mind.* Yes, Paul is saying that when one gives one's self to God wholeheartedly, one of the intended outcomes is the renewal of the mind~ its stimulation, invigoration, inspiration. Certainly I personally have found this to be true. When I have committed myself to Christ and have studied the Bible, I have found I understand it far better and have had far more creative ideas about its meaning and application than I ever did before. It is not hard to understand why. As God's Spirit works in and on the believer, the Spirit sanctifies and illumines the mind, helping one to see the text more clearly, and also clearing out the clutter of sinful and distracting thoughts. Between the Spirit speaking through the Word and the Spirit working in the believer, the end result often is that one gains a great capacity for critical thought, seeing things in depth, understanding even profound things.

C. H. Dodd, one of the great New Testament scholars of the twentieth century, in his book *The Authority of the Bible*, addresses this question, and it will be useful to dialogue with him briefly as we draw this study to a close. Dodd begins where this study begun. Notice his words:

> We *start* with the original writer, what he said, what he had in mind, and what his contemporaries understood him to mean. But to stop there is the part of a pedant. No great literature will stand such treatment. All great writers meant more than they knew. They all welcome the imagination of their readers. But it must be instructed imagination, not fantasy. The imagination of the Christian reader of the Bible should be controlled by intelligent study, and it may be safely inspired by the rich experience of the Christian centuries in their use of the sacred Canon."[1]

Just so. One is invited to use one's imagination and intellect by the text itself, and if one is intelligent one will stand on the shoulders of those wise ones who have gone before us who pondered on the text into the wee hours of the morning. Notice as well that Dodd affirms the notion of authors saying more than they realize. He is right in this.

Dodd then goes on to ask the age-old question: but what if your reason tells you one thing, and the Bible quite another on some topic? What then? Dodd suggests that to simply submit to what the Bible says without deeply wrestling with the question amounts to an abdication of one's moral responsibility, a responsibility affirmed by the Reformation which spoke of the right or even duty of private judgment when it came to reading the Bible, rather than the simple acceptance of what the church hierarchy said about the Bible.[2] He is right about this, but that is not the end of the matter. One may *think* reason tells you one thing, and *think* the Bible says another and one can be wrong on either or both counts due to faulty thinking. One may *think* the Bible makes claims about a subject that in fact it makes no claims about at all. Then what?

One must consult with the good doctors of the church—various of the previous commentators and expositors of God's word. One must not arrogantly think that just because something makes sense to one's self, it then must be a necessary truth of reason. Your experience may be too limited, and your circle of logic too narrow. Interpreting the Bible is not, nor was it ever intended to be, either a purely private matter, nor a matter whereby one allows someone else to do the thinking for you. You must engage the text, but you must also become a dialogue partner with others who engage the text. You must think critically about it, and engage with other good minds in the same struggle and task. Interpreting the Bible is a community as well as a personal affair.

It must be frankly admitted and realized that there are various imperfections in the Bible. There are grammatical and syntactical mistakes, for example. The Bible is not written in Holy Ghost Hebrew or Greek; it is written by real persons, some of whom have much more facility with their language than others. This, however, in no way settles the issue of whether there are errors in regard to truth claims, in regard to matters that the Scripture teaches and not merely in matters of which the Scripture touches. Dodd argues that "the mystery of revelation is . . . the way in which God uses the imperfect thoughts and feelings and words and deeds, of fallible men, to convey eternal truth, both to the men themselves and through them to others."[3] There is some truth in this observation, but what the church has traditionally, and in my judgment, rightly stressed is that on the occasions when an author was inspired by God's Spirit to say something specific, they were guided to speak truly without the admixture of error.

Dodd is right, for instance, that the author of the Letter to the Romans in the first instance is Paul, reflecting his style, thought, concerns, and in a secondary sense "the Word of God" in the words of Paul. But I would insist that God speaks not merely through the words, like through a megaphone, but God speaks in them, having inspired these very words. And what I take this to mean is that when, for instance, Paul wrote Romans, Paul was on his game. He spoke well, truly, accurately, perspicuously—carried along by the Holy Spirit. He was his best self, and so was able to truthfully speak for God. I have no doubt that on other occasions Paul misspoke and made various sorts of mistakes. But in regard to the *content* of his letter (not the grammatical form, but the content), in regard to the theological, ethical, and historical matters he is making claims about, he told the truth. This is what it means to have a high view of Scripture, and it is a view, I believe, validated by intense study of the NT evidence itself.

The issue of the authority of the Bible cannot be settled by saying these books have authority because they are in the canon. It cannot be settled by saying these books have authority because God uses them to exercise divine authority, though that is true. It cannot be settled by saying these books have authority because the church has always said they had authority. No, Dodd is absolutely right in saying "in so far as the Bible possesses authority in religion, it can be only as mediating the truth, or as 'the Word of God.'"[4] Exactly so. When we say these NT documents are the living word of God we mean that they are such because they tell the truth, and have the authority the truth has, but only on subjects on which they intend and purport to make truth claims. Dodd is absolutely right to stress that authority in its primary form is

> the authority of the truth itself, compelling, and subduing. The free-
> dom to investigate passes into a bondservice to truth which is more
> perfect freedom. There are those to whom it will appear meaningless
> subtlety to distinguish between having your own opinion and sub-
> mitting to the truth as it comes to you. But somewhere thereabouts

lies the difference between an irreligious and a religious attitude to life—and men of science are often in this sense more religious than theologians. For it is fundamental to religion to make a distinction between self and God, and to acknowledge the complete dependence of the self upon God. And since God is the source or ground of truth, as of all value, we can know the truth only in dependence on Him.[5]

And here we have finally touched the mother lode. The Bible is intended to lead to a relationship with God, and is most profitably and truly read in the context of a relationship with God. When one presents oneself as a living sacrifice to God, one actually experiences the renewal of the mind, and the Bible, which is always God's living word, also becomes a living word for you. And just as our relationship with God always has the potential for new developments, new depths, and many surprises along the way, so too does our relationship with God's written word.

As John Robinson once said long ago to the pilgrim fathers, "The Lord hath more light and truth yet to break forth out of His holy Word."[6] Indeed, but the question becomes: Will we receive it? Will we believe it? Will we embrace it? Will we internalize it and allow it to change our lives? Do we understand that in this matter believing leads to seeing? The Bible is indeed the living word of God, and we have focused in this book on how the New Testament functions in that way. Like Jesus Christ himself, the New Testament is God's love letter to the world for its salvation. If we embody him, and if we imbibe the good news of the gospel, we too become God's love letter to the world, a living breathing word of God ourselves. It is a consummation devoutly to be wished.

Appendix

BIBLE Q&A

If the Word of God is the Answer, what is the question?

—Anonymous cliché

Since nearly the beginning of the popular Internet Web site Beliefnet.
com, I have been their Protestant Bible Q&A guy. It has been a fun
and interesting avocation that I indulge in, in my spare time. What is
quite amazing is the scope of questions that come my way. They range
from the sublime to the ridiculous. Presupposed behind most of the
questions is that the Bible *is* the word of God, and therefore it ought to
have something to say on a wide variety of subjects from the practical
to the most philosophical. I thought it would be a useful exercise to
present some of that material to a wider audience, after which I discuss
some of the implications of my answers as they have bearing on what
subjects I think the Bible as God's word does legitimately address. I am
of course grateful to those who wrote in and asked probing, puzzling,
perplexing, and just plain playful questions.[1]

I would appreciate any input regarding a situation our church board is facing. A proposal has been made to allow a Christian music studio (instructors giving lessons, mostly to children) to operate from our church. The music instructors are to give a double tithe in return for the use of the church facility. I see many possible conflicts with using the church for this purpose, but my first and compelling objection to approval for this is based on my interpretation of the Scripture regarding the use of the church for a business. It has been argued that this is a ministry because many of the children and/or parents who come into the building for music lessons may be drawn to attend the church as well. Some of the board members have the opinion that Jesus' anger at the time of the cleansing of the temple was due to the excessive charges and unfair money exchange rates involved with the sale of sacrificial animals. However, while I believe he was most likely angered by such practices, I believe first and foremost he was angered by the use of the temple for commerce or business of any kind. Jesus viewed such use as irreverence for the House of God, which is to be a House of Prayer. The temple or church is to be a place "set aside," a holy place. It is my feeling that allowing businesses to function in the church building, whether they may have some value as a ministry or not, compromises the sanctity of the church.

You seem to have misunderstood the story of Jesus cleansing the temple, which has nothing to do with what you are concerned about. Jesus is concerned about activities that interrupt or prevent people from worshiping in the outer courts of the temple, and he is concerned about unethical profiteering in the temple precincts by those who ran the place. If you look carefully at a story like Mark 12:41-43 you will discover Jesus has no problems with holy places taking in money when it is done in the appropriate manner. The church should be engaged in any and all forms of legitimate ministry including musical instruction, and the Bible is perfectly clear that a "workman is worthy of his hire"; in other words, there is no reason that such instructors should not be paid. First Corinthians 10:10 in fact says they should be.

———&ذِ&———

In all my reading of the Bible, I can't seem to find any consensus about what is necessary to attain salvation. The "Judgment of Nations" makes it sound like where we spend eternity is how we treat the "least of these." Paul, in Romans, says that we are justified by faith alone. James seems to disagree, saying that "faith is dead without works." Jesus says that if we don't forgive others, we will not be forgiven. And what happens to one who hasn't accepted Christ, such as Gandhi—one who has forgiven, turned the other cheek, and helped the "least of these"? It just seems like a cosmic injustice to eternally punish someone who is doing their very best to improve themselves, their neighbor, and this world, but who hasn't accepted Christ as their savior. God is love, so to love one's neighbor seems like the ultimate Christian act. Isn't this what ultimately matters?

This is an excellent question, and the answer is somewhat complex. In the first place, initial salvation is by grace and through faith. This is what you called justification. But conversion is not all there is to salvation, and so Paul says in Philippians 2:12-13 that we must work out the salvation that God is working into us, by both our willing and our doing. In other words, our behavior as believers affects our progress in salvation.

Salvation actually has three tenses in the New Testament: I have been saved (conversion), I am being saved (progressive sanctification), and I shall be saved (final salvation). Our deeds do affect both of the latter two stages of salvation, but not because we are saved by the deeds. Instead, it's because they are necessary expressions of salvation if we have time and opportunity to do them (i.e., they are not optional—faith without works is dead, as James says).

Of course it is true that if a person is converted on their deathbed they are simply saved by conversion, but the New Testament is clear that those who live beyond the time of their conversion must behave—look at Galatians 5:19-21. Paul is warning Christians about the consequences of persisting in serious sin. The end result is they shall not inherit the kingdom or receive final salvation.

In short, while good deeds cannot earn the gift of final salvation, apostasy in various forms (moral or intellectual) can forfeit salvation even if one has been a Christian previously. In short, you are not eternally secure until you are securely in eternity. See Hebrews 6:1-4.

I'm hoping to find out the name of one of the thieves who was crucified with Jesus and said, "Remember me when thou comest into thy kingdom." Someone had told me his name a long time ago, but I can't remember it.

The thieves do not have names in the biblical text (see Luke 23:39-43). In fact, they are not thieves; they are revolutionaries. Later Christian tradition made up names for them; for example, the good criminal was called Dismas.

I need to know what this means: "Behold, I show you a mystery." Would the mystery be faith or the word itself?

If you are referring to 1 Corinthians 15:51-52, the answer is neither. The secret Paul is revealing is that all true believers will be transformed into a resurrection condition with a resurrection body when Jesus returns.

I heard that the names "Jesus" and "Joshua" are the same word in Hebrew. Why, then, is Jesus called "Jesus" and not "Joshua"?

Jesus is the English form of the Greek word *Iesous*, which in turn is the Greek rendering of the Hebrew name Yeshua—which we transliterate in English as Joshua. So yes, they are the same name, but the name's form changes as it goes through three languages.

I was wondering where people got the idea of Jesus getting weak and falling down while he carried the cross before Simon took over and carried it the rest of the way. I have studied the Scripture, but could not find this anywhere. I am confused because I have seen many churches perform the crucifixion on Easter, and every time Jesus falls and Simon takes over.

You are right to ask this question. Mark 15:21 simply says that Simon was compelled to carry Jesus' cross. There is nothing about Jesus carrying it and then falling in our earliest gospel. Matthew and Luke say the same. John 19:17, however, says that Jesus carried his own cross. When the medieval church blended these stories together it was assumed that Simon carried the cross after Jesus could no longer do so. The falling of Jesus not once but several times is part of Catholic tradition and not supported by any biblical reference.

In 1 Corinthians 14:22, Paul states that tongues are a sign for unbelievers but prophesying is for believers. Then, in verses 23-25, he goes on to explain how tongues are a sign for believers and prophecy is a sign for unbelievers. Paul seems to contradict himself. Can you reconcile these verses?

There are several issues here in play. What Paul is concerned about when it comes to unbelievers is intelligibility. Speaking in tongues is unintelligible to unbelievers and so is a sign to them that they are not in the right spiritual condition. Here, the term "sign" means a sign of judgment.

Prophecy, however, is intelligible: it is spoken in a known language and can convince and convict an unbeliever. Therefore, it is appropriate communication in a worship service that is attended by both believers and unbelievers.

Paul goes on to say that prophecy is, however, primarily directed to believers and so is of benefit to them. There is no contradiction here; there can be both negative and positive signs, depending on one's spiritual condition. He does not actually say that tongues is a sign for believers (if you read the text carefully in the Greek), and he does indicate that prophecy is primarily directed to and for the benefit of believers. However, there may be collateral benefit to unbelievers since it is in a known language.

Do babies from all nations go to heaven even though their parents are nonbelievers?

Nothing in the Bible speaks to this question. In Mark 10:13, Jesus does say that the kingdom belongs to these little ones and those who are like them. The kingdom Jesus is talking about is on earth, not in heaven.

Does the Bible describe how you should get married? All the Scriptures that I have read only say marriage. It doesn't describe if you should get married in a church or if you are just married by being with the person.

The Bible does not prescribe a special place or locale where one must get married, but it does suggest it needs to be done in the presence of God and witnesses, and it needs to involve vows and promises. In other words, it involves a public commitment where the community of faith recognizes and supports this decision. Simply living together does not constitute being married, nor does privately making promises to each other.

I have been raised Christian, and have always been taught that the Jewish faith does not recognize Jesus as the Son of God. However, I have recently become friends with someone who is Jewish, and he tells me that is not so. I'm confused.

I suppose that the question is, what constitutes recognizing Jesus as Son of God? For example, Genesis 6:1-4 refers to angels as Sons of God, but it is not referring to the Messiah. Elsewhere in the Old Testament, God's children in general could be called sons of God. In Psalm 2, David the king is called God's anointed son. Unless a Jewish person has become a Christian, they generally speaking do not recognize Jesus as the unique and divine Son of God who is the Messiah for Jews and the savior of the world.

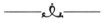

What does the Bible say about seeing God? Does anyone ever "see" God, even after they die?

It depends on whom you are referring to by the word "God." If you are referring to Jesus, the answer is yes: Jesus has been and will be seen when he returns. If you mean God the Father, the answer is no, since God does not have a physical form—though one could claim to have seen him when one sees his glory or brilliance.

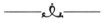

I know wedding vows say "until death do us part." Does this mean that once in heaven you are no longer with your spouse? What about your children or other family members? It saddens me to think that I won't spend eternity with my husband. Also, where in the Bible does it describe what life in heaven is like?

The Bible in fact says very little about life in heaven after death. We could turn to the parable of the Rich Man and Lazarus in Luke

16:19-31, but it is just that, a parable—a form of literary fiction. What this parable shows is that there is a heaven and there is a hell, but it tells us nothing about whom one will spend their time with, in either locale. The book of Revelation says the most about heaven, but again apocalyptic literature is highly figurative in character, being made up of visions. Revelation 4–5 suggests heaven is a wonderful place where the saints dwell with God, but one cannot deduce much more. It is interesting to note, however, that the martyrs are cranky in Revelation 6:9-10, wanting to know how long before God will judge their tormentors.

Paul in Romans 7:1-4 reminds us that when one's husband dies, one is no longer bound to him, which means, among other things, that one can remarry. This makes perfectly clear that marriage is an earthly institution, not a heavenly one. Jesus makes this clear as well when he says in the resurrection there will be neither marrying nor being given in marriage (Mark 12:25), which means marrying will not be going on at the eschaton either.

But perhaps we are asking the wrong question. The focus of the New Testament is not on life in heaven after death but on life after Jesus returns to earth and the dead in Christ are raised. The images of the messianic banquet in the Gospels, or of the new earth after it has been transformed by the new heaven that comes down with Jesus in Revelation 21, make clear that it will be wonderful. Perhaps we can say that the communion we will have with everyone then and there will be as blessed, or more blessed, than even the best moments in earthly marriage.

When you become a Christian and ask for forgiveness for your sins, you are forgiven. I read that after we die and we are in front of God, all of the Book of Life is opened and we are judged by it! Why is that? I thought we were forgiven for all our sins. Why, then, are we still judged for them?

The fact that a person is forgiven does not mean that there are not consequences for sin. We experience this all the time in our broken relationships in this life. We may be forgiven, but the relationship has been irreparably damaged and there are scars. The references to the Book of Life in Revelation about rewards correspond with what Jesus says about rewards in heaven. One could also consult what Paul says in 1 Corinthians 3:10-15 about the testing of even Paul's works. These texts all suggest that even Christians must render account for the deeds they have done in the body, and there will be rewards, or the lack thereof, for their behavior in this life. Salvation is not a reward; salvation is by grace and through faith, but there will be rewards in heaven for works that glorify God and edify others.

Recently in a Bible study group there was mention of the fact that the Bible says there will never be peace in the Middle East. I'm not sure if this just refers to Israel or the entire region. Can you tell me where this Scripture is found if it exists?

Such a text does not exist, but it is true that there will be no final peace until the new heaven and new earth come after the return of Christ, as Revelation 21–22 makes perfectly clear.

I have been working for three Mormon doctors for two years. The owner doctor is angry because the two employee doctors do not see enough patients. I instituted a production-based bonus to encourage the other two doctors. It seemed to help for several months as the clinic had more patients. Recently the two doctors went to the owner doctor and said they should not be so busy—that I am making them see too many patients (they are below national average of optometry benchmarks) and that I am greedy. The owner doctor told me that we should not see too many patients and read me two different passages about greed from the Bible—one was from Timothy and I think the other one may have been Matthew. I have been trained to run offices and feel this was very inappropriate. When I came to the practice it was almost bankrupt. Now we actually have a small profit margin. Does the Bible say that you are greedy when you try to do the best job that you know how? Does the Book of Mormon say anything about greed? The only people who profit from the increase are the doctors. I am on salary and receive the same amount of money whether I do a good job or not. Are there any Scriptures in the Bible that relate to this issue?

Several Scriptures come to mind that could be of relevance, so let's start with the first issue, which is work. Paul is perfectly clear that those who refuse to work, and indeed to work with some industry, should not eat (2 Thess 2:10-13). On the other hand, Paul is also clear that people who do work deserve to be paid according to the work they do—"a workman is worthy of his hire." You may want to quote to them Galatians 6:5—"each person should carry their own load!" You may also want to point them to 1 Thessalonians 5:12-14, which speaks of warning the idle and respecting hard work.

Greed, however, is a very different issue. Sometimes people will bring up the subject of greed simply because they are lazy, or can't be bothered to do their share of the work. Greed is a sin condemned in numerous places in the New Testament (for example, in 1 Tim 6:6-10). The fact that your company now has a small profit margin does not suggest anyone there is getting rich quick.

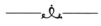

I'm confused. Is drinking alcohol a sin? If it is, why did Jesus turn water into wine? A friend has told me that it wasn't really wine—it was just sweetened water. My belief is that drinking in moderation (e.g., having a glass of wine when having a meal) is fine. Am I wrong?

You are not wrong. Wine in the Bible could range in alcoholic content from about 2 percent if it was "new wine" to much stronger (14 percent), in which case it was classified as "strong drink." The Bible says nothing against having a glass of wine once in a while; in fact, Paul urges Timothy to have a glass to settle his stomach (1 Tim 5:23). Wine was the replacement for water in antiquity for health reasons, as there were no water purification plants in antiquity. It was the normal table beverage.

(In response to a previous column about the translation of the Bible by Jehovah's Witnesses, a reader wrote in upset about my critique of the translation.)

John 1:1 was not falsified by Jehovah's Witnesses in order to prove that Jesus is not Almighty God. Jehovah's Witnesses, among many others, had challenged the capitalizing of "god" long before the appearance of the New World Translation, which endeavors accurately to render the original language. Five German Bible translators likewise use the term "a god" in that verse. At least thirteen others have used expressions such as "of divine kind" or "godlike kind." These renderings agree with other parts of the Bible to show that, yes, Jesus in heaven is a god in the sense of being divine. But Jehovah and Jesus are not the same being, the same God.
Moffatt's translation of John 1:1-3:

> The Logos existed in the very beginning,
> the Logos was with God, the Logos was divine.
> He was with God in the very beginning:
> through him all existence came into being,
> no existence came into being apart from him.

Another inquirer wrote about that same column saying:

Thank you for your recent column in which you comment on "The Jehovah's Witness Bible." There you seem to agree with the contention that the New World Translation is part of "a scholarly conspiracy to amend the Bible to suit particular theological views" of Jehovah's Witnesses. Curiously, the example you chose to cite does not actually "amend the Bible" but simply includes a single solitary indefinite article ("a"), which is completely acceptable to secular Greek scholars. The only real objections to the NWT wording of John 1:1 come from within Christendom, rather than from strict academia. Isn't this an example of intellectual dishonesty on your part, your calling this "amending the Bible"?

I will answer these two queries together. First of all, it is disingenuous to cite Moffatt's translation of John 1:1-3 as if he meant something other than "God" by the word "divine" in that Scripture, when it is perfectly clear from reading the rest of his translation that he takes the two terms "God" and "divine" as synonymous. Moffatt was not a supporter of Jehovah's Witness's ideas about the deity and would have been appalled that his translation might be used to suggest that Jesus ought not to be called God.

Second, there are at least seven or eight places in the New Testament where Jesus is simply called "God," and there is no reason to think the term means anything less than God the Father. A good example of this would be in John 20:28, where Jesus is called both Lord and God by Thomas. Or one could point to Romans 9:5.

As for the second comment made by the enquirer, I must explain the Greek in some detail. We are dealing with a predicate nominative in a sentence where the word order in the Greek would be backward to an ordinary English sentence. It reads literally "and God was the Word." The author certainly does not want to say "and the God was the Word," because that would imply that the one called the Word exhausted the godhead, indeed replaced the Father. Our author's theology is that there are several persons in the godhead, including the Logos, or Word.

The fact that "the Word" is the subject of this Greek clause, but follows the verb, dictates what one does with the object of the verb, "God," which precedes the verb. In such a case in a Greek sentence, the object does not normally take a definite article, and the absence of the article certainly doesn't provide warrant for a translation like "a god" or "divine." In this very same chapter the definite article is omitted in verses 6, 12, 13, and 18, where the term "God" refers not to the Word, but to God the Father. Again, the absence of the article tells us nothing about whether or not we should capitalize the noun *Theos* here.

B. M. Metzger, the leading Bible textual expert of the modern era (head of both the RSV and NRSV teams) stresses that "those who translate 'a god' [or divine] here prove nothing thereby save their ignorance of Greek grammar" (see C. Keener's discussion in his *The Gospel of John: A Commentary*, vol. 1, p. 373). There was a perfectly good Greek term for "divine"—"*to theion*"—which our author could have used if he wanted to merely say Jesus was "divine" in some lesser sense than God is divine. This phrase is never used of Jesus either in John's Gospel or elsewhere in the New Testament. Therefore, I stand by my statement: the New World Translation is meant to bolster an ideology that is at odds with what the New Testament says and means by calling Jesus God.

———— ‿ℓ‿ ————

Research on Luke 16:19-31 indicates that the Pharisees and others of Jesus' day perceived wealth to be a sign of God's favor. Hence, Jesus' story [about Lazarus and the rich man] was intended to correct this thinking. Oddly, research on James 2:5 (particularly from Peter H. Davids's commentary on James) indicates that the popular opinion was that poverty signified God's favor/election. Can you make sense of these apparently contradictory claims?

While it is true, if one reads the book of Proverbs, that wealth is sometimes seen as a blessing from God, poverty is never viewed as a blessing, not even in James. James suggests that wealth is not necessarily a sign of God's blessing, and that the poor can often be closer to God than the wealthy—indeed, that poverty can be the stimulus that drives one to God.

Is there biblical support for withholding charity in certain cases? A year ago a man was hired at my husband's workplace, and at the time the boss told my husband he was doing it as a charitable act because the man has had trouble with drugs and is practically penniless. Without subjecting you to a huge litany of gripes, however, suffice it to say that the man is a very poor worker, usually arrives late and leaves early, often doesn't show up at all, and has a terrible temper. He's a big man, and the other employees are rather afraid of him. They're also demoralized because they know they would have been fired a long time ago if they performed as poorly as he does. The boss is aware of the problems but has done nothing, as far as anyone knows. I seem to recall that the Bible has something to say about this—something about knowing the person you're giving charity to—but I haven't been able to find the verse.

This falls under the category of being wise as serpents and innocent as doves. I would suggest that you look over the Sermon on the Mount in Matthew 5–7. Compassion and charity are acts that should be done wholeheartedly, of course, but giving someone a job that then hurts other workers is not compassionate toward those other workers. Compassion must be exercised wisely and with all concerned in view.

I have a very devoted Christian friend who has taught her kids that when they are sick, it is Satan trying to "get" them. I was shocked at this as her child developed strep throat and was at her bedroom door shivering with sickness and fever, saying, "Satan, Satan." . . . Is this true to Christian belief? And if it is, where in the Bible does it say that getting an organic sickness is due to the devil?

This is certainly not a Christian perspective. Consider, for example, what Jesus says in John 9 about the man born blind. He says that it is neither because he had sinned nor because his parents had sinned that he was in this condition. There is no one-to-one correlation in the Bible between sickness and sin, or between sickness and the devil, for that matter. Satan is linked to one and only one particular condition in the New Testament—namely demon possession—and strep throat definitely doesn't fall under the heading of demon possession. To demonize all illness is to give the devil way too much credit.

Can you give me the verse and Scriptures in the Bible that explain who gets into heaven and under what circumstances?

There is very little discussion about dying and going to heaven in the New Testament, so I am not surprised you have not found the appropriate verses. What is discussed in the New Testament frequently is the means of salvation, which is repeatedly said to be Jesus, whether we think of the Johannine "I am the way the truth and the life, no one comes to the Father but by me" (John 14:6) or "there is no other name under heaven by which we may be saved" (Acts 4:12). Jesus is certainly portrayed in the New Testament as the exclusive means of salvation for anyone.

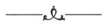

Which of the Ten Commandments was not followed or enforced in the New Testament? I located 1, 5, 6, 7, 8, 9, and 10. But I was having trouble finding 2, 3, and 4.

The Sabbath commandment was not reinforced in the Christian era. See, for example, what Paul says about keeping Sabbaths in Colossians 2:16. Christians worshiped on the Lord's Day, or Sunday, not on the Jewish Sabbath, and did not feel they had to keep the Jewish Sabbath anymore.

———ॐ———

I was brought up to believe that sex before marriage or any man seeing my body before marriage is a sin. I'd like to know what Scriptures there are to back this up. I have made the mistake and lost my virginity. Does this condemn me to hell? Or is there forgiveness for this? I think of it this way: I love the person I am with, I intend to marry him, I am not playing around, nor am I one to sleep around. I need to either calm my mind, or make a decision to change my ways.

There can be no doubt that the New Testament classifies any kind of sexual relationships outside of marriage as a sin, so yes, there needs to be some repentance on your part. But the Lord will forgive you of this if you truly and earnestly repent. Notice how in Matthew 5, Jesus classifies even lustful thoughts as adultery. The basic rule in the New Testament, as Matthew 19 shows, is celibacy in singleness and fidelity in marriage.

The reasons for saving sex for marriage are numerous. First of all, you cannot be sure you will marry this person. Something could happen between now and then. Second, sex is physically the most intimate act you can share, but it needs to be shared in the context of an already extant permanent commitment to each other. You cannot fully love someone you don't yet fully trust, and the trust relationship needs to be fully in place before intimate sharing happens. Third, when you share the marital act outside of marriage you cheapen the special nature of the intimacy of marriage.

———ॐ———

In Matthew 10:34, it reads, "Think not that I am come to send peace on earth; I came not to send peace, but a sword." Then Jesus says somewhere else that "those who live by the sword die by the sword." I can't help but feel a sense of betrayal by these two conflicting passages. God sends the sword, yet he warns us not to live by it?

These two texts are certainly not in contradiction with one another. Matthew 10:34, in its context, has nothing to do with military weapons. It has to do with the division caused in a family when the family is divided over a commitment to Jesus.

As for Jesus' personal stance on fighting and war, it should be clear from Matthew 5–7 that Jesus is a pacifist. He believes in turning the other cheek, in forgiving and loving one's enemies, in leaving revenge in God's hands, and he even condemns the disciples for striking the high priest's slave with a weapon in the garden of Gethsemane when they are seeking to rescue Jesus from his captors.

————⁓————

My daughter passed away almost four years ago from a car accident. Everyone tells me that she is now in heaven, and I believe that. But the Bible states that when the end comes, and Christ returns, he is going to raise the dead believers first to be with him. If she is now in heaven, how would he raise her from the dead? Is she just in eternal sleep now and not really in heaven, or is she in heaven in her new state?

This is a fine question, and you should read closely what 1 Thessalonians 4–5 says on this issue.

Both things are true. As 2 Corinthians 5 says, to be absent from the body is to be present with the Lord (cf. also Rev 6:9 about the saints under the altar in heaven). It is also true, however, that the dead in Christ will be raised. One could envision them coming with Jesus when he returns, but in 1 Thessalonians 4–5, the text suggests that they rise from the earth and go and meet him in the air. In any case, life in heaven is but a prelude to resurrection of the dead, when believers are finally conformed to Christ's image.

————⁓————

Why are there different books in different Bibles? When was this decided anyway? What about the book called Tobit?

In the fourth century AD, the Roman Catholic Church and the Eastern Church agreed on thirty-nine Old Testament books and twenty-seven New Testament books. The thirty-nine Old Testament books did not include Tobit. The Protestant Bible follows the decision of Athanasius in the East and Pope Innocent in the West in about AD 368, which said these sixty-six books and no others. There was, however, a collection of so-called deuterocanonical books that non-Protestant churches recognize as having value and some authority. Tobit is one of those.

Does the Bible itself actually identify exactly on which side Jesus was pierced with the spear? I always thought it was the left side.

No one knows.

Someone who works with me told me that, in the Old Testament, God told the Jewish people to go through the Middle East and destroy everyone and everything in their way. Is this true? I do read my Bible, but I have not seen such a verse.

Perhaps they are thinking of the *haram* or "ban" passages from Joshua, where the Holy Land is to be cleansed of the enemies of God's people. There is nothing in the Bible about Jews going through the entire Middle East and wiping everyone out.

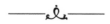

Is it actually said that every believer must have a conversion experience, that is, something that really happened to bring about

repentance? In my own case, I don't have any, other than I grew up hearing and loving the way of Christ and have never had any unnatural experience. It's been two years now since I formally gave my life, and apart from God's intervention in many cases of my life nothing of note has really happened to me. What do you think is my problem? I am not convinced that I am a child of God though people who know me think otherwise.

You seem to have been misled by someone who suggested you had to have some particular kind of experience to be a born-again Christian. This is not true. There are as many different ways to come to Christ as there are believers.

Consider, for example, the story of C. S. Lewis's conversion, in his book *Surprised by Joy.* He says that he had no joyful experience or mountaintop experience or anything like that. Rather for him it was just a matter of giving in, and accepting that God had set him apart. He added, "I became the most reluctant convert in all of Christendom." Yet, as his writings show, he was one of the most profoundly Christian ones.

If you believe in the Lord Jesus Christ, as 1 Corinthians 12 makes clear, no one can truly and earnestly do that unless they are indeed saved, as this requires already having the work of the Holy Spirit within you. The fact of your conversion should not be mistaken for some particular kind of experiential response to the work of God in your life.

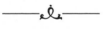

I have been working at my new job for about five months now. I have become really close with one of the men I work with, who is black. He is everything I have been looking for in a man, and he feels the same way toward me. I would like to start dating him, but my parents strongly disagree with interracial dating. They believe the Bible says it's wrong.

The New Testament is perfectly clear on this issue. There can be no problems with interracial dating and marriage, since, as Galatians 3:28 says, "In Christ there is no Jew or gentile, but rather all are one in him."

Matthew's Gospel opens with a list of "begats" tracing Joseph's lineage back through David to Abraham. How is this relevant, considering that the Holy Ghost is the father of Jesus? Why do they not give us Mary's lineage?

The genealogy in Matthew 1 is a royal genealogy, and as such it has several features of such ancient genealogies. For one thing, it is schematized and does not include all the generations. For another, it reflects the Jewish practice that if a man adopted a son, then he was entitled to his stepfather's genealogy, even though he wasn't physically his offspring. In the case of Jesus, this meant that when Joseph accepted him as his son he was entitled to Joseph's genealogy. The author does not give us Mary's genealogy because we are dealing with a patriarchal Jewish culture, where the father's genealogy is all-important.

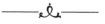

My husband and I have been together for eleven and a half years, we've been married for six and a half. We have two beautiful children. My husband has recently been born again and now thinks our marriage is a sin. He was married before, his wife left him, they did try to get back together and that didn't work. All that happened sixteen years ago. Because he was married before, does God honor my marriage? (This is my first marriage.) Are we living in sin?

Your question is a complex one, and it involves several components. In 1 Corinthians 7, Paul advises a Christian person not to divorce their non-Christian spouse because that spouse might indeed be sanctified by the believing partner, and the children of such a marriage are called holy. In other words, Paul hardly suggests that a Christian married to a non-Christian is in any danger of being defiled or living in sin simply because he has a nonbelieving spouse. If you are also a Christian, but have not had a Christian marriage ceremony, it might allay your husband"s fears if you had a service of consecration of your marriage celebrated by a minister.

Doing a comparison of the twelve tribes listed in Genesis 35 and Revelation 7, what happened the tribe of Dan? Could you explain why Joseph ends up with his own tribe plus the tribe named after his son?

The tribe of Dan, the northernmost tribe, was considered apostate in some circles of early Judaism, and so was replaced in some lists of the twelve tribes that appear around the turn of the era.

Who or what is the immoral woman mentioned in Proverbs 2:16-19?

The woman in question is called a "strange" woman in the Hebrew text. Then, in what follows in Proverbs 2:17-19, it is made clear that she is an adulteress, one who has violated a marriage which was arranged for her when she was a teenager. The advice given may in fact suggest that the woman has gone so far as to become a prostitute, for it speaks of "those" who go to her, referring to more than one. It is also possible, indeed likely, that the term "strange" indicates we are also dealing with a foreign woman.

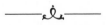

My boyfriend and I have been together for about three years, and when we started the relationship I told him I wanted to wait

until I was married to have sex. He said he was fine with that. But we put ourselves in the position where we were tempted and gave in to that. We now have a sixteen-month-old son. I told him that I am sticking to my guns this time and want to wait until I am married. He feels that I can't make that decision for him and should still give in to him. He says that we have already done it and it doesn't matter. Could you give me some Scripture to back up my decision, also suggest some things that he could read to gain an understanding that just because you sin once doesn't mean you get to go on sinning.

Read carefully what Paul says in 1 Corinthians 7. His advice is that one should get married if one wishes to avoid immoral sexual activities. Your boyfriend is letting his hormones do the talking, and yes it does matter to God. Sex is a gift from God. Indeed, sex is such a great and beautiful gift from God it should be reserved for the person one is prepared to give one's life and love to unconditionally in holy matrimony.

I enjoyed your Beliefnet column on apocalyptic literature. Are you saying that parts of Revelation are a blueprint for the end time and parts are not? Was it because the early Christians were convinced the Parousia was imminent?

The answer to this question is potentially long and complicated. The short answer is that the earliest Christians believed they already lived in the end time, ever since Jesus had been raised from the dead. The book of Revelation does not skip from their day to the end of time, but sees all future events as part of the end time, including events in their own day.

I would urge you to read my little book *Jesus, Paul, and the End of the World* to help you sort this one out. I do not believe that the earliest Christians thought Jesus would definitely return in their lifetimes, as

Jesus himself told them no one knows the timing of the second coming, not even Jesus in his own day (Mark 13:32). It's presumptuous for any of us to think we know better than Jesus did when he said no one knows the time of that event.

Did Jesus appoint Peter as the head of his church, or was the appointment made later by a pope?

The issue about Peter being made the head of the church has to do with one specific New Testament passage, Matthew 16:18-19. If this saying goes back to the historical Jesus, then Jesus said this in Aramaic, which among other things means the word "church" was not involved, as that is a later Christian term.

There were no popes before or during the lifetime of Peter to appoint him. It is Jesus himself who commissions Peter. The phrase here could be rendered somewhat literally as follows: "you are 'rock,' and on this shelf of rocks I will build my community." The point would be that Jesus would build his community on Peter and those like him who make the solid confession about Jesus that we find Peter making on this occasion. In view of the fact that Matthew 16:19 recurs in Matthew 18:18-19, applied to all the disciples, it seems unlikely that Jesus is suggesting some unique role for Peter that could not also be played by other disciples.

Where is the Trinity mentioned in the Bible? Why did Jesus say, "The Father is greater than I" if they are supposed to be equal?

Was the Son always there with the Father in the beginning of the creation? If not, when did the Son come "into the picture" before coming to earth to die for our sins?

Why do so many argue that the Scriptures (Old Testament) makes no mention of a Trinity? An angel, or messenger/ambassador, of the

LORD appeared to Moses. This "angel" of the LORD is later clearly identified as the LORD. How can the LORD be "of the LORD"? (Unless the Scriptures here teach one God in more than one person.)

The Trinity is not really mentioned in the Old Testament. The angel of the Lord is just that—an angel. The angel of the Lord is a special representative or messenger of God to God's people, and according to the ancient concept of agency, he could be considered to be the Lord who sent them, and was to be treated as if he were the one who sent him.

According to Christian doctrine, there was no incarnation of Jesus prior to the Incarnation. This is not to say that the divine son of God was not involved in creation and other things prior to his taking on flesh in Mary's womb; it is simply to make clear that he was no mere angel of the Lord, nor did he manifest himself in some observable form prior to the Incarnation.

Philippians 2:5-11 should be compared with John 1. Both these texts make clear that the divine Son of God existed before he took on flesh. Indeed, John 1 makes clear he existed before the creation of the universe, and even helped in the creation of the universe. Thus, John 1 makes clear that there are at least two persons in the Godhead. Since elsewhere in the New Testament (see, for example, John 14–17), the Holy Spirit is treated as a person distinct from the Father and the Son, not merely as a force or power of God, there is an implicit assumption that the Spirit is also a person within the Godhead. In Matthew 28, the fact that baptism is done in the name of Father, Son, and Spirit is important, for baptism would only be done in God's name. Notice that Matthew 28:19 does not speak of names plural, but of the name of God (singular) being Father, Son, and Spirit—three persons, one Godhead.

Finally, there is a functional subordination of the Son to the Father, and the Spirit to both the Son and the Father, that leads to statements like we find in John's Gospel, where Jesus indicates that he must wait on the leading and guidance of God before acting. The Son acts for the Father and on the basis of the Father's guidance, and the Spirit (called another advocate in John 14–17) acts for the Son. There is thus equality of nature and being between Father, Son, and Spirit, but functional subordination in terms of how the Trinity works.

In Deuteronomy 18:14-19, who is the prophet that Moses is talking about? And if it's Jesus, how is he related to Moses, and how is he like Moses?

Many people have certainly interpreted the prophecy you are referring to—one about the rise of a prophet like Moses—in a messianic way. Of course, in the broad sense Jesus was a Jew, and so was of the same lineage as Moses. But bear in mind that the prophecy in Deuteronomy is not specific; it is more of a character description. The prophet the author has in mind will have certain attributes that Moses also had. Certainly, Jesus had some of these attributes. For example, the feeding of the five thousand is viewed in the Gospels as an event like the miracle of manna in the wilderness during Moses' day. Or again, many would see the presentation of Jesus' teaching during the Sermon on the Mount as similar to Moses giving the law on Mount Sinai.

Nowhere in the Bible does Jesus pray for animals. Is it scriptural to pray for our pets—dogs, cats, etc.?

We have very few of the prayers of Jesus mentioned in the New Testament, and so silence on this matter does not necessarily mean Jesus would not approve. Much depends on what one would pray about in regard to animals. There surely can be nothing wrong with thanking God for the blessing of animals, or praying for their well-being. What we must keep in mind is that animals, like lower life forms, are not created in the image of God. They do not have the same capacity for relationship with God as humans or angels do.

Nevertheless, some Jewish writers of the Old Testament envisioned that when the messianic kingdom comes on earth at the end of history, animals would have a place in that realm, with the "lion lying down with the lamb."

Did Jesus really go down to Hades—Hell—and preach to the saints before his ascension?

The idea that Jesus went down to Hades and preached to the dead is based on a misunderstanding of 1 Peter 3:19. This text is actually about Jesus proclaiming his triumph to disobedient angels who are incarcerated. The angels in question are those referred to in Genesis 6; they came down to earth and sinned, precipitating the flood (compare 2 Pet 2:4-5; Jude 6).

I was told earth is around several million years old. Do you have any idea as to how many years old earth is?

I am not a geologist or any other kind of scientist, but I do have a problem with arguments that fossils and other such evidence only make it *appear* as if the earth is millions of years old. I have a problem with the notion that God would deceive us about the age of things by "planting" fossils and other evidence to fool us about the age of creation. More importantly, the Bible does not try to tell us how old the Earth is. One cannot derive an age for the earth by adding up years in the genealogies in Genesis, for the very good reason that those genealogies are partial and piecemeal. They are not exhaustive or complete. We must always keep in mind that the Bible is not intended to be a scientific textbook. It was written for people who lived long before the rise of modern science.

I'd like to know more about the life of John, one of the Apostles. How did he die and where?

I take it that by John the Apostle you mean John the son of Zebedee. We are not at all sure where and how John died. The Bible does not say. There is one tradition that he moved to Ephesus, lived a long life, and died there. The problem with this tradition is that it is not at all clear that the beloved disciple mentioned in John 13–21 is the same person as John the son of Zebedee, and it also appears unlikely that John the visionary mentioned in Revelation is the same person as John the son of Zebedee.

What was the thorn in St. Paul's flesh?

The literal translation of 2 Corinthians 12:7 is "a stake in the flesh, a messenger of Satan." It seems clear from the context of that verse that this is a reference to some sort of physical malady that plagued Paul from time to time. It is possible that Paul had some sort of eye disease, as Galatians 4:13-15 may suggest.

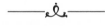

How does the fact that nothing was recorded in Jesus' native language and the language of the people to whom he was speaking affect the canonical Gospels?

This is an excellent question. Jesus' native tongue was Aramaic, and while certainly we have documents from antiquity written in Aramaic (including part of the book of Daniel), we do not have Jesus' teachings in this language. Rather, the New Testament is written in Greek. It is well to remember, however, that many early Jews were bilingual, including, no doubt, some of Jesus' original followers. The accounts in Acts of Peter preaching to all sorts of people, including Gentiles, suggests that he knew some Greek. This is also suggested by his probable authorship of 1 Peter. This being the case, probably not much is lost in translation if at an early juncture one of Jesus' first followers translated his words from Aramaic into Greek.

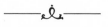

I would like more information on the second coming of Jesus Christ. What are the signs? How will it take place?

There are various prophecies about the second coming in the New Testament. I would encourage you to read Mark 13 in particular. What Mark 13:32 tells us is that not even Jesus himself knew the timing of this event, but he was certain that it would transpire. First Thessalonians 4–5 suggests that we will never be able to predict the timing of the second coming, for it will arrive without warning, like a thief in the night. Thus, the message of the New Testament about this matter is that we must always be prepared, whether it comes sooner or later.

I believe the true Sabbath day to be Saturday and that many years ago the Romans changed this to Sunday to serve their purposes.

You are correct in thinking that the Jewish Sabbath is from sundown Friday until sundown on Saturday. However, it was not the Romans who changed the day of worship. Early Christians began to worship on Sunday even during New Testament times (see, for example, 1 Cor 16:2; Rev 1:10 gives us the first reference to worship on the Lord's Day). Early Christians worshiped on the first day of the week because it was the day Jesus rose from the dead. This practice is even mentioned in a letter from the Roman governor of Asia Minor—Pliny—to the emperor Trajan in the early second century AD.

Recently I decided after much thought and consideration to con-vert from the Roman Catholic Faith into the Church of Jesus Christ of Latter-day Saints. Since my conversion I have found my faith with Jesus Christ to become even greater. I am curious of your thoughts on the Mormon church. Mormons believe, among other things, that Christ appeared in the Americas and that the Book of Mormon is a second companion to the Bible.

Christians in general, and Christian scholars in particular, do not accept the Book of Mormon as a supplement to the Bible. They do not believe it contains historical information, or further revelations from the God of the Bible. Mormonism is a religion that arose in North America in the nineteenth century long after the Bible was written. Christianity had long since been a well-established religion, without a need for a Book of Mormon. The Book of Mormon was probably written by Joseph Smith himself; it has some remarkable similarities to nineteenth-century American novels, which Smith seems to have read. Smith seems to have been concerned that the Bible didn't seem to address the plight of Native Americans and, in general, of the peoples of North America. He was concerned there be a revelation specifi-cally for such peoples. While this is a laudable concern, the Bible is quite specific that the revelation given two thousand years ago is for all peoples in all lands in all times, and needs no supplement.

Why did Peter go into the courtyard of the high priest after Jesus was arrested?

According to John 18:15-18, Peter did not go alone to the high priest's house. He went with the beloved disciple, who was known to the high priest. Perhaps the hope was that they could be witnesses on behalf of Jesus if there was to be a hearing in the high priest's house.

How old was Jesus when he began to preach the Gospel and when he was crucified? Also, what time period was it—AD 30 or 33?

According to Luke 3:23, Jesus was about thirty years old when he began his work. We know he did so probably somewhere between AD 27 and 29, because he died at Passover in April of AD 30. See the chronological discussions in my book *New Testament History* (Baker 2001).

I have read that in Jesus' time it was tradition that the oldest son took financial responsibility of his widowed mother. If this is true, why did Jesus appoint John the beloved to care for Mary while on the cross? I know Jesus had other brothers, James in particular, who could have accommodated this tradition.

The evidence suggests that prior to the resurrection, Jesus' family, perhaps excepting Mary, did not believe in him (see John 7:5 and also Mark 3:21-35). In any case, Jesus believed that the family of faith was the primary family (see Mark 3:31-35). He would certainly have wanted to place his mother into the care of believers once he was deceased. It was only a resurrection appearance to James (see 1 Cor 15:7) that apparently made James believe.

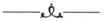

In the original Greek versions of the book of Luke, is the annunciation to Mary brought by an "angel" or by a being described as "a holy messenger all dressed in white"? Does the Greek version of the four Gospels ever use the word "angel"?

In Greek, the word *angelos* can mean either a human or a supernatural messenger, but the attire mentioned in Luke and elsewhere for this messenger is stereotypically associated with angels in the Bible (cf. Matt 28:3).

Looking at the devil from a biblical standpoint, is there any reference from the Old Testament that says he has the power to tempt people into sinning and he is the "king" of hell? Also, are the devil, Satan, Lucifer, the Beast, the False Prophet, and the Dragon all the same?

The term "Satan" probably first appears in the Bible in Job 1-2. It is not a proper name; the word means the accuser, sort of like a prosecuting attorney. In Job 1-2, this is the role Satan plays, bewitching, bothering, and bewildering Job. In the book of Revelation, the beast and the false prophet are not the same as Satan. The beast represents the ungodly empire, which is influenced by Satan (in this case John had in mind the Roman Empire), and the false prophet represents oracles or priests who spread the false propaganda of the Roman Empire, in particular the message that the emperor was a god. Plenty of passages suggest that the Devil tempts people (see Luke 22:31-32).

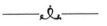

What does the Bible say about reincarnation?

The Bible has nothing directly to say about the matter of reincarnation. However, it indirectly denies such a concept altogether by affirming that each person is uniquely created in the image of God and has his own destiny—a destiny not linked with any other beings in the created order, whether higher or lower beings. In the Bible, every person has one shot—in one lifetime—to sort out their relationship with God. After they die, it is too late (see Luke 16:19-31).

When is the age of accountability? Is it the age of twenty? Is it true that sin doesn't count before the age of accountability?

The New Testament is quite clear that all have sinned and fallen short of God's glory, regardless of age, and that salvation is by grace and through faith for all. The age of accountability has nothing to do with determining whether one is a sinner or not.

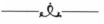

Is Melchizedek Jesus Christ or Christlike? I have read that he is of the Most High God and that he is without predecessor or successor.

Melchizedek is not Christ. What the book of Hebrews suggests is that Christ is rather like this ancient shadowy royal figure. Read the book of Hebrews and compare Psalm 110.

In Genesis 9:18-25, Noah is drunk, and uncovered in his tent. Ham sees him and sends in his two brothers to cover him up. Then Noah awakes and curses Ham's son Canaan. Why does Noah curse Canaan, who wasn't involved in any of the previous doings?

When some sexual matter is a subject of conversation in the Old Testament, a euphemism or a figure of speech is often used to refer to the matter. Thus, for example, the term "foot/feet" is sometimes used to refer to the male genitals (for example, when the Old Testament refers to Saul going into a cave and uncovering his foot). The phrase "uncover or look on the nakedness" of someone usually indicates some kind of sexual assault. This would explain why Noah was so angry about ""what Ham had done to him."" Ham had shamed him by a sexual act when he was drunk. If we compare this to Genesis 6:1-4, we can see how severe the judgments could be for sexual aberrations. It was not uncommon in antiquity to judge someone by placing a curse on their descendants, not least because it was believed that the only way one lived on beyond death was in one's children. All these factors are in play in this text.

I have often wondered what the expression in the Bible, "a reproach to my enemies," or in Psalms, "a reproach to others," means.

The dictionary definition of "reproach" refers to making an accusation so as to make someone feel ashamed, or it can mean to bring shame upon someone and so discredit them. The Bible was written to those who lived in "honor and shame" cultures where public shaming was in many cases far worse than death. If someone was a reproach to their enemies, then they had shamed them or discredited them.

What is the biblical standing on cremation?

There is no "biblical" standing on cremation, but some more conservative Jews and Christians have objected to the burning of the body because of their belief in the resurrection of the body at the end of human history. There are, in addition, some who feel that since their individual bodies are gifts from God, they have no right to destroy them. However, the God who made the material universe out of nothing can certainly create a new body for those who are raised from the dead.

The Holy Bible has been translated into many different languages. In some translations, one word or a group of words can have very different meanings than what the original scripts said. Due to this, is the Holy Bible translated accurately? A group of people are translating the Bible into "gender-neutral" language. Will this change the meaning/accuracy of what the writers wanted to be said?

Gender-neutral translations are not attempts to falsify the biblical data. Rather, they are attempts to make clear that when an ancient androcentric text spoke about men, most of the time what was meant was both men and women. In our own era, terms like "humankind" rather than "mankind" are commonly used to refer to a mixed group of men and women, and there is no reason that such terminology shouldn't be used for translating. My own personal preference would be for the use of gender-inclusive language of a mixed group—so, for instance, if the Greek term "brothers" is used to refer to a group of men and women, it would be more helpful to render this "brothers and sisters"—as, in fact, the NRSV, TNIV, and other modern translations do.

I have become friends with a Native American Eskimo in another community, and we have been discussing Christianity. She wants to know what happens to the souls of her ancestors who died before ever having been told of God. Please refer me to Scriptures that will help answer this question for both of us.

According to Romans 1, there are no human beings who were totally ignorant of the reality or power of God due to their social location or the era in which they lived. God judges persons according to the light they have received and what they have done to respond to it. So Romans 1 says the problem with pagans in the past was not that they were completely in the dark about God, but rather that they had exchanged the truth they could know about God for a lie. In other words they were not totally ignorant; they simply chose to ignore the one true God who made them.

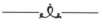

Is the forty days of Lent symbolic of the forty days of the temptation of Christ? If not, can you tell me what the forty days of Lent symbolize and perhaps suggest some Scripture references?

You are right that the forty-day period of Lent is chosen because of the 40 days of Jesus' temptations. The fifty days between Easter and Pentecost, however, reflect the Jewish calendar, which had fifty days between Passover and the Jewish feast of Pentecost.

I am trying to find Scripture related to "the hedge of thorns," or "praying the hedge of thorns" over someone/something. I learned of this from my mother, who told me it was scriptural. Do you know where I can find this in the Bible?

Thorns were indeed used for hedges, and also for fuel, in biblical times (see Judg 9:14-15; Ps 58:9; Hos 10:8; Mark 15:16-18). But the phrase "a hedge of thorns" is also used metaphorically in a text like Hosea 2:6 ("Therefore, behold, I will hedge up her way with thorns") to refer to the way God hems someone in, or makes them go in a particular direction. I suspect Hosea 2:6 is the text your mother had in mind. Perhaps she was referring to praying for the protecting of someone, even against themselves.

Are Christianity and feminism contradictory? Does the Bible really support the notion that men are superior to women or does the Bible provide counterpoints to that argument?

It is anachronistic to refer to the Bible as either feminist or chauvinist, since those are modern terms, but this much can be stated emphatically: the Bible does not support the notion that men are superior to women. Both are created in the image of God, and both can be redeemed in Christ. We are told in Galatians 3:28 that it is God's design for the order of redemption that there be no pecking order based on maleness or femaleness, based on being either Jew or Gentile, or based on one's social position (whether slave or free). All are one in Christ.

Does the Bible prohibit drug use? I've read the passage that says that all animals and plants were created for our use.

Much depends on your definition of drugs. There are, in fact, various places in the Bible where the drinking of wine (clearly an alcoholic beverage in that era; see Prov 20:1) is actually encouraged (for example, in Isa 55:1). Though wine would often be watered down in antiquity, it was nonetheless clearly potent, and is used in several places as a contrast with the powerful effect the Holy Spirit has on someone (see Acts 2:12-16, with its reference to new wine that can make one drunk contrasted with the effect of the Spirit. See also Eph 5:18).

In John 2:1-12, Jesus provides the wine for a wedding. It is clear from the toastmaster's comment ("You've saved the best wine for last") that we are dealing with an alcoholic beverage. The normal procedure in a feast would be to provide the best and most potent wine first, and then the more watered down and less flavorful later as the palate became less discriminating.

There is, however, no endorsement in the Bible to use drugs that have the potential to seriously damage the mind or body. This is why church leaders are to be those not given to too much wine (1 Tim 3:3, 8—not a drunkard, not given to too much wine). There is then condemnation of overindulgence, but not of drinking in moderation.

There is not, however, any encouragement or endorsement of using drugs that do not constitute food or beverage in any age of human history. In fact, there may well be a prohibition of a particular kind of drug, one which produces abortions. In Galatians 5:20, there is a reference to *pharmakeia* (from which we get the word "pharmacy"). This term may, however, refer to the use of drugs in pagan worship ceremonies.

Do you have any idea where the Hail Mary prayer is in the Bible? Someone told me it's in Luke somewhere but I don't know where, so if you know you'd help out a lot.

The beginning of the passage where Mary is greeted with this phrase is found in Luke 1:28ff. It was not originally a prayer, but rather a greeting from an angel to Mary. Praying to Mary using this phrase is a later Roman Catholic practice that finds no endorsement in this text. That practice reflects the later veneration of Mary as a heavenly intercessor for pray-ers who did not feel they could address their prayers to Jesus directly. This practice is in part based on a misunderstanding of Revelation 12, which refers to mother Zion (the people of God in a corporate female image) and also perhaps the mother of the Messiah, using a cosmic apocalyptic symbol.

My mentally ill older brother has schizophrenia, and it's only getting worse for now more than twenty years. He has nightmares of demons wanting him to die, and sometimes he hears them loud and clear. I know Jesus Christ was able to remove demons from people, but obviously it will not happen in this lifetime. Will my brother be free when he dies? Will the demons leave his body when he dies? Will he ever find peace when it is all over?

Actually, if the source of your brother's illness is demonic, it can be removed in this lifetime. If the problem is mental illness, as you suggest, the healing may require both medication and prayer. Demonic possession and mental illness are two very different things, with different symptoms. But in regard to his state beyond death, we are assured that for those who believe in Christ, there will be no more suffering, sorrow, persecution, or the like in the afterlife.

What happens when a person commits suicide? I lost a brother and a son, and they both believed in God and I know one of them had once been saved. But where in the Bible do we look for answers?

There is no teaching in the Bible that condemns people to outer darkness for having taken their own life in despair. The case of Judas is sometimes thought to suggest otherwise, but he was condemned for other reasons, namely the betrayal of Jesus.

The Bible certainly does not encourage anyone to take their life in their own hands, for life is a gift from God. It is not a possession, or the mere property of the individual child of God. None of us are free to do with our lives as we please; we are called to live as God pleases.

Even during points of deep depression and despair, we are called to leave matters in God's hands. In 1 Kings 19:4-6, a despondent Elijah prayed for God to take away his life, but he did not lay violent hands on himself. We too should leave matters in God's hands; this includes leaving the fate of those who commit suicide in the gracious and merciful hands of the Lord.

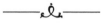

How are Christians supposed to accept homosexuals who say they are believers in Christ Jesus and in all of what God's word in the Bible says about their lifestyle, but do not accept the idea that God in whatever person (Father, Son, and/or Holy Spirit), if only asked, can change their sexuality?

In the first place you are right that homosexual and lesbian sexual behavior are indeed condemned in the Scriptures (see, for instance, Rom 1:26-27). But then so are adultery, theft, and a host of other sins. The Bible does not encourage us to treat homosexual persons with less respect, or as worse sinners, than any other kind of sinner. The old distinction between loving the sinner but not loving the sin is a good one and applies.

We are not called to accept anyone's sinful lifestyle, be they hetero-sexual or homosexual. In regard to welcoming people into the church, everyone is welcome to come as they are. But no one is welcome to stay as they are.

Jesus calls all of us—all sinners—to change. The church is supposed to be a hospital for sick sinners, not a museum for saints. The New Testament clearly teaches that whatever one's sinful inclinations, God's grace is sufficient to help anyone get beyond temptation and resist sin (see 1 Cor 10:12-13). I would remind you as well that homophobia is a sin.

The issue here is not one's inclinations or temptations but one's behavior. The New Testament teaches that one's behavior can be modified with the help of God's grace. Is God's grace powerful enough even to change human nature and its fallen orientations? Yes, indeed, and there are numerous authentic testimonies of former gay and lesbian persons as well as former liars, thieves, heterosexual sinners, and so on who make this evident. Finally, it's not an issue of whether one is "born that way" or not. The Bible is clear that we are all born with sinful inclinations. Just because we are born that way does not mean that was God's highest and best plan for our lives. There are many different kinds of birth defects, some of them moral.

In my view, we need to stop stigmatizing certain particular sins, like same-sex sexual expression, and recognize that all sins are sins for which Jesus has already died and paid the price. Instead of pointing fingers, we need to hold out helping hands, and help each other over-come our sinful proclivities.

———✥———

I have been studying with the Witnesses, who state that December 25 probably wasn't when Jesus was born. They reason that it would have been too cold for shepherds to be out with their sheep in December. They point to the fact that the twenty-fifth was in fact already celebrated as winter solstice and is just used now to make

**things simple. I would appreciate any information you may be able
to give me.**

There is partial truth to this view. The winter solstice, however,
was December 21, not December 25. In the Greco-Roman calendar,
December 25 was the festival of Saturnalia, a holiday during which
masters became slaves and slaves became masters for a day. It was the
day of reversals.

While it is possible that Jesus was born in the winter, this is far
from certain, and the fact that the shepherds and sheep were out in
the fields might well suggest the birth occurred during some other season of the year. If Jesus' birth was heralded by a partial conjunction of
planets, it might be possible to be more certain as to the time of year.
But the Magi story in Matthew suggests something more supernatural
than an ordinary cosmic event.

The church probably began to celebrate the birth of Christ when
they did in order to replace pagan holidays with Christian ones. Beginning with the Emperor Constantine, who converted to Christianity,
there was a decided movement in this direction.

What we can say with certainty is that since Jesus was born during
the reign of Herod the Great, and we know that Herod the Great died
in or before 2 BC, we also know that Jesus was not born right at the
turn of the era (in the "year zero"). The monk who set up the calendar
was clearly off a few years.

**In the history of the Bible, how many times was the holy book
revised? During the revision, is there any possibility that God's verses
were amended to suit the needs of the scholars concerned?**

The Bible has not really been revised over the ages, as you are suggesting. However, words and passages have at times been miscopied or
mistranslated.

If you are wondering if there has been a scholarly conspiracy to amend the Bible to suit particular theological views, the answer is basically no. But bear in mind that every translation is already an interpretation of the original language text, and scholars do debate what the proper translation of this or that foreign word or phrase may be. Words only have meaning in context, and as with English, many Greek or Hebrew words have multiple possible meanings. Only careful study of the context helps determine what the inspired author may have meant.

I would like you to explain how the concept of the Trinity came about and comment on the acceptance of it in various Christian denominations. Are there things about the Trinity that certain denominations believe and others don't?

The Trinity has been an accepted doctrine of the Christian Church in all its major branches (Catholic, Protestant, and Orthodox), and indeed was an accepted doctrine even before it was officially ratified at major church conclaves in AD 325 (at Nicea) and in AD 450 (at Chalcedon).

All Christian denominations affirm the Trinity as an essential doctrine of the faith. Some offshoots from the church (for example, the Jehovah's Witnesses or the Unitarians) have not accepted this concept, but they have chosen to go their own way, and are not part of the fellowship of Christian churches worldwide.

I have a friend who believes adamantly that all Jews are going to hell. I confronted her on this to ask where in the Bible it says this. She couldn't answer me exactly, but stood firm in her belief that this was in the Bible.

Fortunately the Bible doesn't consign Jews or anyone else to hell simply because of their ethnic or religious background. What the New Testament does say is that all have sinned and fallen short of God's glory, and therefore salvation is by grace and through faith in Christ alone. You might want to read carefully through Romans 1–8 on these matters. If you continue to Romans 9–11, Paul argues that, in fact, after the full number of Gentiles are saved, also "all Israel will be saved" (see Rom 11:25ff). By this Paul likely means that a very large number of Jews will be saved when Christ returns.

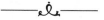

The word "God" is used without regard for meaning. In most formal religions, the texts that talk about "God" use the male, singular term and follow it with pronouns "he, his, him." Why?

Words only have meaning in contexts, not in the abstract. All of the major world religions came to us in the context of patriarchal cultures, and the texts themselves were all—or almost all—written by men.

In the biblical tradition, the Jewish and Christian writers wanted to avoid any suggestion that they were referring to some sort of fertility religion, and so they did not refer to God as a female, by and large. In the Christian tradition, God is called "Father" because it is believed that God was indeed the father of Jesus, and Jesus taught his followers to address God as he had done, in the famous Lord's Prayer (see Matt 6:9-13).

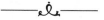

Since so much of the Bible takes place in Egypt, why is there no mention of the pyramids? To this day we don't know for sure how they were constructed, so why no mention of them?

Some of the pyramids surely existed during the time of Moses (around 1300 or so BC), but most of the time that Israel spent in Egypt was not spent near the Giza plateau, where the great pyramids are. The Israelites seem to have lived in Egypt's northern grain storage cities, so Moses would have visited the palace in Memphis, which is not at the Giza plateau.

We also need to remember that the Israelites (including Moses) were nomads, not great building constructors, until well into their history. Such structures may not have impressed them very much. Remember the negative judgment passed on such human constructions in the early tradition about Babel (Gen 11:1-9).

What is the best speculation as to what language was spoken in Eden?

It has been the time-honored tradition in Judaism that the language spoken in the garden was Hebrew, which was also seen as the language of God. If the rivers mentioned in Genesis 1–2 are any clue, it would definitely have been some sort of Semitic or ancient Near Eastern language.

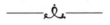

Is it wrong for a born-again, spirit-filled Christian to be cremated?

While it is probably not unethical for a Christian to be cremated, some Christians have strong reservations about it because it involves a living person choosing to have their own body immolated or destroyed, rather than simply allowed to decay in the earth. To some, this suggests a denial of God's right to determine the end of our life and our life processes. Still others object because of the Christian belief in the resurrection of the body or in the body, which is promised in Scripture (see 1 Cor 15).

How are Protestants able to discard the belief in the Petrine Doctrine and a fifteen-hundred-year history so quickly? Do they not believe that Christ left behind a church with a teaching authority, or what we Catholics call the Magisterium?

The notion of Petrine supremacy seems to overlook the biblical account that James, not Peter, was the head of the earliest church in Jerusalem (see Acts 15). Peter, James, and John were all considered co-leaders, according to Paul (see Gal 1–2).

While Protestants certainly believe that God left behind teaching authorities such as the apostles and prophets, the final authority rests with the canon of Scripture and not with church tradition about Peter or anyone else, especially if that tradition is not well grounded in Scripture. Protestants usually understand Matthew 16:18-20 (Jesus' statement, "On this rock I will build my church") to refer to Peter's faith as the basis of the church, not necessarily some Petrine personal authority.

But even if it is the latter, the word "rock" here should be translated "shelf of rocks," and refers to Peter as a person of faith, and those like him having such authority. Peter was certainly not the first great church leader in Rome, historically speaking.

———————

What is the biblical standpoint on divorced church leaders, like pastors, youth pastors, and so on?

Some scholars would interpret 1 Timothy 3:1-12 to rule out the possibility of divorced clergy. However, the key phrase here—"the husband of one wife"—could refer to a prohibition of polygamy, or it could refer to an endorsement of only serial monogamy (that is, one wife at a time). Certainly it is true that religiously mixed marriages were viewed differently than Christian marriages (see, for example, what Paul says about a mixed marriage in 1 Cor 7:12-16). Nowhere in the New Testament is divorce called the unforgivable sin. So it would be difficult to talk about the """biblical""" view on divorced clergy when the key texts are interpreted differently by equally devout and careful scholars.

There is a Scripture that says, "be perfect as your father in heaven is perfect." I know I am not perfect, and I don't know anyone who is perfect. Please explain this. I do try to do right, but I cannot attain to what I want to be.

You are referring to the verse in Matthew 5:48, which needs to be read in light of Matthew 5:43-47. Jesus is referring to loving others as God the Father loves us—in other words, following God's example and behavior, rather than that of others.

Jesus is probably not referring here to inward moral perfection, or even perfect execution of all the good things we intend to do. He seems to be referring to our intent and attempt to emulate God"s love. Those things are attainable goals if we rely on God's grace to help us.

St. Augustine once said, "Give what you command, Lord, and then command whatever you will." In this case, we should pray for God to fill us with his love, and then share it with others. This is the perfection Jesus had in mind.

I have heard that your name can be blotted out of the Book of Life. Is this true? I have found several verses that say our name can never be erased but am still searching for the verse that proves otherwise (if there is one).

You are thinking of Revelation 3:5 (see Rev 17:8; 20:12; 21:27). This passage involves a stern warning to Christians in Sardis that they must be faithful to Christ until the end of their life, even if that means martyrdom. The warning reminds us that we are not eternally secure until we are securely in eternity. We must rely on God's grace every day to remain faithful until the end. Apostasy is a possibility for Christians, and so this passage warns against it.

During a recent Bible study, the leader told the group that before Satan was thrown out of heaven, he was the chief musician in heaven. We have searched and searched and cannot find any reference to this. Can you help us?

You are quite right. There is no reference in the Bible to Satan being the chief musician in heaven. The only real passage that discusses Satan's role in heaven is Job 1–2, where Satan is presented as the accuser of believers in the heavenly court.

Why did Jesus always call the Blessed Virgin Mary "lady" and not "mother"?

This is an excellent question (see John 2 and 19). My view is that Jesus calls his mother "woman" (not lady) rather than "mother" because he is disengaging from her parental authority. As a text like Luke 2:41-52 shows, Jesus had to follow the dictates of his heavenly father rather than his earthly mother if they did not correspond.

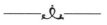

I have been considering getting a tattoo. Is there anything in the Bible that I should consider before taking this step?

You are thinking of Leviticus 19:28. Notice that this text first says that it is wrong to make gashes in one's flesh for the dead. We are talking about cutting or marking the flesh as part of some religious ritual (see, for example, the gashing of the wrists in 1 Kgs 18:28). This text is probably not a general prohibition against tattooing, since that act in antiquity always had specific religious associations.

Still, it is fair to say that if you choose to get a tattoo, it should not involve an inscription that is inappropriate for a believer to display.

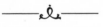

In the Bible, God told Adam and Eve that they would die if they ate from the tree. The snake told Eve that she would gain knowledge between right and wrong. Isn't that what did happen? I mean, they didn't die, so does that mean that the snake was telling the truth and God lied?

Actually, your interpretation is incorrect. Adam and Eve did go on to die, as God said they would. God did not say they would die instantly. The awareness that Adam and Eve gained from eating the apple was not proper moral knowledge of good and evil but rather an awareness that they had sinned. Also, an extreme form of self-consciousness and self-centeredness resulted from this sinful act.

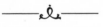

My friend and I were talking about whether or not animals go to heaven. He heard someone speak about the animals in heaven, as stated in the Bible; did that mean all our animals or a selected few? It is my belief that animals have a soul/spirit too. But he won't believe me until I have proof from the Bible that states this.

The Bible is quite clear that only human beings are created in the image of God. Nothing in the Bible suggests that other parts of the creation have eternal spirits. Nor are there any texts about animals dwelling in heaven. What we do find is a promise that in the new creation at the end of human history there will be animals present, with even the wolf lying down with the lamb (Isa 11:6-7). Since Revelation 21–22 speaks of a new earth as well as a new heaven, there is no reason that God might not renew the animal kingdom as well as the human one when the final kingdom of God comes here on earth.

———ه———

How do evangelical Christians justify their view that abortion is "murder" when there is nothing in the Bible to indicate human life begins at conception rather that birth? Other Christians see birth (or a midway point) as the starting point of a sentient human.

The psalmist in Psalm 139:13-14 speaks in a personal way of his own life beginning at conception, with God forming him in his mother's womb. Furthermore, God reminds the prophet Jeremiah, "Before I formed you in the womb I knew you, and before you were born I consecrated you; I appointed you a prophet." In other words, Jeremiah is a person whom God knew and whom God had plans for well before Jeremiah was born.

———ه———

Reference the Rapture: If the dead will rise up first, where are they now? I thought the souls and spirits of believers were already with Christ. Also, how does this relate to believers who have been cremated?

Paul says that those who are deceased or presently absent from the body are present with the Lord in heaven (2 Cor 5:8). However, Paul clearly believes, as in 1 Corinthians 15, that the final form of the afterlife involves having a resurrection body that is received after the Lord returns. As for the cremated, this is hardly a problem, since the God who made all creation out of nothing can certainly make a new body for a cremated person he raises from the dead.

———ه———

In Matthew 1 there is a genealogy of Jesus that ends with Joseph the carpenter, and in Luke 3 the same, but all other names are different. Would you please explain why there are these two different genealogies?

These two genealogies differ in various respects, and the traditional answer is that Matthew's genealogy is that of Joseph's family, while Luke's is that of Mary's family. Another possibility would be that we have the paternal and maternal genealogies of either Joseph or Mary. Whatever the case, the focus of the Matthean genealogy is to show that Jesus is a son of David, while the focus of the Lukan genealogy is to show that Jesus is a son of Adam, a son of humanity. The purposes of the two genealogies differ.

———✦———

I am wanting to become a Christian, but I was wondering if God ever said it was sinful to have a same-sex relationship.

There are several passages in the Old and New Testaments that forbid same-sex sexual activities: Leviticus 18:22, Romans 1:26-27, and 1 Corinthians 6:9, among other texts. The concept stressed is that, by God's grace, any and all sinful inclinations can be resisted, whether homosexual or heterosexual in nature.

———✦———

Ever since I read in St. James that women should not braid their hair, I've haven't done it. Is it OK or not? And why?

There is actually nothing in the Epistle of James about hair at all, but when in the New Testament there are instructions to women about hair, the function of those instructions is to make certain that only God's glory is reflected in worship (see 1 Cor 11). Since in Paul's culture a highly adorned hairdo was considered a woman's glory, Paul said it ought to be covered in worship. Perhaps you have 1 Timothy 2:9 in mind, but the point of that text is not so much to forbid braiding of the hair but to encourage wearing your hair in a way that does not distract from worship by drawing attention to yourself.

———✦———

Does the Bible directly oppose witchcraft? Does it make any dif-ference if it is white or black?

The Bible is unequivocal about prohibiting witchcraft in any and all forms. For example, Leviticus 19:26-28 makes evident that witch-craft was prohibited for God's people even in Old Testament times. Furthermore, in 1 Samuel 28 we have the story of how King Saul expelled all mediums and wizards from the Holy Land and then him-self consulted a medium, which the narrator of the story makes clear is a very grave sin. In the New Testament, Paul lists sorcery as one of the sins that can keep a person out of the kingdom of God (Gal 5:20).

Why is it thought that Christ was poor? In fact, Jesus was rich, his uncle being Joseph of Arimathea. Joseph had his wealth in ship-ping. That is how Christ was able to have transportation whenever he required it.

Nothing in the NT suggests that Joseph of Arimathea was related to Jesus at all. Jesus himself, of course, says at one juncture that he has nowhere to lay his head, and when asked his judgment on paying taxes to Caesar, he does not even have a coin to examine so he can discuss the matter. The evidence we have certainly suggests that Jesus was poor by any culture's standards.

What is the role of a prophetess specifically? How do you claim this calling upon your life?

The role of the prophetess, like the role of the prophet in the Bible, was to be God's mouthpiece. Sometimes this involved simply proclaiming a revelation you had received from God (see 1 Cor 11 and 14). Sometimes it involved offering up an exhortation to God's people or making a wise judgment, based on some revelation from God. See Judges 4-5 about Deborah.

In regard to claiming such a calling in your life, you must first have been called by God to do this and accordingly granted the gift of prophecy, as recognized and attested in the faith community. It's not a matter of simply going out and claiming to be a prophetess. There must be fruit and evidence in your life that you have been gifted in this way.

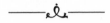

The doctrine of *sola scriptura* (or "the Bible alone") is the sole and only authority in Protestantism. Where is this foundation of all of the Protestant beliefs given to us by a revelation from God? How do we infallibly know that this doctrine is true? If it is true, where in the Bible is it taught, and where was it taught by the apostles?

This is an excellent question. Second Timothy 3:16 focuses on the fact that all the Old Testament Scriptures are inspired by God and thus are truthful. There was, of course, not yet a New Testament canon during the NT era itself; the books were still being written. But the principles of holding a very high view of Scripture, and basing your life on God's word as the final authority, are clearly present in texts like Psalm 119. Because of such texts, and also because of the ecumenical church counsels in the fourth century AD—which said these twenty-seven books are our NT canon— the Protestant churches have held up the notion of *sola scriptura*: of Scripture alone being the final arbiter of truth.

What race was Jesus? Some believe that he was African American or white. The Bible talks about him having hair like wool, and I believe that he was African American.

Jesus was a first-century Jew, and so neither black nor white, but rather a Middle Eastern person. His mother Mary was a Jew from

Nazareth in Galilee, not an African. The fact that Jesus' family fled into exile in Africa briefly to escape the wrath of King Herod tells us nothing about his genetic heritage or appearance.

You are perhaps thinking of the "white as wool" passage in Revelation 1:14, which is most likely an allusion to Jesus. However, it is based on the description of God in Daniel 7:9, and certainly the author of Daniel was not thinking of an African genetic trait. In any event, in antiquity both Semitic and African peoples were known for their "wooly" or tightly curled hair.

———ﷺ———

During the first century AD, Mithraism is the dominant faith in the places Paul travels to. Is it not probable that early Christianity was mirrored after this pagan faith in order to gain new converts?

Mithraism was indeed a rather popular religion in the first century A.D., but there is no evidence that it influenced early Christian practice or doctrine at all. Early Christianity was a development out of early Judaism. It is indebted to the various forms of early Judaism, not to pagan religions.

———ﷺ———

As one reads through these exchanges it becomes clear rather rapidly that not only do people expect the Bible to answer all kinds of questions, but in general they also think that the OT is just as relevant as the NT for Christians in such matters. The questions seldom reflect much understanding of the concept of progressive revelation. What is also very interesting is that many of the questions are not just informational ones about what the Bible says on this or that subject. Many of the inquirers were looking for practical help in the application of truths they already knew were in the Bible and with which they were struggling.

I proceeded in answering these questions in a way that I hope accords with the spirit and ethos of God's word. First of all, I do not assume that the Bible answers all questions we might like to ask it. Nor do I assume that even in regard to questions we could ask, that I have all the answers. In many cases that are not reflected above, I had to say I don't know. But what I did assume is that since the Bible is God's truth, I needed to be absolutely honest and truthful and not deceptive in answering these questions. I assumed that the Bible addresses some things directly, and some things indirectly, and the task of a good teacher is to explain not only what the text says and means but what its implications and applications ought and ought not to be. Rightly dividing or interpreting the word of truth is only the first task. Rightly applying it today is a far more delicate and difficult task. Of course, since I think we are dealing with the living word of God, I believe it is not a matter of making the text relevant for today. It is a matter of showing its relevance, since truth is always relevant and important. One must respect the questioner just as one respects the biblical text, honoring both in the process.

In sum, I think these exchanges show the range and scope of topics the Bible can address, and I mentioned as well some of the scientific topics I do not think the Bible attempts to address. Trouble comes when an exegete or pastor or teacher "over-eggs the pudding," as the British would say, trying to read more into the biblical text than is there, or extract more from it than one can legitimately deduce or infer.

All too often we come to the Bible with some urgent or emergency matter and demand an answer. Why did God allow my relative to die so young? Why do I have cancer? Am I being punished? Why is it that I work so hard and can never get out of debt? The truth is that sometimes the Bible does not answer such questions directly. A teacher or preacher of the word must walk carefully and prayerfully through such questions without either trivializing the pain of the questioner or dismissing the Bible as a resource for help and succor in times of need.

But my experience has been that God can write straight even with a crooked stick. God can take a text that might not seem immediately helpful and provide some much-needed solace. We also have to learn that sometimes what people need most is not an answer to their questions but a solution to their problem, or even just some companionship on an arduous journey into the presence of God. As the psalmist says, however, we are never alone on such journeys, and indeed we may count on the word of God to be a light unto the path, and a lamp to carry on the journey that illumines more than the path; it illuminates the journeyer and also sheds light on the destination as well. Can we truly ask for more than this? God through his word reveals enough of the future to give us hope, but not so much that we do not need to have and exercise faith.

NOTES

Chapter 1

Epigraph. 2nd **c.** BC inscription from Macedonia. See *New Documents Which Illustrate Early Christianity*, vol. 1, ed. G. H. R. Horsley (Sydney: Macquarrie University, 1981), 10–11.

1 *New Documents Which Illustrate Early Christianity*, vol. 9 (Grand Rapids: Eerdmans, 2002), 37–38.

2 Nor is it likely that the word "writings" in the previous verse refers to both the OT and the gospel message, which at this stage was not yet a written Gospel in all likelihood. "Sacred writings" is simply a collective noun for the works we call the OT.

3 The full text is cited in *New Documents Which Illustrate Early Christianity*, vol. 1, 10–11.

Chapter Two

Epigraph. Peter Enns, *Inspiration and Incarnation* (Grand Rapids: Baker, 2005), 109.

1   I. H. Marshall, *Biblical Inspiration* (Grand Rapids: Eerdmans, 1982), 33. This statement is interesting for a variety of reasons, but one thing that stands behind it is a particular theory of how God relates to human beings—namely personally. One can imagine that this might comport better with a certain sort of Arminian view of how divine sovereignty works in relationship to human will and actions than with some kinds of Calvinist views that are strongly predeterministic in character.

2   See p. xiii above.

3   Marshall, *Biblical Inspiration*, 33.

4   Ben Witherington, *Jesus the Seer* (Peabody, Mass.: Hendrickson, 1999).

5   Marshall, Biblical Inspiration, 37. See Achtemeier's discussion of the very same subject in his *Inspiration and Authority: Nature and Function of Christian Scripture* (Peabody, Mass.: Hendrickson, 1999), 91–120.

6   Michael Green, *2 Peter, Jude* (Downers Grove, Ill.: InterVarsity, 1987), 90–91.

7   Richard Bauckham, *Jude, 2 Peter* (Waco, Tex.: Word, 1983), 230–31.

8   Bauckham, *Jude, 2 Peter*, 230.

9   J. B. Mayor, *Jude, 2 Peter* (repr.; Grand Rapids: Baker, 1967), 197.

10   J. N. D. Kelly, *A Commentary on the Epistles of Peter and Jude* (London: A. & C. Black, 1981), 324.

11   N. T. Wright, *The Last Word: Beyond the Bible Wars to a New Understanding of the Authority of Scripture* (San Francisco: Harper Collins, 2005), 1.

12   John Webster, *Holy Scripture* (Cambridge: Cambridge University Press, 2003).

13   Wright, *Last Word*, 14.

14   Wright, *Last Word*, 29.

Chapter Three

Epigraph. Rodney Stark, *Cities of God* (San Francisco: Harper Collins, 2006), 2.

Epigraph. Karl Donfried, *Who Owns the Bible*, (New York: Herder, 2006), 14-15.

1   Peter Enns, *Inspiration and Incarnation: Evangelicals and the Problem of the Old Testament* (Grand Rapid: Baker, 2005).

2   Enns, *Inspiration and Incarnation*, 18; emphasis mine.

3   Enns, *Inspiration and Incarnation*, 20.

4   Enns, *Inspiration and Incarnation*, 40.

5   Enns, *Inspiration and Incarnation*, 55.

6   Enns, *Inspiration and Incarnation*, 66.

7   Enns, *Inspiration and Incarnation*, 76.

8   Enns, *Inspiration and Incarnation*, 80.

9   Enns, *Inspiration and Incarnation*, 87.

10   Enns, *Inspiration and Incarnation*, 94.

11   Enns, *Inspiration and Incarnation*, 96.

12   Enns, *Inspiration and Incarnation*, 99.

13   Enns, *Inspiration and Incarnation*, 108–9.

14   Enns, *Inspiration and Incarnation*, 110.

15   Enns, *Inspiration and Incarnation*, 115–16.

16   See, especially, R. B. Hays, *Echoes of Scripture in Paul* (New Haven, Conn.: Yale University Press, 1989).

17   See, rightly, R. N. Longenecker, *Biblical Exegesis in the Apostolic Period*, 2nd ed. (Grand Rapids: Baker, 1999).

Chapter Four

Epigraph. C. S. Lewis, *A Preface to Paradise Lost* (Oxford: Oxford University Press, 1942), 1.

1   On all of what follows, one may want to consult for more details my *The New Testament Story* (Grand Rapids: Eerdmans, 2004), 74–95.

2   Which makes extremely problematic the whole modern attempt to treat one or more of the Gospels as literary fiction, even if it is considered to be some sort of "true fiction." This is not how these documents present themselves, nor are their authors conforming to such conventions.

3   See Witherington, *The Problem with Evangelical Theology* (Waco, Tex.: Baylor University Press, 2005).

4   Donfried, *Who Owns the Bible*, 4–9.

Chapter Five

Epigraph. Enns, *Inspiration and Incarnation*, 170.

1   Bart Ehrman, *Misquoting Jesus* (San Francisco: Harper Collins, 2005).

2   Maurice Casey, *Aramaic Sources of Mark's Gospel* (Cambridge: Cambridge University Press, 1998). Casey is no conservative or evangelical scholar, as anyone who has read some of his other works will know. He cannot be accused of special pleading in order to spare Jesus or the Bible an error.

3   See A. N. Sherwin-White, *Roman Society and Roman Law in the New Testament* (Grand Rapids: Baker, 1978), 168–69.

4   I have dealt with historical issues and problems in far more depth in my *New Testament History* (Grand Rapids: Baker, 2001)

5   On this point see now Donfried, Who owns the Bible? Pp. 11-13.

6   See my *What Have They Done with Jesus?* (San Francisco: Harper Collins, 2006).

7   Stark, *Cities of God*, 181.

8   In fact the head of the household is rarely addressed in such codes at all. But see Seneca, *Epist.* 94.1, and notice how Seneca says the proper philosophy will "advise how a husband should conduct himself toward his wife, or how a father should bring up his children, or how a master should rule his slaves" (there are no matched pairs of advice here, only a focus on the head of the household), cf. Dionysius of Halicarnassus, *Ant. Rom.* 2.25.4-26.4.

9   N. T. Wright, The Epistles of Paul to the *Colossians and Philemon* (Downers Grove, Ill.: InterVarsity, 2007), 147.

10   For Jewish treatment of the household relationships see Philo, *Decal.* 165–67 and Josephus, *C. Ap.* 199–210; Sir 7:19-28. Doubtless this tradition has affected what is being done in this Christian code as well.

11   Andrew Lincoln, *Ephesians* (Waco, Tex.: Word, 1990), 657.

12   Wright, *Colossians*, 151.

Chapter Six

1   I have discussed Jesus' and Paul's views on the Parousia at length in *Jesus, Paul, and the End of the World* (Downers Grove, Ill.: InterVarsity, 1992).

2   See Kevin Vanhoozer, *The Drama of Doctrine* (Louisville, Ky.: Westminster/John Knox, 2005).

3   L. T. Johnson, *The First and Second Letters to Timothy* (New York: Doubleday, 2001), 422–23.

4   P. Achtemeier, J. B. Green, and Marianne Meye Thompson, *Introducing the New Testament and Its Literature* (Grand Rapids: Eerdmans, 2001), 589.

5   See now the fascinating discussion in Ramsay MacMullen's *Voting about God in Early Church Councils* (New Haven: Yale University Press, 2006).

6   See M. Hengel, *The Septuagint as Christian Scripture* (Grand Rapids: Baker, 2002).

7   L. T. Johnson, *The Writings of the New Testament* (Minneapolis: Fortress, 1999), 601.

8   Achtemeier, Green, and Thompson, *Introducing the New Testament and Its Literature*, 608, italics added.

9   I was privileged to see the Peshitta in a recent exhibit in the Smithsonian in Washington, D.C., along with other early papyri and codexes containing some portion of the Bible.

10   This quote is found in the very fine study of my friend Alistair

McGrath, *In the Beginning* (New York: Doubleday, 2001), 20. In what follows in this section, I will largely be following his lead.

11   See McGrath, *In the Beginning*, 164.

12   McGrath, *In the Beginning*, 176–77.

13   McGrath, *In the Beginning*, 189.

14   McGrath, *In the Beginning*, 190.

15   See p. xiii above.

16   Quoted in McGrath, *In the Beginning*, 192.

Chapter Seven

Epigraph. Gordon D. Fee, *Gospel and Spirit* (Peabody, Mass: Hendrickson, 1991), 26.

1   On this, see B. Witherington and L. Ice, *Shadow of the Almighty* (Grand Rapids: Eerdmans, 2006).

2   See pp. 125–27 above.

Chapter Eight

Epigraph. Fee, *Gospel and Spirit*, 34, 27.

Epigraph. Donfried, *Who Owns the Bible*, 154

1   This point has been helpfully reinforced recently by my friend Richard Hays's SBL lecture in 2006 on whether narrative criticism can preserve the unity of scripture.

2   See Witherington and Hyatt, *The Letter to the Romans* (Grand Rapids: Eerdmans, 2004).

3   Reader-response criticism is a form of creative reading of the biblical text based on a theory of meaning which does indeed suggest that since all readers are active readers, then we are bound to, and indeed need to, read things into the text. In short, meaning is largely in the eye of the beholder. Whatever else one says about this highly subjective theory of meaning, it does not accord with what the biblical authors thought about meaning. On these sorts of epistemological questions, see K. J. Vanhoozer, *Is There a Mean-*

ing in *This Text?* (Grand Rapids: Zondervan, 1998). As the blurb for the book on Amazon says, "Vanhoozer defends the concept of the author and the possibility of literary knowledge. . . . He argues that there is a meaning in the text, that it can be known with relative adequacy, and that readers have a responsibility to do so by cultivating 'interpretive virtues.'"

4   Leslie Poles Hartley, from the prologue to *The Go-Between* (repr.; New York: New York Review of Books Classics, 2002).

5   I learned these principles under G. D. Fee. See his helpful summary of his teaching on these things in *New Testament Exegesis*, 3rd ed. (Louisville, Ky.: Westminster/John Knox, 2002).

6   See now Ben Witherington, *Troubled Waters: The Real NT Teaching on Baptism* (Waco, Tex.: Baylor University Press, 2007).

7   This is from his essay "How Can the Bible be Authoritative," which is posted on his Web site,   www.NTWrightpage.com (accessed April 26, 2007).

8   Quoted in Fee, *New Testament Exegesis*, v.

Chapter Nine

Epigraph. This is quoted in Brian McLaren's *The Secret Message of Jesus* (Nashville: W Publishing Group, 2006), 194, but without citing the source.

1   Richard Bauckham, "Reading Scripture as a Coherent Story," in *The Art of Reading Scripture*, eds. E. Davis and R. Hays (Grand Rapids: Eerdmans, 2003), 44.

2   Bauckham, "Reading Scripture as a Coherent Story," 46.

3   Bauckham, "Reading Scripture as a Coherent Story," 52.

4   See the variety of quotations at Wikipedia, s.v. "Postmodernism," http://en.wikipedia.org/wiki/Postmodernism#Term. My personal favorite is that postmodernism is "weird for the sake of [being] weird" (Moe Szyslak, of The Simpsons).

5   David Harvey, *The Condition of Postmodernity: An Enquiry into the Origins of Cultural Change* (Cambridge, Mass.: Basil Blackwell, 1990).

6   Donald Miller, *Blue Like Jazz: Non-Religious Thoughts on Christian Spirituality* (Nashville: Nelson, 2003).

7   Rob Bell, *Velvet Elvis* (Grand Rapids: Zondervan Press, 2005), 21.

8   Miller, *Blue Like Jazz*, 59.

9   Bell, *Velvet Elvis*, 46.

10   A speaker at a Christian conference a couple of years back came to me in distress about McLaren's publicly expressed views at the conference on this subject.

11   See two of his more popular books: *A Generous Orthodoxy* (Grand Rapids: Eerdmans, 2004) and *The Secret Message of Jesus* (Thomas Nelson, 2007).

12   This is quoted in the foreword by John Franke to McLaren, *Generous Orthodoxy*, 14, 18.

13   Don Carson, *Becoming Conversant with the Emerging Church* (Grand Rapids: Zondervan, 2005).

14   This is the first featured review on Amazon on the page where Carson's book is for sale. Kellerman is a professor at Capital Bible Seminary.

15   Carson, *Becoming Conversant with the Emerging Church*, 186-87.

16   Davis and Hays, *Art of Reading Scripture*, 1-5.

17   See pp. 51-81 above.

18   Davis, "Teaching the Bible Confessionally in the Church," in *Art of Reading Scripture*, 9-26.

19   Davis, "Teaching the Bible Confessionally in the Church," 11.

20   Davis, "Teaching the Bible Confessionally in the Church," 21.

21   Bauckham, "Reading Scripture as a Coherent Story," in *Art of Reading Scripture*, 38-53, 39.

22   Bauckham, "Reading Scripture as a Coherent Story," 40.

23   Bauckham, "Reading Scripture as a Coherent Story," 43.

24   Bauckham, "Reading Scripture as a Coherent Story," 44.

25   W. S. Johnson, "Reading the Scriptures Faithfully in a Postmodern Age," in *Art of Reading Scripture*, 109-24.

26   Johnson, "Reading the Scriptures Faithfully in a Postmodern Age," 112.

27 Hays, "Reading Scripture in Light of the Resurrection," in *Art of Reading Scripture*, 216–38.

28 Hays, "Reading Scripture in Light of the Resurrection," 232–33.

Afterword

1 C. H. Dodd, *The Authority of the Bible* (London: Collins, 1960), 18–19.

2 Dodd, *Authority of the Bible*, 24.

3 Dodd, *Authority of the Bible*, 27.

4 Dodd, *Authority of the Bible*, 264.

5 Dodd, *Authority of the Bible*, 31.

6 Quoted in Dodd, *Authority of the Bible*, 274.

Appendix: Bible Q&A

1 I am thankful to my friends at Beliefnet for letting me use this material. I especially want to thank my friend Laura Sheahan. It's been a great pleasure working with her. All this material is reprinted with permission of Beliefnet, the leading website for inspiration and faith.

INDEX OF BIBLICAL AND OTHER REFERENCES

AUTHOR INDEX